Haflin Creek Trail | *Trent Bona*

Indian Ridge/Colorado Trail | *Kennan Harvey*

Colorado Trail | *Kennan Harvey*

The Rim Trail | *Scott DW Smith*

Coal Creek Trail | *Holly Annala*

Missionary Ridge | *Trent Bona*

Corral Draw | *Howie Schultz*

Colorado Trail/Section Point | *Howie Schultz*

Colorado Trail/Rolling Pass | *Howie Schultz*

Dalla Mountain Park | *Scott DW Smith*

Colorado Trail/Kennebec Pass | *Scott DW Smith*

Skyline Trail | *Scott DW Smith*

Raider Ridge/Snake Charmer | *Trent Bona*

Extended Extended Ridge | *Scott DW Smith*

Telegraph Trail | *Scott DW Smith*

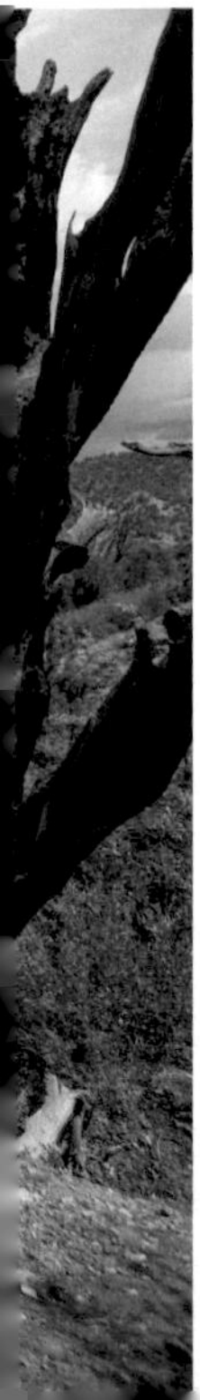

Colorado Trail/Sliderock | *Dodson Harper*

ACKNOWLEDGEMENTS

Writing this guide would not have been possible without many helpful people and organizations. I would like to extend a very sincere thank you to all who have participated in making my inspiration become reality:

Farid Tabaian of Singletrack Maps for so much work to make perfect maps and elevation profiles. Chris Hanna for his design skills and endless patience through the layout and corrections. Scott DW Smith, Trent Bona, Kennan Harvey, Howie Schultz, Paul Adams, Bill Koons and Dodson Harper for their great photos. My awesome Durango friends Kurt Smith, Kelly McCormick, Bob, Miko and Sue who helped me with obscure trails in the area, accompanied me on several rides, offered local knowledge and proofed rides. Trails 2000, Southwest Colorado Cycling Association and all the volunteers for doing the hard work year after year to keep the trails open and in great shape, and for working on future trails! Jeff Fox (Osprey Packs and SWCCA), Jeff Hemperley (El Freako from Rico,) and Scott Darling (co-owner of Kokopelli Bike and Board) helped me immensely to know which rides in the Dolores and Rico areas to include. To my husband Rob who always has enthusiasm for my projects. To my mom for shuttling me to some of the rides and helping me in any way she could, as always. To both of my parents for encouraging me. Thanks to Lena for her thorough proofreading. To the San Juan National Forest Service and Cathy Metz of the City of Durango for helping me out with accurate details on the trails. To San Juan Cycles and Lizard Head Cycles for fixing my bike immediately when I was running short of time. To Rob and all my friends who encouraged me throughout the process of riding, writing, researching and the seemingly endless process of proofreading and checking details! And to all the good people that contribute to mountain biking in so many different ways,

THANK YOU ALL!

Cover Photo by Scott DW Smith, Colorado Trail
Back Cover Photo by Scott DW Smith, Skyline Trail

Design & Layout by, Crested Butte Publishing & Creative
Printing by Crested Butte CPC Solutions
Maps & profiles by Farid Tabaian, Singletrack Maps

AREA OVERVIEW

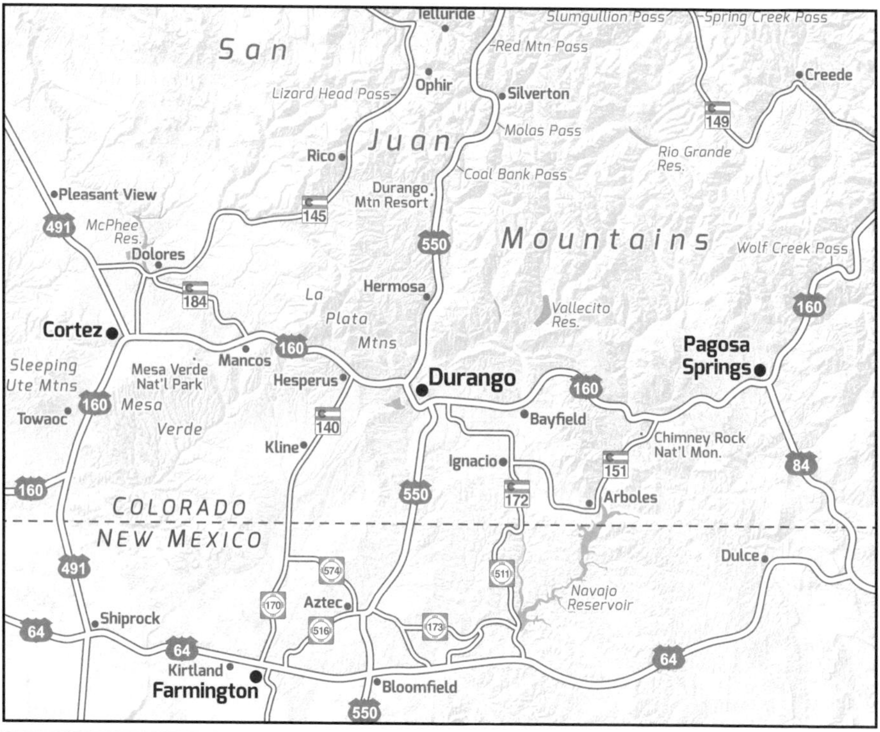

Map Legend

Trail (Singletrack) .... ·······

Trail (Old Road, Double Track, ATV, Wide Path) .... ----

Paved Trail

Primitive Route (Includes hiking only trails) .... ·······

Trailhead

Campground

Gate (Access Okay. Only shown to aid in navigation.)

Spot Elevation .... • 7484'

Wilderness Area .... _._._.

Major Road

Intermediate Road

Minor Road

Gravel Road (2WD, High Clearance or 4X4.) .... =====

Forest Service Road 201

County Road 201

Some maps have been simplified for ease of reading. Motorized trails are not differentiated on these maps.

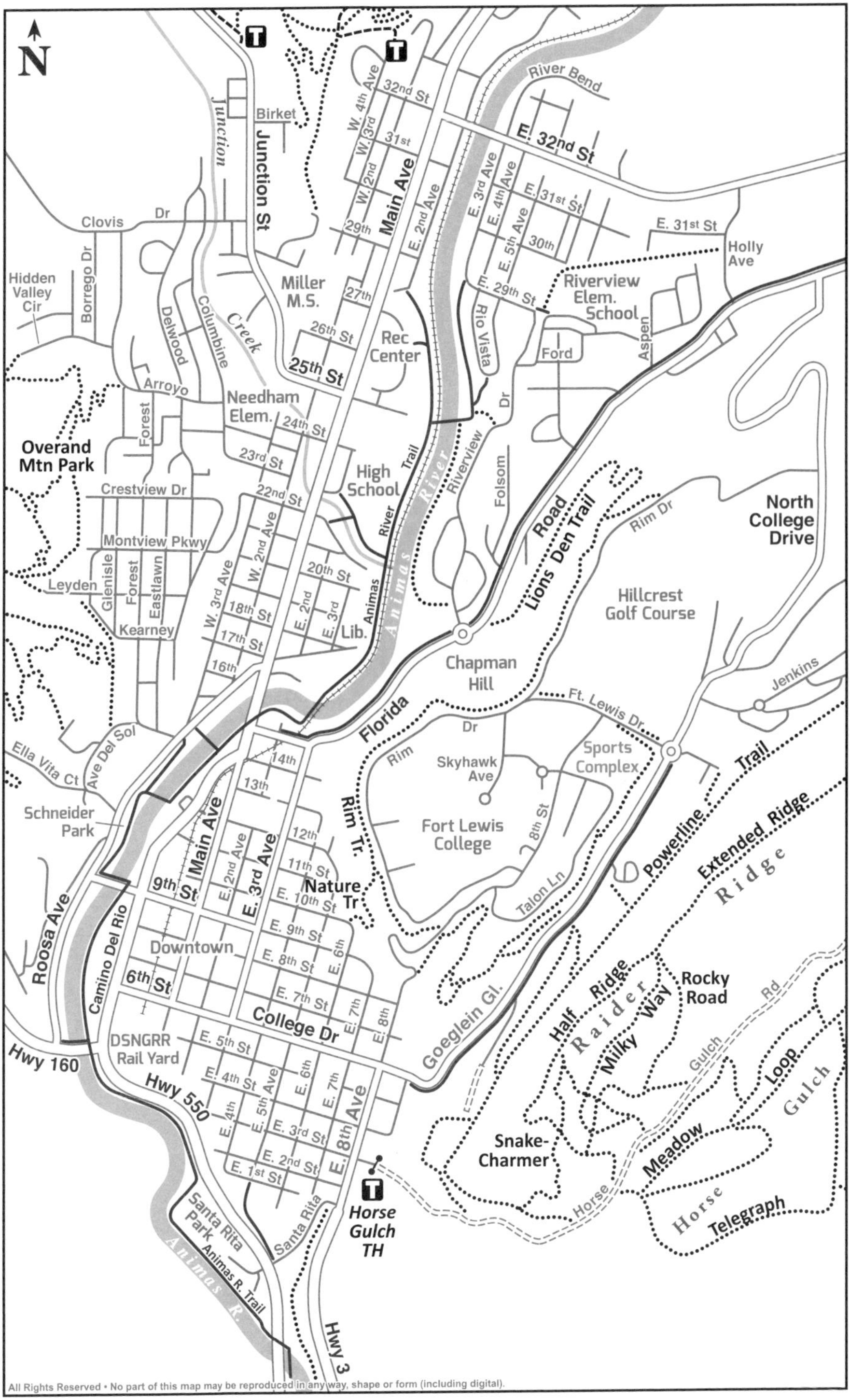
N
Junction St
Birket
W. 4th Ave
32nd St
W. 3rd
31st
W. 2nd
Main Ave
River Bend
E. 32nd St
E. 2nd Ave
E. 3rd Ave
E. 4th Ave
E. 31st St
E. 5th Ave
30th
E. 31st St
Holly Ave
Clovis Dr
Hidden Valley Cir
Borrego Dr
Delwood
Columbine
Creek
Junction
Miller M.S.
29th
27th
26th St
25th St
Rec Center
E. 29th St
Rio Vista
Riverview Elem. School
Aspen
Ford
Arroyo
Forest
Needham Elem.
24th St
23rd St
22nd St
Overand Mtn Park
Crestview Dr
Montview Pkwy
Leyden
Glenisle
Forest
Eastlawn
Kearney
High School
River Trail
Animas River
Riverview
Dr
Folsom
Road
Lions Den Trail
Rim Dr
North College Drive
W. 2nd Ave
W. 3rd Ave
20th St
18th St
17th St
16th
E. 2nd
E. 3rd
Lib.
Animas
Hillcrest Golf Course
Chapman Hill
Florida
Jenkins
Ft. Lewis Dr
Rim Dr
Ella Vita Ct
Ave Del Sol
Schneider Park
14th
13th
Main Ave
Rim Tr.
Skyhawk Ave
Sports Complex
Fort Lewis College
8th St
Powerline Trail
Extended Ridge
Ridge
12th
11th St
E. 2nd Ave
E. 3rd Ave
Nature Tr
9th St
E. 10th St
Talon Ln
Roosa Ave
Camino Del Rio
E. 9th St
E. 6th
Downtown
E. 8th St
6th St
E. 7th St
E. 7th
E. 8th
College Dr
Goeglein Gl.
Half Ridge
Raider
Milky Way
Rocky Road
Rd
Gulch
Loop
Gulch
DSNGRR Rail Yard
E. 5th St
Hwy 160
Hwy 550
E. 4th St
E. 5th Ave
E. 6th
E. 7th
E. 4th
E. 3rd St
8th Ave
E. 2nd St
E. 1st St
Snake-Charmer
Meadow
Horse
Horse
Telegraph
Horse Gulch TH
Santa Rita Park
Santa Rita
Animas R. Trail
Animas R.
Hwy 3

THE RIDES

After each ride is listed the difficulty of the ride or rides: Beginner (B), Intermediate (I), Advanced Intermediate (A), Expert (Ex) or Epic (Ep). More than one rating may be listed for different loops and options in the same area.

THE RIDES

DURANGO, CORTEZ, DOLORES AND RICO COLORADO

From high altitude epic summer rides above treeline to semi-desert rambles for the cooler months, it is all here within a two hour drive from Durango. These southwest Colorado and northern New Mexico towns have an amazing variety of trails for all abilities of mountain bikers, and there is quality riding nearly every month of the year. This book is written for folks who want to experience the singletrack in the area, and includes Durango, Molas and Coal Bank Passes, Cortez, Dolores, Rico, Farmington and Aztec trails. Enjoy spectacular views of the San Juan and La Plata Mountains, wide open Pinyon-juniper country, meadows of wildflowers, archeological ruins, and miles of excellent singletrack. The trail descriptions in this guidebook help you decide on a ride that fits your ability, desires, and time schedule, and it fits in your pack for easy reference out on the trail. Have fun out there!

HELPFUL INFORMATION BEFORE HEADING OUT ON THE RIDE

High Altitude: The town of Durango is at an altitude of 6,523 feet, Molas Pass is 10,900 feet, Coal Bank Pass is 10,680 feet, Cortez is 6,200 feet, Dolores is 6,936 feet, Rico is 8,827 feet, and Farmington and Aztec are 5,300 and 5,650 feet. Many of the rides in the higher areas climb above 10,000 and up to 12,500 feet. If you are from lower altitudes or unaccustomed to mountain biking, even the lower altitude rides of this book should be considered high altitude. Spend a few days riding shorter and lower rides before attempting higher and more strenuous rides. Drink extra water before, during and after rides. If you aren't feeling well, it could be the altitude.

Weather: A storm can blow in quickly in the mountains, so check the weather before starting your day and plan a ride accordingly. The San Juan and La Plata Mountains have more severe weather and are a lot cooler than the lower areas near the towns of Durango, Cortez, Dolores, Aztec and Farmington. If the weather looks threatening, ride a lower and shorter ride. Get started very early during the summer thunderstorm season for higher altitude rides, so you can be off ridges and passes when afternoon thunderstorms roll in. Get off your bike and off high points if there is lightning. Be prepared with warm clothes and raingear and plan exits from longer rides in case the weather turns. If you are caught in a severe storm and there is no quick exit, wait out the worst of it in a lower, thickly forested area, staying as dry as possible. Summer can be a different story on the lower rides; they can be very hot. Ride early in the morning and take a lot of water, or ride up higher near Rico, Molas or Coal Bank Passes.

Trail Conditions: Check with a local bike shop or Trails2000.org for current trail conditions before setting out on unfamiliar rides, as trails change with storms, the season, and from year to year. Many of the high mountain trails aren't clear of mud and snow until June or July, and after heavy rains these trails stay muddy for several days. Horse Gulch, Overend Mountain Park, Phil's World, Farmington and Aztec all have clay mud that really sticks to your bike with heavy rain. Often one big early snowstorm in September or October will close higher altitude trails for the winter. The trails that hunters use horses on (Coal Bank Pass, Cascade, Hermosa and Elbert Creek, Priest Creek and Calico areas) can be damaged in the case of an early snowstorm during hunting season. The semi-desert trails in Durango, Aztec, Farmington and Cortez can be fun and rideable early on winter mornings while still frozen, but very muddy by afternoon. Many of the trails near Mancos, Rico and Dolores are great fall rides because of the huge aspen groves in the area. Some of these trails can be littered with downed aspens after high winds, snow or heavy rains and in the spring.

Trail Closures for Wildlife: Near Durango, several trail systems or parts of them are closed for wintering wildlife. These trail closures are when wildlife is most vulnerable to human disturbance, and give these animals a much better chance of survival. The trails that are closed are in the Grandview Ridge area of The Telegraph/Horse Gulch Trail System (Sale Barn, Big Canyon, South Rim, Skull Rock, Telegraph, Carbon Junction, and Sidewinder Trails,) Animas Mountain, and Twin Buttes. They are closed from as early as December 1 until sometime between March 1 and April 15, depending on snow conditions in the high country. For more information call the San Juan Forest Service, 970-247-4874.

Creek Crossings: Several rides in this book have creek crossings which can be swift and dangerous in the spring and early summer, and even late in the summer or in the fall after heavy rains. Most of the bigger creeks of concern are listed in the ride descriptions, or consult your maps. Check with local bike shops for advice on water levels and turn back if you have any doubts when faced with a big or swift looking creek. If you attempt to cross, keep your shoes on. Don't cross alone!

Route Finding: Longer, more remote rides often require route finding and you might not see anyone else. Take this book and an accurate, updated map (listed in the descriptions) with you on every ride. Before heading out, read the entire description and plot it on your map. Keep track of trail signs and the surrounding terrain and landmarks. Always stay on the marked trails; you could get in worse trouble by bushwhacking or riding unknown spurs. Many user created trails exist and may not be on your map. If you think you are getting lost, turn around and retrace your route back to your starting point. If you are not confident with map reading and route finding, ride the trail systems close to the towns. Or, hire a local guide.

Clothing and Gear: Being caught in a severe rain or snowstorm is not unusual even in the summer months in the higher altitudes of Colorado. Always carry a jacket and warm layers on the higher altitude rides in this book, or on all the rides in cooler weather. Bring leggings or tights, a warm long sleeve top, a waterproof jacket and full finger gloves. Also bring rain pants, a hat that fits under your helmet, and a first aid kit on big rides at high altitude. Always wear a good fitting helmet and eye protection! Hydration packs are the best for carrying enough water and all your gear and food on longer rides. On long rides in unfamiliar areas, throw in a headlamp.

HELPFUL INFORMATION

Water and Food: Always take water and food! Even on the shortest rides in this book, you will probably want a snack and some water. On the big rides take a full 100 oz. of water in your pack, an extra water bottle, and high energy protein foods. Sugary foods alone are not enough for longer rides. Drink extra water at high altitude, and eat often to retain your energy. Filter or treat all surface water if you refill on the ride, and check your maps and get local bike shop advice to make sure there are year round streams on the epic day ride or overnight you have planned.

Tools: Always take along basic tools and know how to use them. Carry a good pump in your pack, an extra tube (even with tubeless tires), tire levers, a patch kit, a tire patch, allen (and/or star) wrenches, a screwdriver, a chain tool, quick link, lube, a rag and a stiff brush to clean your chain. Local bike shops can help you with these tools. Take an extra derailleur hanger and cleat bolts on bigger rides.

Maintenance: Keep your bike and gear in good condition at all times! Check it over before every ride to make sure everything is tight and in good shape. If you don't know how to do basic maintenance and repair, take it to a shop regularly, get a good book or take a clinic and learn to be prepared.

Additional Maps: The maps in this book may not cover a large enough area to orient yourself if you take a wrong turn or need to abandon a ride. Bring along one of the recommended maps that is listed in ride's overview. When using older maps, be aware that trails may have changed. Buy the most updated version of the map possible.

- Singletracks Maps Durango Trails is the best map for all the local Durango rides, the Hermosa area, and Coal Bank and Molas areas. It is easy to read (large scale and clear,) and lightweight. It does not cover Missionary Ridge.
- Latitude 40 Southwest Colorado Trails is an accurate overview map for the wider Durango, Cortez, and Rico area. It has almost all the rides in this book, but some important details are very small and hard to see. I suggest carrying a larger scale map also.
- The Latitude 40 Durango Trails is detailed and accurate, and covers many of the Durango, Molas, Missionary and some of the Rico area rides. For longer rides it is easy to use, but for areas where the trails are dense (Overend Mountain Park) it is hard to see important details.
- The National Geographic/Trails Illustrated Durango, Cortez is detailed, easy to read, and good for the Hermosa, Rico and Bear Creek areas, but covers a limited area and has some inaccuracies.
- Mountain Bike Map for Cortez, Dolores, Mancos and Rico is an accurate map, covers most rides in the Cortez/Rico area and is available at Kokopelli Bikes in Cortez. It is the best for Boggy Draw and Sage Hen. This map is slightly difficult to read. Beware of some suggested trails on this map, some are mostly hike-a-bike and difficult to follow, reference this book for the best rides in the area.

- Singletrack Maps Phil's World is the easiest to use for Phil's World. It has a helpful Farmington ride map, but several trails on the map are no longer there, and there are new paved and dirt roads near the trailheads and routes. Be sure to bring this book and the map along for a Farmington ride.
- Trails 2000 has several single area maps that are helpful for areas near Durango: Overend Park, Horse Gulch, Dalla Mountain Park, Animas Mountain.

Hunting Seasons: You may encounter hunters anytime between September and late November, especially on trails in the mid and high country areas. Wear hunter orange when in these areas, or stay on popular trails near towns. I suggest avoiding heavily hunted areas in rifle season. Call the San Juan Forest Service for more information, 970-247-4874 or Dolores Public Lands 970-882-7296.

Stay in control to be courteous, to avoid injury to yourself or others and to avoid a serious mechanical: Keep your speed down on trails near town or in busy areas, as you may need to stop for another user. Some other rides are quite isolated, and you may not see another person if you need help. Cell phone service is spotty at best on rides farther from the towns.

Don't ride trails closed to bikes and respect no trespassing signs: Sections of many trails travel across private property; respect the owners and protect public access by staying on the trail and passing courteously. Riding in wilderness is illegal and carries a fine or your bike can be confiscated. Stay on existing roads and trails. Close all gates behind you, gates keep livestock where they belong.

Respect other users, keep singletrack single, and create a feeling of peace on the trails: Be polite to all users! Always yield to hikers and horses. Don't ride up quickly on horses, calmly ask permission to pass, or dismount to let them pass. Don't chase or spook livestock or wildlife, and let them get off the trail. Yield the right of way to motorcyclists. It is easier for mountain bikers to step off and it keeps the trail from being widened with passing. Uphill riders have the right of way. Step to the side to let others pass, don't ride off the trail. Slowly pass others. Keep your speed down in tall vegetation to avoid running over small animals and birds. Pack out your trash and leave no trace that you've been there.

Getting to the trails: Some rides require a shuttle or driving, but many close rides are enjoyable to ride to. A road warm-up improves your riding ability on the trail, and is more environmentally friendly than driving. Ride to the trailheads in Durango on the Animas River Trail, side streets or dirt roads, if possible. Stay on the shoulder when on roads. Camino del Rio, Main Avenue, College Drive, and Hwy 550 South/Hwy 160 East are too busy and unsafe to ride on. Cross busy roads only with the lights and follow traffic rules. If you drive to a trailhead, please slow down and pass riders and hikers slowly. Avoid riding Hwy 145 during busy times.

HOW TO USE THIS GUIDEBOOK

DISCLAIMER:

I assume you know: how to ride your bike, your own and your riding partners' limits, when to turn back from a ride, navigation and route finding, bike repairs, and what to do in case of an emergency. This book is only a trail guide, intended to help you pick out and locate rides. It is not intended to replace knowledge of mountain biking and backcountry travel, map reading, navigation skills, or common sense. Inaccuracies may be present within the ride descriptions. The descriptions may become obsolete even in a short period of time, so always double check the information with other resources including trail signs and detailed maps of the area where you are riding. The author, the producer, the designer, the cartographer, the publisher of this book, and anyone mentioned in or associated with this book is in no way responsible or liable for anyone using this book and the suggested routes within this book. Mountain biking is a hazardous sport with unforeseen risks and dangers, including but not limited to: getting lost, injured, heat stroke, frostbite or hypothermia, struck by lightning, hit by a vehicle, attacked by an animal, or drowning while crossing a creek, crashes by your own mistake or another person's mistake, and even death. Cyclists assume responsibility for themselves when using this guide. Be careful and responsible, and think about the consequences of your decisions beforehand.

HOW TO USE THIS GUIDEBOOK

Important statistics and a description are listed for each ride, so you can decide which rides suit your ability, time frame, and fitness level. Here is a short explanation of each.

Time: A general guide. The time listed is a range for the level of rider that matches the ride's difficulty rating, or a rider of a higher level of expertise. Ride times can fall greatly in either direction of this range due to weather, trail conditions, route finding, mechanicals, long breaks, riders unaccustomed to high altitude or riding, and physical condition of riders, to name a few factors. To be safe, always allow extra time for a ride, and start early.

Difficulty: Beginner, intermediate, advanced intermediate, expert, expert with very difficult/extreme sections, expert/epic. Distance, difficulty and length of climbs, descents, and technical sections, and the difficulty following the trail are considered in the rating. Beginner and easy intermediate rated rides are for those with limited experience mountain biking on singletrack. Intermediate rides are for riders who have ridden quite a bit of singletrack and are in good physical condition. Advanced intermediate rides are a step up in difficulty. The expert rating is for very experienced riders who can handle many hours in the saddle and very strenuous and technical trails, possible long hike a bike sections, route finding and rough trails. Rides rated expert with very difficult/extreme sections are very technical or steep. Rides rated expert/epic are the most difficult of expert rides.

Aerobic Effort: Whether the ride demands easy, moderate, moderately high, high, very high or strenuous aerobic output. If you are from a lower altitude, a ride may seem more difficult to you than the aerobic rating suggests. Most rides in the Molas and Coal Bank Pass, La Plata Mountains, Hermosa Park, Missionary Ridge and Rico areas challenge even experienced riders because of the long climbs at high altitude. If you are concerned about the aerobic difficulty of the rides, start with shorter and lower altitude rides, near the towns.

Elevation: Top: The highest elevation on the ride in feet. **Gain:** The total gain in elevation in feet. **Loss:** The total loss in feet, for shuttle rides with more loss than gain.

Season: This is a general guide. Visit a local bike shop to find out if trails are in good condition and dry before riding them. Trail conditions change frequently with storms, seasons, or from year to year.

Finding Route: Easy, moderate, difficult, or variations of these ratings. This rating assumes you carry this book and at least one of the maps suggested in the description for the ride, and that you have knowledge of route finding, map reading, and navigation.

Maps: The map or maps that best illustrate the ride. See **Additional Maps** heading on page 24 for more information on specific maps.

Description: A general overview of the ride.

Point by Point Mileage: Measured with a GPS. These mileages could vary significantly from your GPS or computer measurements for various reasons. I have included descriptions of landmarks along the routes, to help you decipher where you are. Some of the mile points have (approx. mileage) after, this is to alert you to a possible greater difference. Use maps, a compass, trail signs, landmarks, a GPS or a cycling computer, and this guide to help you be sure of your location. Read through the description before the ride, plot it on your map and a quick check of trail signs will keep you rolling.

Star Rating: Subjective, to help you decide between similar rides. Great views and scenery, quality and length of singletrack, and character of the ride add stars. A ride may or may not suit your group's ability, desires or time frame, despite having a certain number of stars. Even two star rides are good rides! Always read the entire description before choosing a ride.

Abbreviations in this book: FS 686 is Forest Service Road 686. Hwy is Highway. CR is County Road.

A Note on Elevation Profiles: Due to the huge range in elevations (5,300 to 12,500 ft.) and lengths of rides (4-40 miles) in this guide, shorter rides appear steeper than they are. Read the description to get a clear picture of the length and difficulty of climbs.

HORSE GULCH/TELEGRAPH TRAIL SYSTEM/RAIDER RIDGE

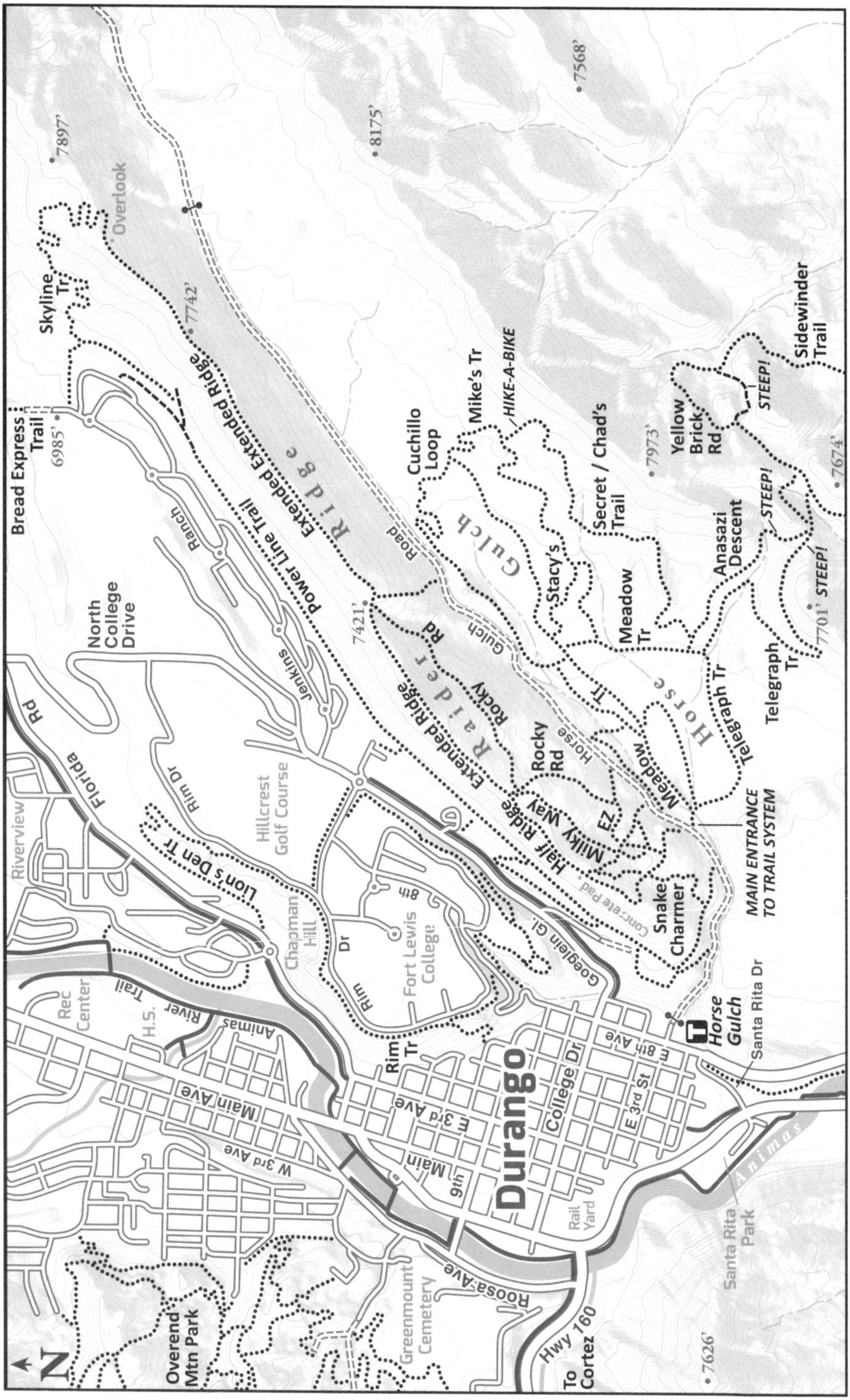

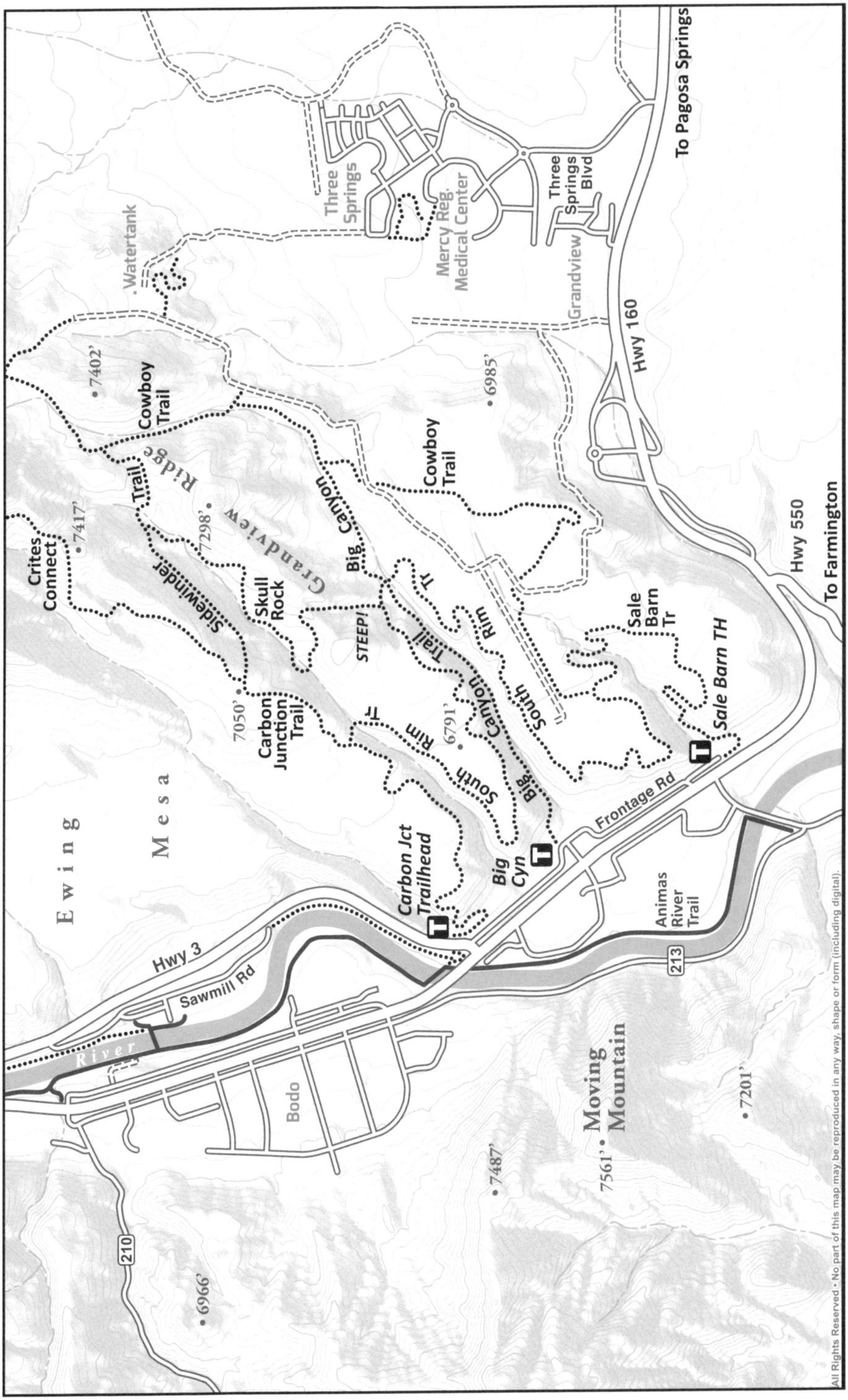
To Pagosa Springs
Three Springs
Mercy Reg. Medical Center
Three Springs Blvd
Grandview
Watertank
Hwy 160
7402'
Cowboy Trail
6985'
Cowboy Trail
Grandview Ridge
Trail
7417'
7298'
Crites Connect
Sidewinder
Skull Rock
Big Canyon
Tr
STEEP!
Rim
Trail
Hwy 550
To Farmington
Sale Barn Tr
Sale Barn TH
South
Canyon
7050'
Carbon Junction Trail
Rim Tr
6791'
South
Big
Frontage Rd
Ewing
Mesa
Carbon Jct Trailhead
Big Cyn
Animas River Trail
Hwy 3
Sawmill Rd
River
213
Bodo
Moving Mountain
7561'
7487'
7201'
210
6966'
All Rights Reserved • No part of this map may be reproduced in any way, shape or form (including digital).

HORSE GULCH/RAIDER RIDGE DETAIL

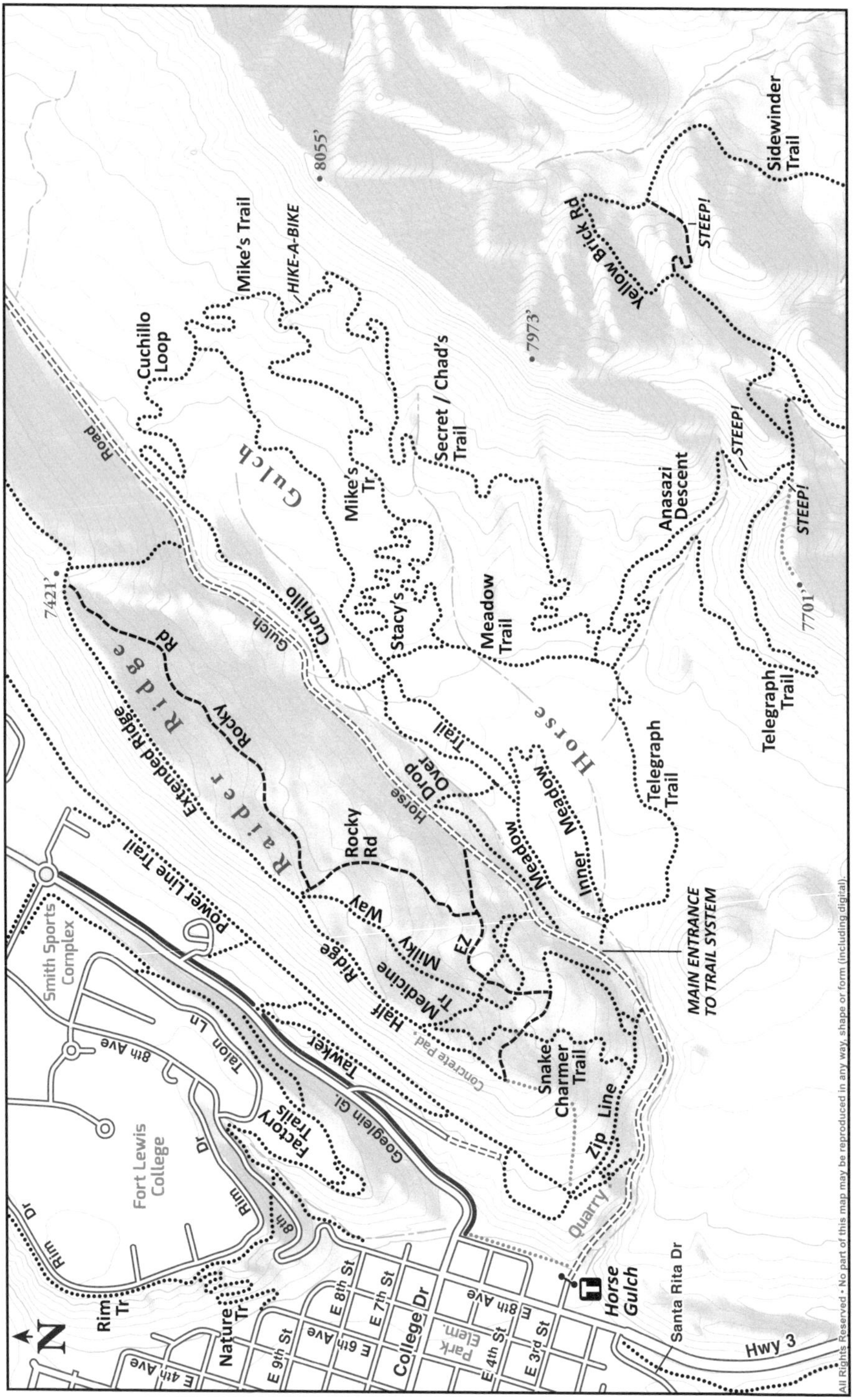

HORSE GULCH/TELEGRAPH TRAIL SYSTEM

Overview and Trailheads

The Telegraph Trails, commonly known as Horse Gulch, are a really fun system of singletracks next to Durango. The trails wind through Pinyon-juniper hills in Horse Gulch, on Raider Ridge, and south to Grandview Ridge. The La Plata Mountains are in view from several of the trails and the area is closed to motorized use. There are many ways to link the stacked trails to create a short loop or a full day of singletrack riding, with only short sections of dirt or paved road for access. Many of the trails are smooth and fast, but there are also plenty of choices with steeper climbs and descents or big sandstone outcrops for fun technical riding if you prefer more challenge. Most of the trails ride well in both directions with the exception of Anasazi Descent, Snake Charmer, Secret Trail (aka Chad's), and the most southern portion of Half Ridge. Several other trails have a recommended direction so there is less chance of collision or congestion. The Horse Gulch Trails are generally dry and rideable from about mid-April through November. Some trails in the system are closed in winter for wildlife, see page 23 for details. It can be very hot in the summer. The Telegraph Trails can be accessed from six trailheads, listed below. Also listed is a short description for each trail, a description of the Fort Lewis College Trails as access to Horse Gulch and five loops in the system. Route finding takes patience if you are new to Horse Gulch/Telegraph Trails, with many junctions and trail spurs. Many junctions are signed with maps and most trails lead back to Horse Gulch Road, Durango or Highway 550. Singletrack Maps Durango Trails is the best map to bring to Horse Gulch. The Trails 2000 Telegraph Trails map is helpful but is missing a few trails. Trails 2000 and the City of Durango have been instrumental in the development and maintenance of the Telegraph Trails system.

TRAILHEADS:

Horse Gulch Trailhead: This main trailhead is located at the southeastern end of Durango, at the junction of East 8th Avenue and East 3rd Street. There is limited parking and a big map. Santa Rita Park is only ½ mile away with plenty of parking, some shade, and restrooms. Cross Hwy 550 from this park and ride up Santa Rita Drive, turn left on East 8th Avenue/Hwy 3, and turn right on East 3rd to the trailhead. To ride to the trailhead from the east parts of town, ride on streets east of East 3rd Avenue. If you are in the north part of town, take the Animas River Trail all the way to Santa Rita Park and cross the highway to ride to the trailhead.

Carbon Junction Trailhead: To drive to the trailhead, take East 8th Avenue to Hwy 3 and go south from Durango 2 miles. The small parking area and trailhead are on the left just before the junction with Hwy 550. To ride to this trailhead go south on the Animas River Trail 2 miles from Santa Rita Park, cross the pedestrian bridge to the singletrack before the Hwy 550/160 underpass, and climb up to cross Hwy 3 to the trailhead. To return to town from the trailhead on singletrack, cross Hwy 3 and descend toward the bike path and turn right on the unsigned River Trail singletrack. Ride upriver ½ mile on the east side and turn right to climb switchbacks to Sawmill Road. Turn left and ride 3/10ths mile and turn left on an unsigned road just past ProBuild and before the Rivergate Center. Ride downhill 1/10th mile and turn right just before a private road and fence on doubletrack that turns into a bike path. Ride straight ahead on bike path and doubletrack through Rivergate Park to town, or cross the bridge to the left and take the Animas River Trail.

Big Canyon and Sale Barn Trailheads: Drive three miles south from Durango on Hwy 550/160 and turn left on Dominguez Drive, across from Wal-mart. Drive uphill to the stop sign. Turn left on the frontage road to the parking area for Big Canyon, on the left in 1/10th mile. For Sale Barn, turn right on the frontage road and continue ½ mile to a side road on the left to the trailhead, just before the end of the frontage road. To ride to the Sale Barn Trailhead, take the Animas River Trail south 3.3 miles from Santa Rita Park, turn left and ride up to River Road. Turn left and ride up and cross Hwy 550, turn left and ride 2/10ths mile to the frontage road, and turn right two times to the trailhead. Ride back from the Sale Barn and Big Canyon Trailheads by taking the frontage road Hwy 3, crossing the highway and returning to town on the River Trail singletrack or The Animas River Trail. See Carbon Junction Trailhead, above, for details. I suggest not crossing Hwy 550 at Dominguez Drive as it is a dangerous intersection. These trails and trailheads are closed in wintertime for wildlife, for details see page 23. Be very careful on all the highway shoulders and crossings, as these roads are very busy.

Goeglein Gulch Trailhead: Located 7/10ths mile up Goeglein Gulch Road from the junction of East 8th Avenue and College Drive. Ride on side streets north of College Drive to East 8th Avenue and turn left onto Goeglein Gulch Road. Ride one block to the bike path, and climb to the singletrack on the right. There is a pedestrian sign and a break in the curb. This is the Tawker Trail. Or ride to this trailhead via the college trails, see page 33. There is no parking on Goeglein Gulch Road.

Bread Express/Ball Lane Connector: From the corner of East Animas and Florida Roads, go up Florida Road ½ mile and turn right on Ball Lane, by the Sunridge Apartments. Ride up Ball Lane 3/10ths mile and turn left on the unsigned singletrack. Climb steeply 3/10ths mile to a gravel road, and ride straight up to the pavement. Across and left is the Bread Express Trail. Climb 2/10ths mile to intersect Skyline/Powerline Trails.

ANIMAS RIVER TRAIL: This concrete recreation path is good access to many trailheads in Durango, without riding on busy streets. In the north part of town it starts on 32nd Street and East 3rd Avenue, (or from 32nd ride south on East 2nd Avenue 4/10ths mile, uphill and left to join the trail on the west side of the river.) These two segments connect via a bridge just south of the Recreation Center. South ½ mile from the Rec Center a spur splits off west in Rank Park, and is a good place to cross Main Avenue at 22nd Street. (Cross Junction Creek left on the path and turn right to the light.) The main path continues south and right, under Main Street, along the river and across to Schneider Park. It continues under or over 9th Street, under Hwy 160W and on to Santa Rita Park (Horse Gulch access,) and under Hwy 550/160 East. Two miles south from Santa Rita Park, it crosses the Animas River (access to Carbon Junction and Big Canyon Trails,) and 3.3 miles south of Santa Rita Park the path ends on River Road (access to the Sale Barn Trail.)

FORT LEWIS COLLEGE TRAILS (access to Horse Gulch/Telegraph Trails)
There are several singletracks up to and around Fort Lewis College. These short trails are a fun, advanced way to access Horse Gulch and Raider Ridge by riding up to the college, down to Goeglein Gulch Road and crossing to the Tawker Trail. There are currently no signs on the College Trails. Be aware these trails are heavily used by walkers with dogs. Keep your speed down.

The Nature Trail to the Rim Trail: Advanced intermediate. At the top of East 10th Street and East 6th Avenue is the Centennial Nature Trail, which switchbacks up to the Rim Trail in 4/10ths mile. Cross a ditch trail at an angle on the way up. Turn right on the Rim Trail (with an "F" sign post,) stay right at the next junction, and ride 2/10ths mile and cross College Drive. Stay left and climb 2/10ths mile, turn right on the trail just before Talon Road. The trail widens to a doubletrack. Follow this 2/10ths mile to the end, turn left on singletrack on the east side of the rim and ride about 3/10ths mile, staying right through braided trails until you see an unmarked but obvious singletrack on the right. Descend to Goeglein Gulch Road. Cross to the Tawker Trail and climb to The Horse Gulch/Telegraph Trails. A left on the Rim Trail at the top of the Nature Trail has some exposure over a steep hillside, and has great views. It adds 8/10ths mile of singletrack between The Nature and Lion's Den Trails.

Lion's Den Trail: Advanced intermediate. Access to this trail is from the corner of Riverview Street and Florida Road, next to the Chapman Hill Ice Rink. Florida Road has a bike lane. To access Lion's Den from the Animas River Trail, cross the bridge 2/10ths mile south from behind the Durango Recreation Center, and turn right on the singletrack next to the river, on the east side. Ride downstream, and climb a hill to end on Riverview Drive. Turn right and ride downhill, turn left on Florida Road, and right into the parking area at Chapman Hill. Ride to the north of the building to the unsigned start of the Lion's Den Singletrack. Climb, staying left immediately, up long switchbacks to a fork in the trail by a bench (7/10ths mile) and turn right on the Rim Trail. Pass a double left at 1 mile. At 1.2 miles, right before a power pole, turn left and ride up to cross Rim Drive on the cross walk. Follow the trail along a chain link fence. At 1.5 miles, cross Fort Lewis Drive to the right and turn left on the singletrack, and then curve around the rim to the right. Continue to 2.2 miles where an obvious left turn leads down to Goeglein Gulch Road. Descend 3/10ths mile and cross to the Tawker Trail.

Chapman Hill Bike Park: Approved and hopefully to be constructed with flow trails and features for all levels of riders.

HORSE GULCH/TELEGRAPH TRAILS:

Horse Gulch Road: Intermediate. This doubletrack is one of the main access routes for the Telegraph Trail System and is direct and quick access to the Meadow Loop, the Telegraph Trail, and Raider's Ridge areas.

Meadow Loop: Beginner/easy intermediate, 2 miles. Add 7/10ths mile of Horse Gulch Road each way to access it. This is an easy rolling trail through the lower areas of Horse Gulch. Recommended counter clockwise.

Stacy's Loop: Intermediate, 1 mile. An extension to the Meadow Loop with rolling terrain and a fun winding downhill. Counter clockwise.

Cuchillo: Advanced intermediate, 2 miles. An extension to the Meadow Loop and Stacy's. Moderate climb and winding descent with a few short technical sections. Counter clockwise.

Mike's: Advanced intermediate, 2.5 miles. This is a scenic extension to the Meadow and Stacy's Loops, with a sustained steep climb, rolling and winding downhills, and some short technical sections. Counter clockwise.

Secret (aka Chad's) Trail: Expert, 1.5 miles. A non-system trail, unsigned, not maintained. Start with a hike a bike from the summit of Mike's Trail (clockwise,) then short steep climbs and descents lead to the bottom of the Telegraph climb. Challenging, fun, great views.

Telegraph Trail: Advanced intermediate, 1 mile to ridge, 1 mile down to Sidewinder. Steady climb to the ridge above Horse Gulch with views of the La Plata Mountains. Telegraph is a moderate descent back to Horse Gulch to avoid Anasazi.

Anasazi Descent: Expert, ½ mile. Steep, rocky, and at times after rains, rutted. Fast flow down lower. Downhill only.

Yellow Brick Road: Intermediate, 4/10ths mile. A singletrack connector from the Telegraph Trail to Sidewinder, good up or down, better than the steep, eroded doubletrack it replaces.

HORSE GULCH/TELEGRAPH TRAIL SYSTEM

List of Trails

Sidewinder: Intermediate, 2 milcs. A smooth and fast descent from Yellow Brick Road and Telegraph south. Access to Cowboy, Crites, Skull, and South Rim Trails. Good in reverse but hazardous due to blind corners.

Crites Connect: Advanced Intermediate, 1.4 miles. Moderately hard climb on the way up from Sidewinder to Telegraph, with a couple fun technical sections. Fun descent in reverse.

Cowboy: Beginner/easy intermediate, 2.7 miles. Nice singletrack, but not the most pristine as it passes a gravel pit, gas wells and power lines. Closed in winter for wildlife.

Grandview Ridge: Gas well road. Closed in winter for wildlife.

Carbon Junction: Advanced intermediate, 2 miles. Rocky climb, bumpy downhill.

River Trail Singletrack: Intermediate, 7/10ths mile. Unsigned. Connects the Carbon Junction Trailhead to Sawmill Road near Hwy 3, on the corner.

Big Canyon: Intermediate, 1 mile. Smooth and fun both directions through a fun little canyon. Access to South Rim and Cowboy Trails. Not great above the junction with the South Rim Trail, just a gas line road. Closed in winter for wildlife.

Skull Rock: Advanced intermediate/expert, 1.3 miles. A fun way to descend from Sidewinder to Big Canyon. It has a very steep section at the end, but is meandering and moderate through the middle. Closed in winter for wildlife.

Sale Barn Trail: Intermediate, 1.7 miles. Gradual switchbacking trail. Access to the Grandview Ridge area. Closed for wildlife in winter.

South Rim Trail: Intermediate, 4.4 miles. Connects the southern and central trails of the Telegraph Trail System. Not much elevation gain or drop, partly smooth and partly rocky.

Raider Ridge (aka Extended Ridge and Half Ridge): Expert, 1.4 miles. Really fun technical singletrack on a sandstone ridge outcrop interspersed with a bit of smooth riding. Some short exposed sections, great views. Access by Rocky Road or Extended Extended Ridge.

Rocky Road: Advanced intermediate/expert, 1.3 miles. Narrowing old doubletrack, access to Extended and Half Ridge. Rocky and technical.

HORSE GULCH/TELEGRAPH TRAIL SYSTEM
List of Trails

Milky Way Trail: Expert, 7/10ths mile. Fun descent from Raider Ridge, smooth and winding with some technical rock drops.

Snake Charmer: Expert, 7/10ths mile. Access this downhill-only trail from Half Ridge from Raider Ridge. Progress your skills on slickrock and rock gardens. All rollable cross country lines, and expert alternative lines for lovers of big drops and air.

Medicine Trail: Expert, now a system trail. A progressive trail located between Milky Way and Snake Charmer off Half Ridge. One hike a bike section.

Extended Extended Ridge: Expert with extremely difficult sections, 1.6 miles. On a beautiful ridge outcrop with great views and continuous technical riding. Access from Goeglein Gulch and Powerline or Bread Express/Ball Lane and Skyline, and continue to Extended and Half Ridge after. It is more rideable north to south.

Skyline: Advanced intermediate with a few expert switchbacks, 1.6 miles. Out and back to great viewpoint, or continue on Extended Extended Ridge. Skyline has lots of switchbacks. Access Skyline from the Tawker and Powerline Trails, or from Bread Express/Ball Lane Connector.

Tawker: Intermediate, 4/10ths mile. Moderate climb from Goeglein Gulch Road. Singletrack access to Powerline, Skyline, and Horse Gulch.

Powerline: Intermediate, 3.2 miles. Mostly level doubletrack, access to Skyline.

Bread Express (aka Ball Lane Connector): Advanced intermediate, ½ mile singletrack. Access to Skyline Trail from Florida Road and Ball Lane.

Stacy's Loop | *Holly Annala*

★★★☆☆

MEADOW LOOP, STACY'S AND MIKE'S TRAILS

See map pages 28-30

Horse Gulch/Telegraph Trail System

Description: The Meadow Loop is a moderate ramble through the lower sections of the Telegraph/Horse Gulch Trail System. Beginning riders with some fitness can ride this scenic loop, and more advanced riders will also enjoy the smooth singletrack and the many options to lengthen the ride. The ride starts with a short grind up Horse Gulch Road, but quickly levels to an enjoyable spin. The Meadow Loop winds through sage meadows and Pinyon-juniper forest. I recommend adding on Stacy's Loop for additional moderate singletrack and a fun, longer downhill. For more challenge add Mike's or Cuchillo Loop, see option below.

Distance: 4.8 mile loop, 3.2 miles of singletrack, 1.6 miles of dirt and paved road
Time: 1 to 2 hours
Difficulty: Beginner/easy intermediate with optional advanced trails
Aerobic Effort: Moderate
Elevation: Top: 7,047' **Gain:** 450'
Season: Mid-April through November or mid-December
Finding Route: Moderate, most junctions are signed but there are many turns.
Map: Singletrack Maps Durango Trails
Location: The Horse Gulch Trailhead on East 3rd Street and East 8th Avenue in southeast Durango, see page 31 for directions to the trailhead.

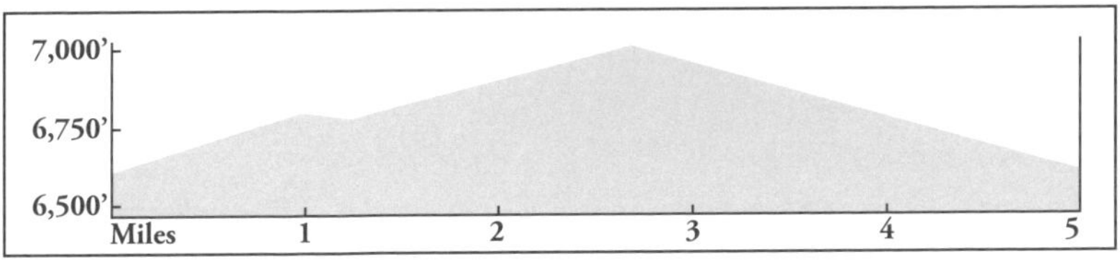

Mileage Log:

0.0 Start up Horse Gulch Road, and ride around the gate. Pass a quarry and a singletrack on the left on the way up.

0.7 Turn right on the Telegraph Trail at a major intersection with a map and benches. Cross the draw, staying right at two forks in the trail. In 1/10th mile stay left at a cable gate and climb gradually through sage meadows.

1.4 Turn left on the Meadow Loop at the signed intersection, as the Telegraph Trail turns right. Ride straight ahead and pass another trail on the right.

1.8 Turn left as Stacy's goes right at a signed intersection. (Or add on Stacy's or Mike's, see option, below.)

1.9 Turn left and descend, passing Cuchillo. Stay left again and pass Cuchillo return.

2.3 Trails merge, cross a dip and climb to a small ridge.

MEADOW LOOP, STACY'S AND MIKE'S TRAILS
Horse Gulch/Telegraph Trail System

2.5 Trail splits, go left. These trails merge again soon.

2.7 Turn right, pass the other trail and ride back to Horse Gulch Road.

2.8 Turn left on the road and descend for 1/10th mile. Turn right on an unsigned singletrack, across the ruts. Climb a small steep hill and turn left on Zipline as another singletrack merges in. Ride past Snake Charmer on the right and two spurs to the left to the quarry.

3.1 Turn right into the trees at a junction, then left and right on the signed Powerline Trail. Climb the wide trail, in a meadow. Pass a road to the left.

3.5 Turn left on the Tawker singletrack, by a power pole, and descend.

3.9 End on Goeglein Gulch Road. Turn left and descend on the bike path (left.)

4.6 As you round the corner before the junction of College Drive and East 8th Avenue, look for a hidden trail on the left to the Horse Gulch Trailhead.

4.8 Back to the trailhead.

Option: For Stacy's, turn right at mile 1.8 and climb for 4/10ths mile. Turn left at the next junction and wind downhill for 6/10ths mile. Next stay left to rejoin the Meadow loop. Stacy's is easy intermediate and fun! For a more advanced loop, add on Mike's by staying right after the climb on Stacy's. This adds more climbing and a fun descent. Or take Stacy's to mile 2.8 and turn right to ride the Cuchillo Loop, also more advanced.

★★★★☆

TELEGRAPH, SIDEWINDER, CRITES, ANASAZI, MIKE'S TRAILS
SECRET (AKA CHAD'S) TRAIL
Horse Gulch/Telegraph Trail System

See map pages 28-30

Description: This is a tour of some of the best trails in the Horse Gulch/Telegraph Trail System, starting just a few minutes from downtown Durango. This well maintained system of non-motorized trails roll through Pinyon-juniper forested hills and small canyons. This figure 8 loop combines the bigger climbs of Horse Gulch with super fast, smooth and flowing descents, some moderately technical sections, one steep technical descent (easily bypassed,) and great views of the La Plata Mountains and Durango. There are many options if you want to ride farther or shorten the ride in the description below.

Distance: 12.5 miles: 11.5 miles of singletrack, 1 mile of dirt road.
Time: 2 ½ to 3 ½ hours
Difficulty: Advanced intermediate with expert options.
Aerobic Effort: Moderately high

TELEGRAPH, SIDEWINDER, CRITES, ANASAZI, MIKE'S TRAILS
SECRET (AKA CHAD'S) TRAIL
Horse Gulch/Telegraph Trail System

Elevation: Top: 7,549' **Gain:** 2,025'
Season: Mid-April through November
Finding Route: Moderate, most trails are signed but there are many junctions.
Maps: Singletrack Maps Durango Trails
Location: The Horse Gulch Trailhead on East 8th Avenue and East 3rd Street in southeast Durango. See page 31 for directions to the trailhead.

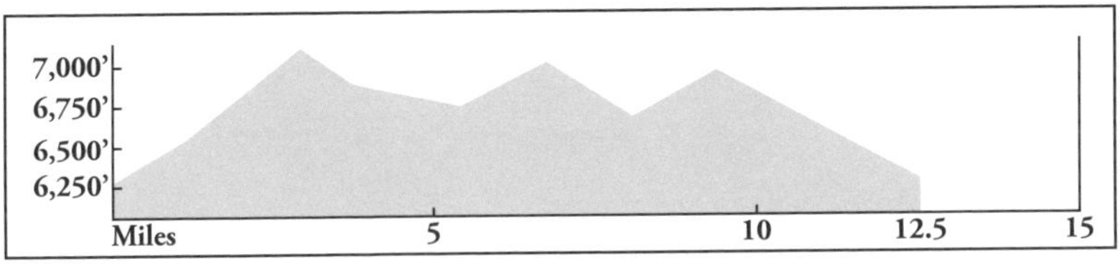

Mileage Log:

0.0 Ride up Horse Gulch Road, past the green gate. Pass a quarry road and a singletrack on the left on the way up.

0.7 Turn right at a major intersection with a map and benches, on the Telegraph Trail. Cross a small draw and stay right as the trail splits two times. Turn left at a cabled gate in 1/10th mile and climb gradually toward the ridge.

1.3 Stay right on Telegraph at a signed junction. Meadow Loop is left. In 1/10th mile, again stay right. Climb moderately for one mile, with a steep kicker at the end.

2.6 Top out and ride left, then straight past a stone bench and then pass a sharp left to Anasazi Descent (a quick way back.) The trail splits again, stay left.

2.9 Merge left at a signed intersection on an old road. Turn left on an unsigned trail in 2/10ths mile, Yellow Brick Road. (Right and down the doubletrack ends at the same intersection, but is steep and eroded.) At the bottom of the hill stay right as the trail levels, passing the faint Old Car Loop on the left.

3.6 Turn left onto Sidewinder; the steep doubletrack merging in on the right. Stay right at all intersections on the way down Sidewinder.

4.2 Pass an inconspicuous left to Grandview Ridge.

4.6 Stay right at a signed junction, passing the Cowboy Trail.

5.0 Pass an inconspicuous steep left to Skull Rock.

5.7 Turn right on Crites Connect Trail and climb. Straight ahead is the Carbon Junction Trail.

7.1 Turn left off Crites, an old road at this point, onto a singletrack. Descend, and climb up the old telegraph line. Merge left on Telegraph, and turn right on Anasazi, a steep and rocky trail. (Or go down Telegraph for a more moderate descent.)

7.8 Turn right at the bottom, then stay left and pass the unsigned Secret Trail. In 1/10th mile, turn right on the Meadow Loop.

8.2 Turn right on Stacy's. (Left on the Meadow Loop is the fast way back.)

8.6 Stay right and pass an unsigned trail. Climb steadily and then steeply.

9.3 Level out and descend left on Mike's. (Straight ahead and steeply up is the unsigned Secret Trail. See option, below.)

9.7 Stay right at the intersection with Cuchillo.

10.9 After a short steep climb, turn right at the junction.

11.2 Ride straight ahead, passing an unsigned trail to the right. Merge right, roll through a dip and ride up on a small ridge.

11.5 Stay right (or left) at a fork in the trail.

11.6 Turn right and ride back to the main intersection.

11.7 Turn left and descend Horse Gulch Road 1/10th mile, and turn right across the ruts, to a singletrack. Climb a short hill and turn left on Zipline. Pass Snake Charmer on the right.

12.1 Turn left at the split and descend to the quarry.

12.3 Turn right on Horse Gulch Road.

12.5 End at the trailhead.

Option: The Secret Trail (aka Chad's) is a 1.6 mile non-system trail. It has some too-sharp corners and steep grades, but is a fun, challenging expert trail to ride. It is best clockwise from the highest point on Mike's Trail (9.3 above.) Ride straight ahead and then hike a bike up the steep, loose hill. Turn right and descend and wind around toward Telegraph. In 9/10ths mile, turn sharp left, descend, and climb to a fun ridge ride and another descent. 6/10ths mile farther the trail turns left and heads to the bottom of Anasazi and Telegraph.

★★★★☆

EXTENDED RIDGE, MILKY WAY, SNAKE CHARMER TRAILS

Horse Gulch/Telegraph Trails System/Raider Ridge *See map pages 28-30*

Description: This is one of my favorite rides in the Horse Gulch area. It is short and sweet, but can easily be connected to many other trails for a longer ride. It is unique for the area and has a lot of character, being similar to some Moab style riding with big slabs of rock, singletrack on a narrow ridge, and some technical drops and rock obstacles. It is challenging, but nothing extreme, all rideable for an expert cross country rider. It has great views of Fort Lewis College, the Animas Valley, and the La Plata Mountains. The Extended Ridge to Milky Way loop flows best in a counter-clockwise direction, rideable in reverse but more of a grind. The descent on Milky Way is mixed moderate, smooth and winding with a few advanced technical sections. An alternative descent, The Snake Charmer Trail, is great for riders to progress their downhill skills with everything from open slick rock fields and full speed sections, to rock gardens. There are all rollable technical lines for cross country riders, as well as three optional expert lines. See option 2 below. For a shorter uphill ride to Snake Charmer or Milky Way, see option 1 below. For a very challenging technical ride on Raider Ridge, see Extended Extended Ridge, page 43.

Distance: 4.3 miles, 2 miles singletrack, 2.3 miles doubletrack.
Time: 1 to1 ½ hours.
Difficulty: Expert
Aerobic Effort: Moderately high for short distances.
Elevation: Top: 7,486' **Gain:** 915'
Season: Mid-April through November or mid-December
Finding Route: Moderately difficult. There are a lot of junctions, and several unmarked trails, but all trails lead to Horse Gulch Road or town.
Map: Singletrack Maps Durango Trails
Location: Start at the Horse Gulch Trailhead on East 8th Avenue and East 3rd Street. See page 31 for directions to the trailhead.

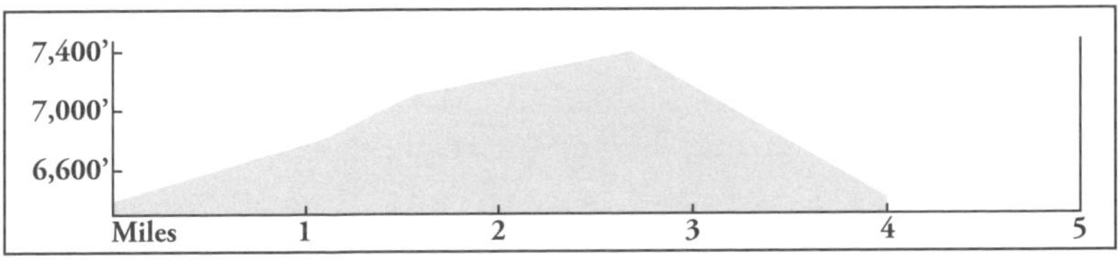

Mileage Log:

0.0 Ride up Horse Gulch Road and around the green gate. Pass the quarry and a singletrack on the left on the way up.

0.7 Pass a major intersection to the right, with benches and a map. Continue up the road. Pass a hidden singletrack on the right, Cap's Trail.

EXTENDED RIDGE, MILKY WAY, SNAKE CHARMER TRAILS

Horse Gulch/Telegraph Trails System/Raider Ridge

1.0 Turn left on Rocky Road and climb rutted road and broken slickrock. In 1/10th mile, stay right and climb, passing a doubletrack on the left, EZ.

1.2 Take the singletrack on the right at a fork.

1.4 Turn right at a fork in the doubletrack in a black dirt area. The doubletrack is loose and mostly climbs but has a few short downhills. (See option 1 below, for the shorter version to the left.)

2.2 Top out on the Extended Ridge Trail. Turn left and climb a bit more and roll along the ridge, looking for fun lines. (Right leads to Extended Extended Ridge, see page 43.)

3.0 Reach the black dirt area from mile 1.4, and a trail sign. Ride about 100 feet and turn left on the unmarked Milky Way singletrack. If you start to climb the ridge, you have passed the trail. There are more options further along the ridge, see Snake Charmer, option 2 below, or see the Singletracks map.

3.5 Turn right at a junction on EZ, then immediately left. Descend. Pass a couple spur trails. (Straight at this junction, and then left, will also end on Horse Gulch Road.)

3.7 After a short, steep, slickrock section, end on Horse Gulch Road. Turn right and descend 2/10ths mile, passing the major intersection, and then turn right across some ruts, up a short hill on singletrack, and left onto the Zipline Trail.

4.0 Turn left and down through the quarry, and right on Horse Gulch Road. (Right at the top leads to Powerline, Tawker and Goeglein Gulch.)

4.3 Back to the trailhead.

Option 1: At mile 1.4, turn left and climb the black dirt steeply, turn left at a trail sign and in about 100 feet turn left on the unsigned Milky Way Trail. This cuts 1.5 miles, 360' feet of climbing, and about 1/2 hour from the ride.

Option 2: To descend Snake Charmer:

3.0 At the black dirt area ride straight ahead past the Milky Way Trail and climb shortly. In about 2/10ths mile the trail splits, take either.

3.4 Ride into another black dirt area. Look for the "Progressive Trail" sign to the left just before a big concrete slab, which is Snake Charmer. Once over the ridge, stay right on the slickrock, following the signs and cairns. Cross an old road.

4.1 End on Zipline. Merge right, then left on the next singletrack. Ride down through the quarry, then right on Horse Gulch Road.

4.5 Back to the trailhead.

★★★★☆

SKYLINE, EXTENDED EXTENDED RIDGE

Horse Gulch / Telegraph Trail System/Raider Ridge *See map pages 28-30*

Description: The Skyline Trail switchbacks up to an amazingly scenic section of Raider Ridge above Fort Lewis College, with views north up the Animas Valley, south down the ridge into Horse Gulch, and west to the La Plata Mountains and Durango. Skyline has some shady areas on the climb that stay cooler on hot summer days. It is a really fun advanced out and back ride on quality singletrack, if you enjoy switchbacks. It is also the best access to Extended Extended Ridge. Extended Extended Ridge is continuously technical on big slabs of broken sandstone, with some exposure. It is best ridden in this direction as the technical sections tend to be downhill. It is a very challenging ride, all rideable for very technically savvy expert riders only. Extended Extended Ridge ends at the top of Rocky Road and the start of Extended Ridge. Extended Ridge is also best in this direction and leads to several different ways down, including Milky Way, described here, and Snake Charmer, see page 41. Be courteous to hikers on the Skyline Trail; the shade makes it popular.

Distance: Skyline Out and Back: 9.0 miles: 5 miles of singletrack, 4 miles of doubletrack. **Loop:** 9.0 miles, 6 ½ miles of singletrack, 2 ½ miles of doubletrack. Add at least one mile to ride to the trailhead and back.
Time: 2 to 3 ½ hours
Difficulty: **Out and Back:** Skyline is advanced intermediate with expert sections. **Loop:** Extended Extended Ridge is expert with very difficult/extreme sections; Raider's Ridge, Milky Way and Snake Charmer are expert.
Aerobic Effort: Moderately high
Elevation: Top: 7,882' **Gain:** 1,566'
Season: May through November
Finding Route: Moderate. Lots of turns, most are signed.
Map: Singletrack Maps Durango Trails
Location: Start at the Goeglein Gulch Trailhead and the Tawker Trail, no parking here. Or from Florida Road and the north end of town, ride up Bread Express and intersect the ride at mile 2.9. See page 32 for directions to these trailheads.

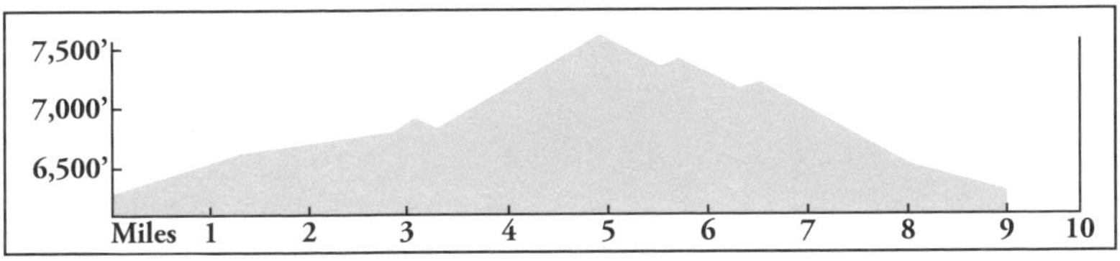

Mileage Log:

0.0 Turn right onto the Tawker singletrack, stay right, and climb.

0.4 Turn left on the Powerline Trail. Pass Shocker and several left turns down to neighborhoods and Fort Lewis on this fairly level doubletrack.

SKYLINE, EXTENDED EXTENDED RIDGE
Horse Gulch/Telegraph Trail System/Raider Ridge

2.1 Shortly after passing a water tower, ride straight ahead onto the gravel road.

2.3 Turn right and ride uphill on the gravel road. Left leads to private.

2.5 Turn left on a signed singletrack, Powerline.

2.9 Turn right at the junction on the signed Skyline Trail and climb, crossing a user-created trail several times. Left is Bread Express.

4.5 Top out and turn right on the ridge, to a great viewpoint. The trail becomes very technical beyond this point. (Turn around if you aren't up for difficult technical riding and enjoy the descent on Skyline.)

6.0 Turn sharp right at an unsigned junction on the more used trail. Left quickly descends to Horse Gulch Road.

6.1 The trail ends at the top of Rocky Road and the start of Extended Ridge. Stay right and climb. (Descent on Rocky Road is uninteresting and rough. Extended Ridge has just a bit of climbing and is a lot more fun.)

6.8 Arrive at a trail sign at the top of a black dirt area. Ride about 100 feet and turn left on an unsigned singletrack, Milky Way. Swoop through tight trees and down short technical sections. (or ride straight ahead onto Half Ridge and descend Snake Charmer, see page 42.)

7.4 At the T-intersection, turn right and immediately sharp left. Pass a couple trails on the right and then the left, closed with rocks. (If you miss this turn, descend and turn left to Horse Gulch Road.)

7.6 Turn right on Horse Gulch Road and descend.

7.8 Pass the main intersection to the Meadow Loops. In 1/10th mile, turn right across the ruts and up a short climb on singletrack, then left on Zipline, as a trail merges in from the right. Pass the bottom of Snake Charmer to the right and two trails to the quarry on the left.

8.2 Turn right at a fork, then left, and then merge right on the signed Powerline Trail and climb. Pass a road spur.

8.6 Turn left and descend Tawker.

9.0 Back to Goeglein Gulch. Turn left and down the bike path, or cross the road and ride the college trails for more singletrack. See page 33 for details.

★★★☆☆

SALE BARN, COWBOY, SIDEWINDER, SOUTH RIM, SKULL, BIG CANYON TRAILS

Horse Gulch/Telegraph Trail System/Grandview Ridge *ee map pages 28-29*

Description: This smooth, all singletrack ride connects several trails in the southern section (Grandview Ridge) of the Horse Gulch/Telegraph Trail System. The singletrack is good quality and there are nice views of the La Plata Mountains. The loop described here starts with a moderate climb on the Sale Barn Trail, meanders gradually through Pinyon-juniper forest, descends a smooth, flowing section of the Sidewinder Trail, and rolls along the South Rim Trail to finish the loop. The climbs and descents are more moderate than many on the trails that start at the Horse Gulch Trailhead, making it a good option for those newer to mountain biking or from low altitude. This ride is also fun in reverse, but be careful of fast riders coming down Sidewinder when you ride up it. An alternative would be to ride up Crites Connect, down Yellow Brick Road and Sidewinder to Cowboy instead of riding up Sidewinder. Adding these trails makes the climbing more difficult and adds two miles. To add an exciting advanced descent to the loop, try the Skull Rock Trail, see option 1 below. Sections of this ride are not very pristine, as the trails pass by a gravel pit and gas wells, under power lines, by a re-vegetated mine, and above Highway 550/160.

Distance: 12.2 miles, all singletrack.
Time: 2 to 2 ½ hours
Difficulty: Intermediate
Aerobic Effort: Moderate
Elevation: Top: 7,186' **Gain:** 1,406'
Season: Mid-April through November. Closed in winter for wildlife, see page 23 for details.
Finding Route: Moderate. Most junctions are signed and the trails easy to follow, but there are many turns and some junctions are unmarked.
Map: Singetrack Maps Durango Trails
Location: Start at the Sale Barn Trailhead, three miles south of Durango. See page 32 for directions to the trailhead.

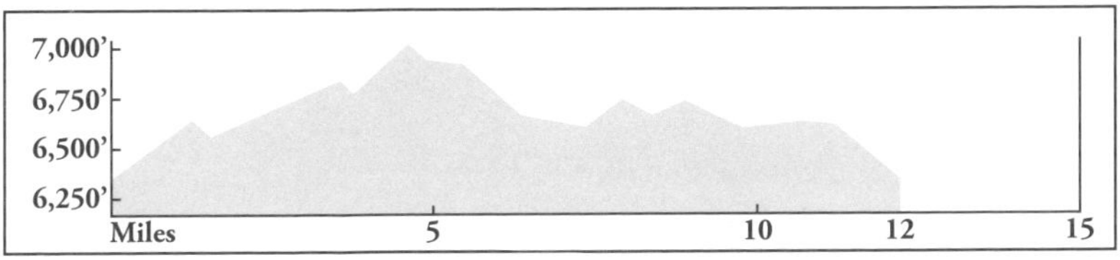

Mileage Log:

0.0 Start up the signed wide trail at the southern end of the parking area. The trail turns to singletrack and switchbacks up 8/10ths mile, and rolls along the mesa top.

SALE BARN, COWBOY, SIDEWINDER, SOUTH RIM, SKULL, BIG CANYON TRAILS

Horse Gulch/Telegraph Trail System/Grandview Ridge

1.7 Stay right at an unmarked Y intersection onto the Cowboy Trail. Left is the South Rim Trail (to ride the loop in reverse.)

2.2 Cross a gas well road and continue on singletrack.

3.3 Merge right onto a powerline road briefly, then turn left and continue on singletrack. Ride under the powerlines and descend to the next intersection.

3.6 At re-vegetated pipeline road, cross and turn right on singletrack on Cowboy.

3.9 Swing left on the more defined singletrack at the split. Turn left at the next intersection in less than 1/10th mile. Climb more steeply and be alert for riders coming down.

4.4 Turn left on Sidewinder and start downhill.

4.8 Pass the unmarked Skull Rock Trail on the left. This more advanced option leads to Big Canyon and South Rim Trails, see option 1, below.

5.5 Ride straight ahead onto the Carbon Junction Trail, passing Crites Connect on the right. Ride past a reclaimed mine, and descend a rocky section of trail.

6.1 Turn left at the signed Y intersection onto the South Rim Trail.

8.3 Pass Skull Rock Trail coming in on the left. Continue straight ahead to a several-way intersection under the powerline. Right and down is Big Canyon, a fun descent in an interesting little canyon. See option 2 below. The two trails to the left rejoin and climb Big Canyon. To continue on South Rim back to the Sale Barn Trailhead, ride straight ahead and climb to the rim.

9.5 Ride straight ahead at the unmarked intersection passing a less used trail.

10.5 Back to the unsigned Y intersection and the Sale Barn Trail. Turn right.

12.2 Back to the trailhead.

Option 1: Turn left on the Skull Rock Trail at mile 4.8 of the above description. Descend and ramble through an interesting draw, climb to a small ridge and descend steeply to the South Rim Trail. Turn left on South Rim to a signed junction of many trails (mile 8.3 above.) This is 2.2 miles shorter than the description above, more advanced with an expert section of descent, and more fun in my opinion.

Option 2: If you take Big Canyon at mile 8.3, descend 1.1 miles to the bottom. Turn left and follow the frontage road 6/10ths mile to the Sale Barn Trailhead.

Option 3: For a shorter ride, turn left on the South Rim Trail at mile 1.7, ride two miles to the Big Canyon Trail, turn left and head down Big Canyon 1.1 miles to the frontage road, and left 6/10ths mile to the Sale Barn Trailhead.

Animas River Trail | *Holly Annala*

Ned Overend at Overend Park | *Scott DW Smith*

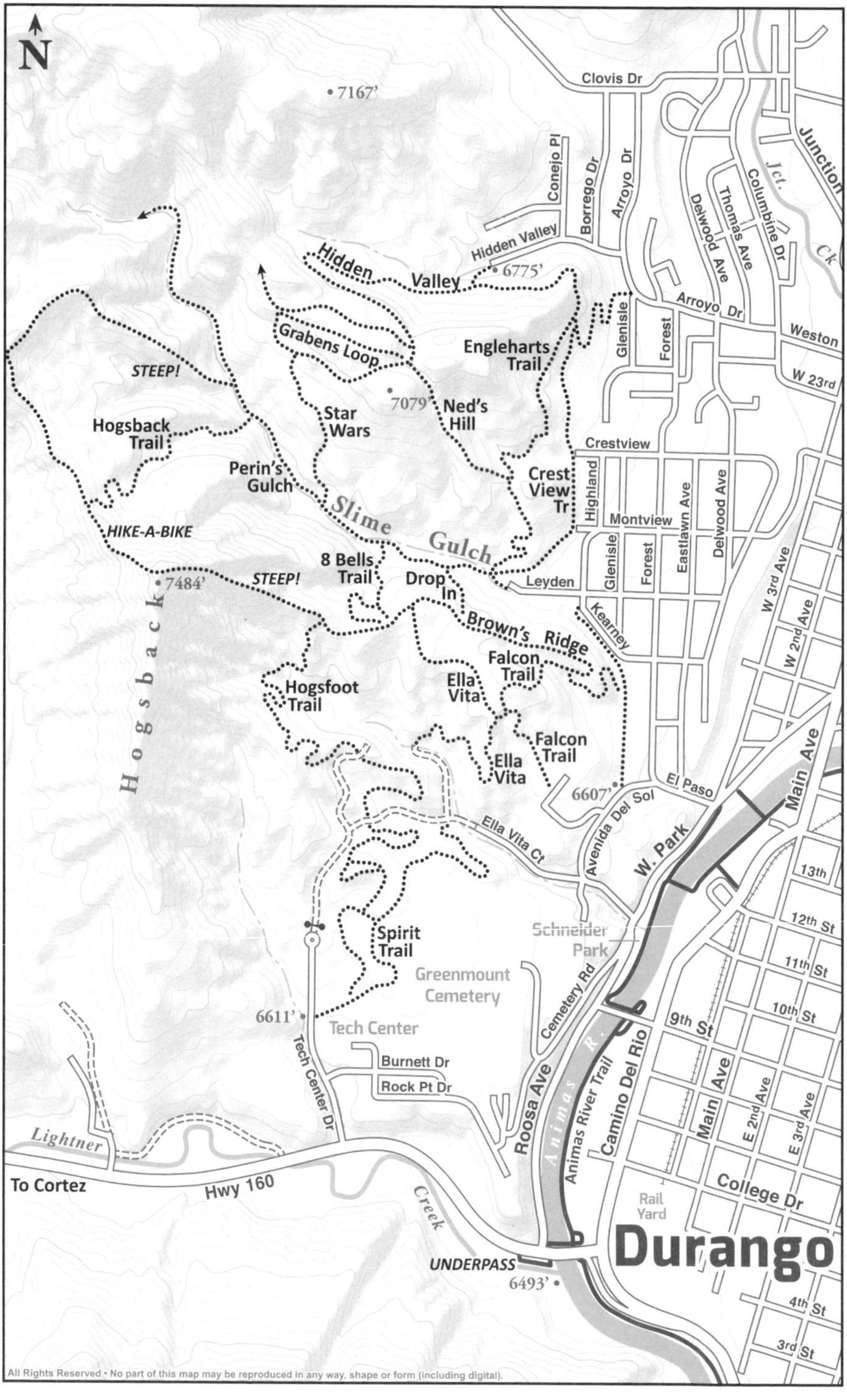
N
7167'
Clovis Dr
Conejo Pl
Borrego Dr
Arroyo Dr
Junction
Jct.
Ck
Columbine Dr
Thomas Ave
Delwood Ave
Hidden Valley
Hidden Valley
6775'
Arroyo Dr
Weston
W 23rd
Glenisle
Forest
Grabens Loop
Engleharts Trail
STEEP!
7079'
Ned's Hill
Star Wars
Hogsback Trail
Perin's Gulch
Crestview
Crest View Tr
Highland
Eastlawn Ave
Delwood Ave
Montview
Slime Gulch
HIKE-A-BIKE
8 Bells Trail
Drop In
Leyden
Glenisle
Forest
7484'
STEEP!
Kearney
W 3rd Ave
W 2nd Ave
Brown's Ridge
Falcon Trail
Ella Vita
Hogsfoot Trail
Hogsback
Falcon Trail
Ella Vita
6607'
El Paso
Main Ave
Avenida Del Sol
Ella Vita Ct
W. Park
13th
12th St
Spirit Trail
Schneider Park
11th St
Greenmount Cemetery
10th St
Cemetery Rd
6611'
Tech Center
9th St
Tech Center Dr
Burnett Dr
Rock Pt Dr
Roosa Ave
Animas R.
Animas River Trail
Camino Del Rio
Main Ave
E 2nd Ave
E 3rd Ave
Lightner
To Cortez
Hwy 160
Creek
College Dr
Rail Yard
Durango
UNDERPASS
6493'
4th St
3rd St

★★★★☆

OVEREND MOUNTAIN PARK (AKA TEST TRACKS)

Description: Overend Mountain Park is a fun and flowy, non-motorized, all singletrack area to ride, located adjacent to Durango. This local favorite has interesting geography and a lot of character. There are lots of ways to connect the loops once you get to know your way around, and there are several access points to the trail system. The trails are forested with Pinyon-juniper, Ponderosa Pine, and even fir trees, and are slightly more shady and cool than the Telegraph/Horse Gulch Trail System. Route finding is a challenge the first time you ride here, but if you lose your way you will end in town. It can be very hot in the summer. There are lots of hikers in the area, be courteous. Below is a list of trailheads, and a tour of the best trails. The two main trailheads are located at the tops of Avenida Del Sol and Leyden Street and have very limited parking, so it is easier to get to them on your bike. If you are driving to town, park at Schneider Park on the corner of Roosa Avenue and 9th Street, or Santa Rita Park on Hwy 550 and ride to the trailhead. Trails 2000 helped raise funds to purchase land for the park, and continues to build, sign and maintain the trails in Overand Park.

TRAILHEADS:

Leydon Street Trailhead: Best access to the trails. At the top of Leydon Street, west from Eastlawn Avenue and Crestview Drive.

Avenida del Sol: Located uphill from Schneider Park on Ella Vita Court, or uphill on El Paso and left on Avenida del Sol, then right on Ella Vita to the top.

Arroyo Drive: At the top of Arroyo Drive (and North Glenisle) is a singletrack to the Hidden Valley Trail. Go by the fence and switchback steeply up 3/10ths mile.

Tech Center: Located 2/10ths mile up Tech Center Drive, on the right. This is a good connector to Twin Buttes (1.3 miles from here.) Or continue up Tech Center Drive 7/10ths mile to access the Spirit Trail, on the right.

TRIPLE CROWN LOOP:
Hidden Valley, Star Wars, Hogs Back, 8 Bells and Spirit Trails

Description: The loop incorporates many of the best trails in the park into a two hour ride. It has two moderate climbs on the Hidden Valley and 8 Bells Trails, and one longer and at the top challenging climb on Hogsback. Star Wars is a fun banked descent. The Spirit Trail descent is fast and has great flow. Since the loops are interconnected, it is easy to skip the advanced Star Wars descent or the expert Hogsback loop for an easier ride. See option below. This loop and most of the trails in the area are good in either direction, with the exception of the expert section on Hogsback, which is only rideable in a clockwise direction from Perin's Gulch; and Star Wars, Ned's Hill and Falcon, which are fun downhill only.

Distance: 6.7 miles point to point, all singletrack. Connect the loop with one mile of paved road, the Ella Vita singletrack, or see directions below for an alternative singletrack connector.

OVEREND MOUNTAIN PARK (AKA TEST TRACKS)

Time: 1 ½ to 2 hours.

Difficulty: Advanced intermediate with expert sections. See option below for an intermediate loop.

Aerobic Effort: Moderate, moderately high with the Hogsback section.

Elevation: Top: 7,024' **Gain:** 1,465'

Season: Late April through November or mid-December

Finding Route: Moderately difficult, but hard to get lost. Signed with maps at intersections (thanks to Trails 2000 and the City of Durango), but there are many turns and many spur trails with no signs. Read over the directions before your ride to plot your route, and a quick glance at the trail signs should keep you rolling.

Map: Singletrack Maps Durango Trails, Trails 2000 Overend Park Map

Location: This loop starts at the Leydon Street Trailhead. Ride city streets to the trailhead, or ride from Schneider Park to the Leydon Street Trailhead on singletrack: Ride north out of the parking lot on the bike path, straight past the bridge and up past the skate park. Ride straight across the intersection of Roosa and West Park, and up the steep hill on El Paso Street. Continue up and left onto Avenida del Sol. Just past a dry canal and fence, turn right on a singletrack, starting in a private drive. Stay left along the bank and ride straight ahead, past two spurs on the left. Cross the canal to the right and swing left on the opposite bank. Descend onto the sidewalk to Leyden Street. Turn left and uphill to the trailhead at the top of the street.

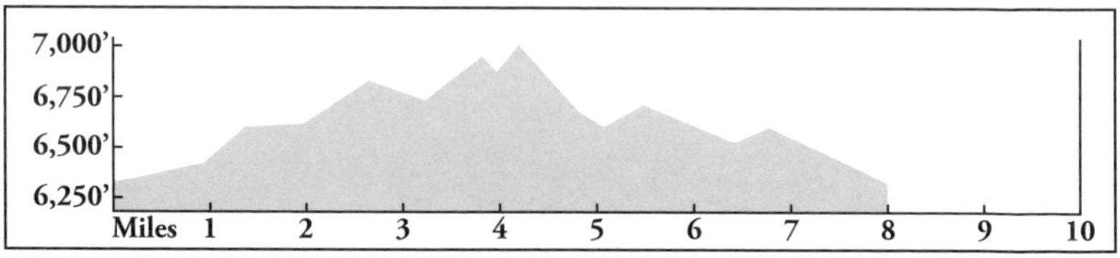

Mileage Log from Leydon Street Trailhead:

0.0 Ride on the wide path, turn right behind the homes (straight ahead is Perin's Gulch) and toward a signed fork. Turn left and climb Ned's Hill.

0.2 Top out in a flat area. Turn left and descend, and turn right at the next intersection before the trail climbs again, on Englehardt's.

0.6 Merge left onto the Hidden Valley Trail, and contour. Cross a spur in 2/10ths mile.

0.9 Stay left at an unmarked junction. Wind through the forest and climb.

1.4 Turn right at a signed intersection and climb a short distance, and descend. (Left is Ned's Hill.) Pass spur trail on the left.

1.7 Roll through a wide area and pass a trail to the right. Ride over the berm ahead and start steeply down Star Wars (no sign), passing another trail to the left on top of the berm (part of the Graben's Loop.) Pass the Graben's Loop again on the left in 1/10th mile and continue down and right.

OVEREND MOUNTAIN PARK (AKA TEST TRACKS)

2.1 Reach an intersection with Perin's Gulch. Turn right to add on Hogsback. (To skip the Hogsback loop, turn left and descend for 2/10ths mile to the next signed intersection, and turn right and continue the loop, up 8 Bells. See mile 4.0, below. Or ride an out and back to the viewpoint on Hogsback, avoiding the more difficult loop section.)

2.3 At the next signed intersection turn left, ride over a bridge and climb.

2.8 Turn right on the ridge. Descend and climb on exposed trail to a higher ridge and to a steep, loose descent.

3.6 Stay right and merge onto Perin's Gulch. Cross a bridge and pass the uphill from 2.3 on the right. In 2/10ths mile, stay right, passing Star Wars.

4.0 Pass a steep right, then turn right at the next signed intersection and climb 8 Bells. In 1/10th mile, stay right and climb on the main trail.

4.3 Turn right at the signed intersection on Brown's Ridge. (To cut the ride shorter, turn left on Brown's Ridge, then right in 1/10th mile on Ella Vita. Next turn left on Falcon Trail to Leydon Street, or turn right on Ella Vita to Avenida del Sol.) Climb and descend and stay left at the next three intersections with Hogsback. Contour around a big re-vegetated area.

5.1 Ride straight across a road and look for the unsigned Spirit Trail. In 3/10ths mile, cross another road.

5.7 After a climb, the singletrack splits. Turn right or left as the trails join shortly. Continue downhill in 1/10th mile.

5.9 Turn sharp left before dirt piles and the city storage. Right is the Tech Center Trail.

6.3 End at a road. Go straight down Ella Vita Court to Schneider Park. (Or, to keep riding turn left and cross the dirt road and climb a doubletrack to Ella Vita. Turn right and contour and climb 4/10ths mile and turn left to climb to Brown's Ridge. Turn left, then right to return on 8 Bells and Perin's Gulch.)

6.7 End of Avenida del Sol. Schneider Park is straight ahead. Turn right on Roosa Avenue, and carefully left at the park entrance to your vehicle.

Intermediate loop option: Go straight from the Leydon Street trailhead 2/10ths mile up Perin's Gulch to 8 Bells and turn left. Continue the loop from here (mile 4.0 above.) This cuts off the advanced sections of the ride.

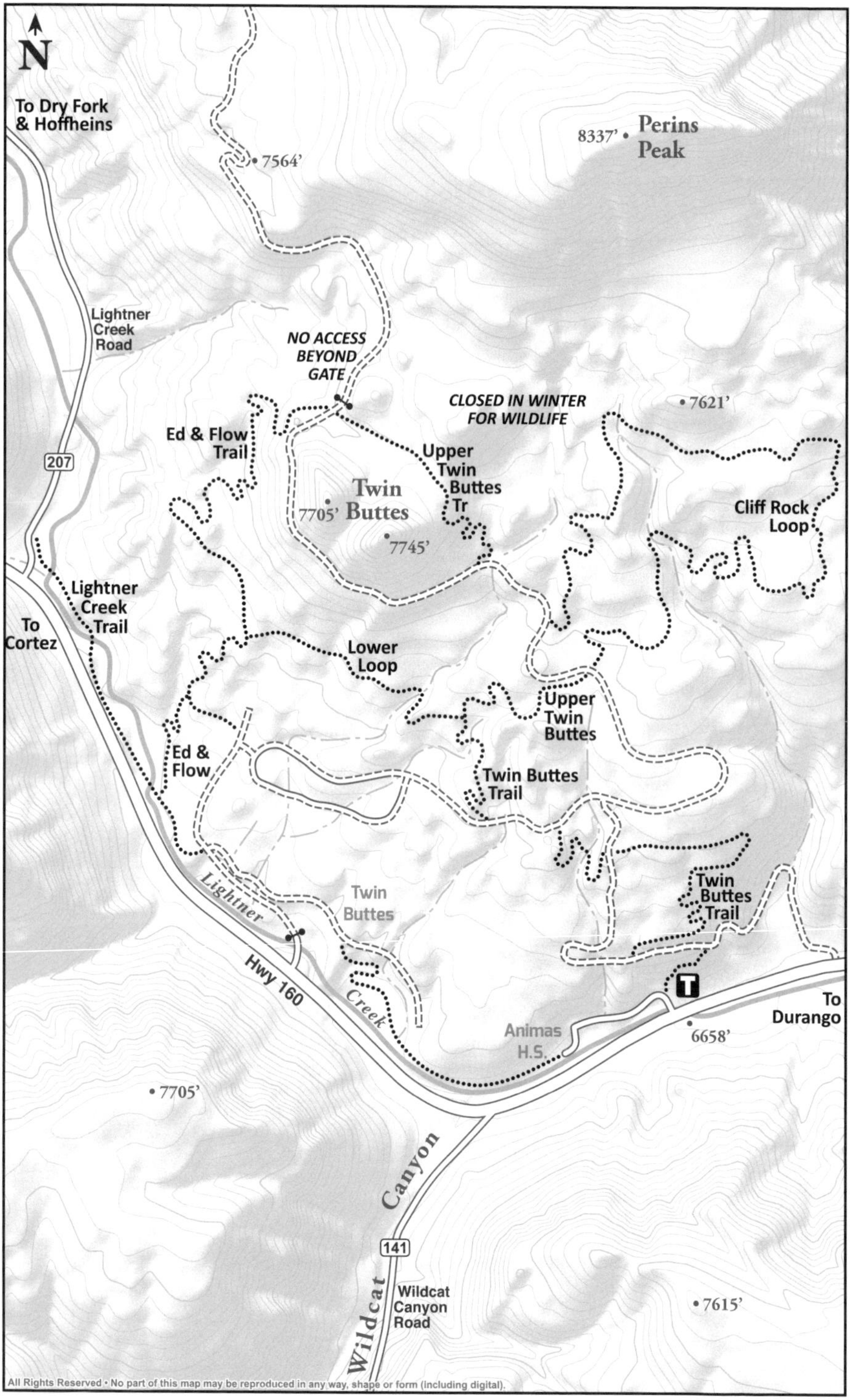
N
To Dry Fork & Hoffheins
Perins Peak
8337'
7564'
Lightner Creek Road
207
NO ACCESS BEYOND GATE
CLOSED IN WINTER FOR WILDLIFE
7621'
Ed & Flow Trail
Upper Twin Buttes Tr
Twin Buttes
7705'
7745'
Cliff Rock Loop
Lightner Creek Trail
To Cortez
Lower Loop
Upper Twin Buttes
Ed & Flow
Twin Buttes Trail
Twin Buttes Trail
Lightner
Twin Buttes
Hwy 160
Creek
To Durango
6658'
Animas H.S.
7705'
Canyon
141
Wildcat Canyon Road
Wildcat
7615'

TWIN BUTTES

Description: Twin Buttes is a newer flow trail system 1 ½ miles west of downtown Durango. There are several moderate and fun trails to link up a short or medium length loop. It is located where the old classic Perin's Peak Loop was, but now there is a lot more singletrack. The uphill trail winds back and forth through Pinyon-juniper forest and into the Ponderosa Pines on its way to the base of Perin's Peak. The shorter loop is moderate and has no steep sections, and begins downhill at mile 1.8. The longer loop (including Cliffrock and Upper Twin Buttes) has great views and a few challenging switchbacks on the way to the top, but otherwise moderate climbs. The descent from Upper Twin Buttes starts with fast trail and a few rough switchbacks. Next, Ed and Flo is smooth, with many banked swoops and a few optional features that will make you giggle. Ride back on the short loop's descent for more downhill the way you came up, or on the mostly gradual Lightner Creek Trail. This trail is also a great way to ride back from the Colorado Trail/Dry Fork Loop. See page 63. The Twin Buttes area will have intermittent construction closures on the lower trails until 2016 while the infrastructure of the subdivision is finished. Follow temporary signs to access the trails. In the future look for new trail sections and alignments. The loops are recommended counter clockwise.

Distance: Short loop: 4 miles **Long loop:** 9 miles, 8 miles singletrack, 1 mile doubletrack
Time: 1 to 2 ½ hours, depending on loop.
Difficulty: Short loop: Intermediate
Long loop: Advanced intermediate, with a few short expert sections.
Aerobic Effort: Short Loop: Moderate **Long loop:** Moderately High
Elevation: Short loop: Top: 7,075' **Gain:** 350'
Long loop: Top: 7,467' **Gain:** 1,479'
Season: May through November. The upper trails are closed in winter for wildlife, see page 23 for details.
Finding Route: Easy to moderate. The route flows easily and a few small signs mark the way, but one important turn at mile 1.3 has no sign. Construction closures will change the route often until 2016/2017.
Map: Singletrack Maps Durango Trails

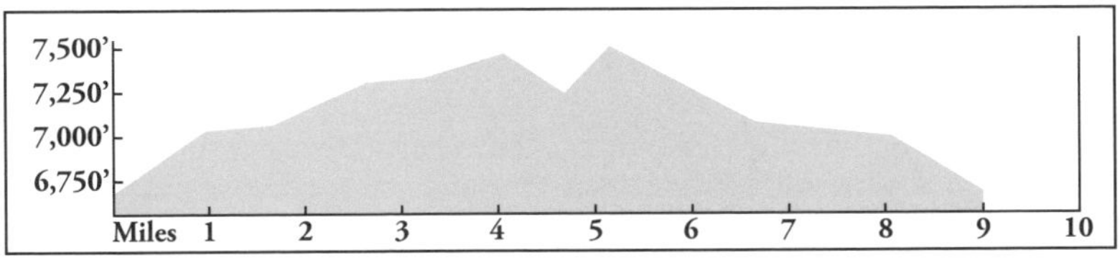

Location: The Twin Buttes Trailhead is located 1.6 miles west of Durango on Hwy 160 (toward Cortez,) just past the Giant Station. Ride out on the highway shoulder (access from Roosa Avenue and turn right; ride under the Hwy 160 bridge to Roosa on the way back) or there is a parking area at the trailhead. Another option is to ride a loop in Overend Mountain Park to the Tech Center Trail (exit by the city storage area.) Go left and ride down Tech Center Drive 2/10ths mile, right on Hwy 160 and ride 1.1 miles to the Twin Buttes Trailhead.

Mileage Log:

0.0 Start riding up the switchbacks from the trailhead.

0.2 Turn left onto the doubletrack and continue climbing.

0.3 Turn right onto the singletrack.

1.1 Cross a doubletrack.

1.3 Turn left on a wide path through a narrow gully (right quickly ends on a road.) In less than 1/10th mile, turn right on a doubletrack, and then again right on singletrack in 1/10th mile.

1.8 Junction. Stay right for the longer loop. Left is a shorter version, see option below.

2.1 Cross another doubletrack. Continue climbing.

3.5 Lookout on the right. Contour left across the hillside, climb, and descend a steep doubletrack.

4.6 Merge right onto a road. Left would bypass one of the best parts of the loop.

4.7 Turn right on the singletrack with a sign, climb steeply and switchback up.

5.1 Reach the top, with great views of the La Plata Mountains. Start a fast downhill through meadow and Ponderosa forest behind the Twin Buttes.

5.4 Cross a road with a gate to the right, and go down and left onto another road.

5.6 Turn left onto the singletrack, then wind down, on and off road, following the singletrack.

6.6 At the junction you have two choices: Turn left to ride back and join the uphill trail in ½ mile, then turn right and head back the way you came up, and back to the trailhead at 9.1 miles. Be careful of uphill riders. Or continue straight downhill for more fun flow.

6.9 Stay right at the junction.

7.1 Turn left on the Lightner Creek Trail, following signs and new trails.

7.5 Pass a singletrack on the left.

9.0 Back to the trailhead.

Option: For the shorter version, turn left at mile 1.8. In ½ mile turn left and descend ½ mile, and go left on the Lightner Creek Trail to ride back to the trailhead.

Twin Buttes | *Holly Annala*

The Rim Trail | *Scott DW Smith*

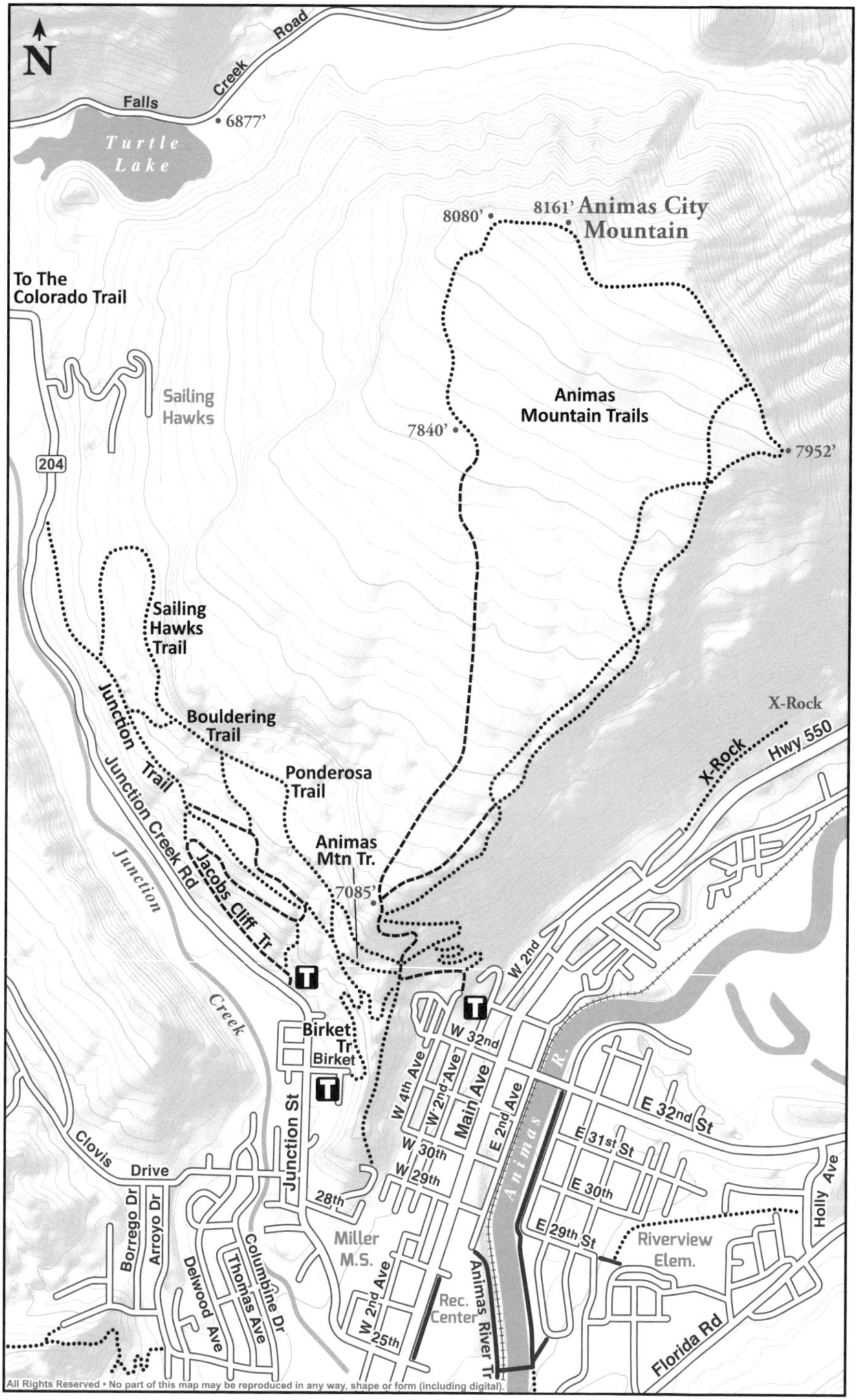
N
Falls Creek Road
6877'
Turtle Lake
8080'
8161' Animas City Mountain
To The Colorado Trail
Sailing Hawks
204
Animas Mountain Trails
7840'
7952'
Sailing Hawks Trail
Junction Trail
Bouldering Trail
Ponderosa Trail
Animas Mtn Tr.
Junction Creek Rd
Jacobs Cliff Tr
7085'
Junction
Creek
X-Rock
X-Rock
Hwy 550
W 2nd
Birket Tr
Birket
W 32nd
W 4th Ave
W 2nd Ave
Main Ave
E 2nd Ave
Animas R.
E 32nd St
E 31st St
E 30th
E 29th St
Clovis Drive
Junction St
W 30th
W 29th
28th
Borrego Dr
Arroyo Dr
Delwood Ave
Thomas Ave
Columbine Dr
Miller M.S.
W 2nd Ave
25th
Rec. Center
Animas River Tr
Animas
Riverview Elem.
Holly Ave
Florida Rd

★★☆☆☆

ANIMAS MOUNTAIN

Description: Animas Mountain is a short ride with a big climb, a great strength workout! At the top are amazing views of the Animas Valley, the La Plata Mountains, and Hidden Valley. I prefer the loop clockwise: up the southwest side, which has some smoother sections and is less of an uphill grind (it is an old road closed to motorized,) and down the singletrack, which is quite rocky in sections. Some prefer to ride Animas Mountain counterclockwise to enjoy the smoother, fast and wide descent. It is a popular hiking trail, be courteous and prepared to give other users the right of way. The climb can be very hot in the summer. For a longer ride, add on Sailing Hawks (Dalla Mountain Park,) see option 2 below. Animas Mountain Trails are closed to motorized, and are closed in the winter for wildlife, see page 23 for details.

Distance: 5 ½ to 6 mile loop, depending on which trails you descend. 4 miles singletrack and wide trail, and 2 miles doubletrack.
Time: 1 to 1 ½ hours
Difficulty: Expert
Aerobic Effort: High
Elevation: Top: 8,182' **Gain:** 1,618'
Season: Late April or May through November
Finding Route: Moderate, many junctions at the start of the ride; easy once you get past the first 7/10ths mile. Most junctions are signed with maps, thanks to Trails 2000 and the City of Durango.
Map: Singletrack Maps Durango Trails
Location: There are two trailheads. The first is on West 4th Avenue. To get here, take 32nd Street west (uphill) from North Main Avenue. Go to the top and turn right on West 4th to a parking area at the end. Ride north to this trailhead from downtown on West 2nd Avenue. The other access is from 25th Street/Junction Creek Road, 7/10ths mile from Main and right on Birket Drive. See option 1 below for details.

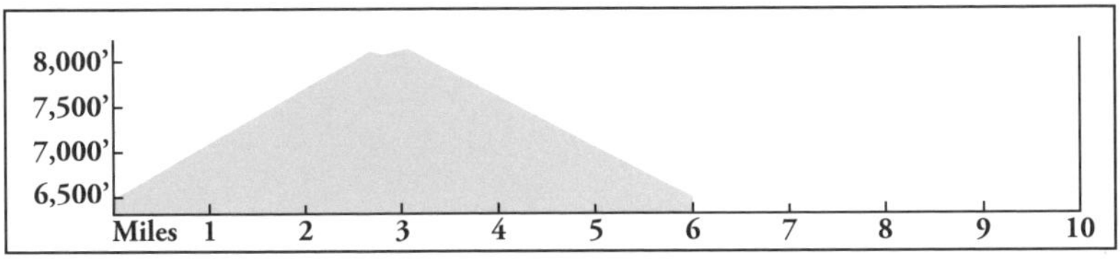

Mileage Log from West 4th Avenue:

0.0 Ride through the gate and up the road. In 200 ft, turn right at the signed start of a singletrack and climb gradual switchbacks. (Left is heinous, steep old road.)

0.3 Turn left at a signed fork in the singletrack. Right rejoins the route at mile 0.7, but left is the easier route.

0.4 Arrive in a wide area where several trails merge on the saddle. Turn right and uphill on the old road. (Left and up, and then right leads to Birket Drive, straight ahead is the Ponderosa Trail and Dalla Mountain Park.)

0.7 Continue straight ahead and up the old road, passing two signed singletracks to the right. Grind your way up several steeper rocky sections. At two miles the road levels and narrows to a singletrack.

2.5 Enjoy great views of the La Plata Mountains. Turn right at the sign and continue climbing on singletrack.

2.6 Turn right and continue up the ridge. Left is a viewpoint. Pass a couple more side trails to view points.

3.3 After starting down along the rim, pass a signed intersection. Stay left along the rim for great views and a wider, rocky trail. Or turn right and try the inner loop, which is a narrower and slightly less rocky but doesn't have the views. In the future some sections of these duplicate trails may be closed.

3.7 Stay left as the two trails rejoin. Or turn sharp right for the inner loop.

4.2 Turn left at the sign and begin a more technical, interesting section. Right turns into a doubletrack that goes to the intersection at 0.7 of the climb.

5.2 Turn left at a signed intersection, on narrower trail.

5.5 Turn left for challenging switchbacks.

5.8 Stay left and ride past the first intersection.

6.0 End at the trailhead.

Option 1: Ride up Birket Drive to the signed singletrack. Climb, and stay right as two trails turn left, one signed, one not. These go to Dalla Mountain Park. At the top, swing left and ride down into a wide area with trails heading off in all directions. This is the same junction as mile 0.4 above, but adds 2/10ths mile. Continue straight up the old road.

Option 2: To add on Dalla Mountain Park, turn right at 5.8 miles. Climb a little to the flat junction area (mile 0.4 above) and take Ponderosa, the signed singletrack under the power pole, and ride the Sailing Hawks loop. See page 59 for details.

★★★☆☆

PONDEROSA AND SAILING HAWKS TRAILS

Dalla Mountain Park

See map page 56

Description: Dalla Mountain Park is a unique system of trails located on the northwestern edge of Durango, next to the Animas Mountain Trails. The trails here wind around giant boulders and through Ponderosa Pine and Pinyon-juniper forest. All of the trails have technical sections, some quite long, but nothing extreme. Although challenging, the trails are all rideable by expert cross country riders with good technical skills. There are no beginner singletracks in Dalla Mountain Park. Ponderosa and Sailing Hawks are the best trails in the park for linking up a really fun and magical singletrack loop through the boulders, and ride best in a counter clockwise direction from the Birket Drive or Animas Mountain Trailheads. (If you start from the Dalla Trailhead and ride clockwise, riding uphill on The Junction Trail has some hike a bike, and the alternative, Jacob's Cliff, is wide logging road with little character.) The Dalla trails are a nice addition after riding Animas Mountain, or as a way to ride more singletrack on the way to the Colorado Trail or Log Chutes, see option below. All the trails are non-motorized.

Distance: 4 mile loop, all singletrack.
Time: 30 to 45 minutes
Difficulty: Expert
Aerobic Effort: Moderately high for short distances
Elevation: Top: 7,152' **Gain:** 658'
Season: Mid-April through November or mid-December
Finding Route: Moderately difficult but hard to get lost as all trails lead back to the trailhead or Junction Creek Road. The main intersections are signed with small maps, but several spur trails are not signed.
Map: Singletrack Maps Durango Trails
Location: Start at the Birket Drive Trailhead. Ride to the trailhead from West 2nd Avenue to 25th Street, avoiding Main Avenue. Turn left (west) and ride 7/10ths mile out 25th Street/ Junction Creek Road to Birket Drive, and turn right to the trailhead. If you drive, park at The Dalla Mountain Park Trailhead, 2/10ths mile past Birket, on the right. Ride back to the Birket trailhead. In the northern part of town, you can ride up from the Animas Mountain Trailhead on West 4th Avenue to mile 0.4, which is the same as 0.6 in this description, see page 57 for details.

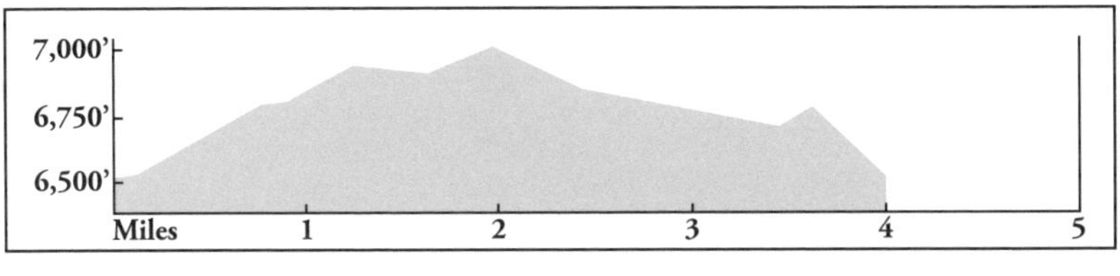

Mileage Log:

0.0 Ride up Birket Drive 1/10th mile to the signed trail. Climb and stay right as two trails turn left, one signed, one not.

0.6 Swing left and down into a wide area with trails heading off in all directions.

PONDEROSA AND SAILING HAWKS TRAILS
Dalla Mountain Park

Ride straight up to the powerline and turn left on the signed Ponderosa singletrack, next to a big power pole. Climb and ride through a few rocky areas, staying on the main trail as a spur turns right, and through a braided section.

1.3 Stay right at a signed intersection and start the really fun and technical part of the ride through giant boulders, on the Bouldering Trail.

1.5 Stay right at the signed intersection, now on Sailing Hawks. Climb and descend more technical sections, and curve back toward town, on easier terrain.

2.3 Ride straight ahead and pass a signed right, Junction Trail. (This exits to Junction Creek Road and on to the Colorado Trail (CT) and Log Chutes, see option below.) In 1/10th mile, merge right on a wider trail.

2.5 At the junction, stay right on a rocky doubletrack section. The trail descends, climbs, and then becomes narrow and technical.

2.7 The trail widens to a smooth flat road, Jacobs Cliff. In 1/10th mile, turn right at a junction in the road (Jacob's Cliff continues left and uphill) and immediately turn left on an unsigned singletrack. This is the continuation of Junction, and is technical.

3.2 Back to the road, Jacobs Cliff, and a signed intersection. Ride straight across to another signed singletrack, Animas Mountain. In 2/10ths mile stay left at a signed intersection. Right leads down to the Dalla Trailhead.

3.5 Back to the wide saddle. Turn right, go uphill a few feet and turn right to get back to Birket. (Or across, slightly left, and down to the Animas Mountain Trailhead.)

4.1 Back to the Birket Trailhead.

Option: To ride Sailing Hawks to the Colorado Trail (CT): Ride to mile 2.3, above, and turn right on the Junction Trail. Descend 3/10ths mile to Junction Creek Road and turn right. Ride out the paved road, staying left when the road forks in 7/10ths of a mile, and continue 6/10ths more to the CT Trailhead. To ride to Log Chutes, ride the first mile of the CT to a signed junction and turn right, then left on Junction Creek Road. Climb 1 mile on the road to Log Chutes, on the right.

Animas Mountain | *Holly Annala*

Jones Creek Trail | *Bill Koons*

COLORADO TRAIL, DRY FORK AND HOFFHEIN'S TRAILS

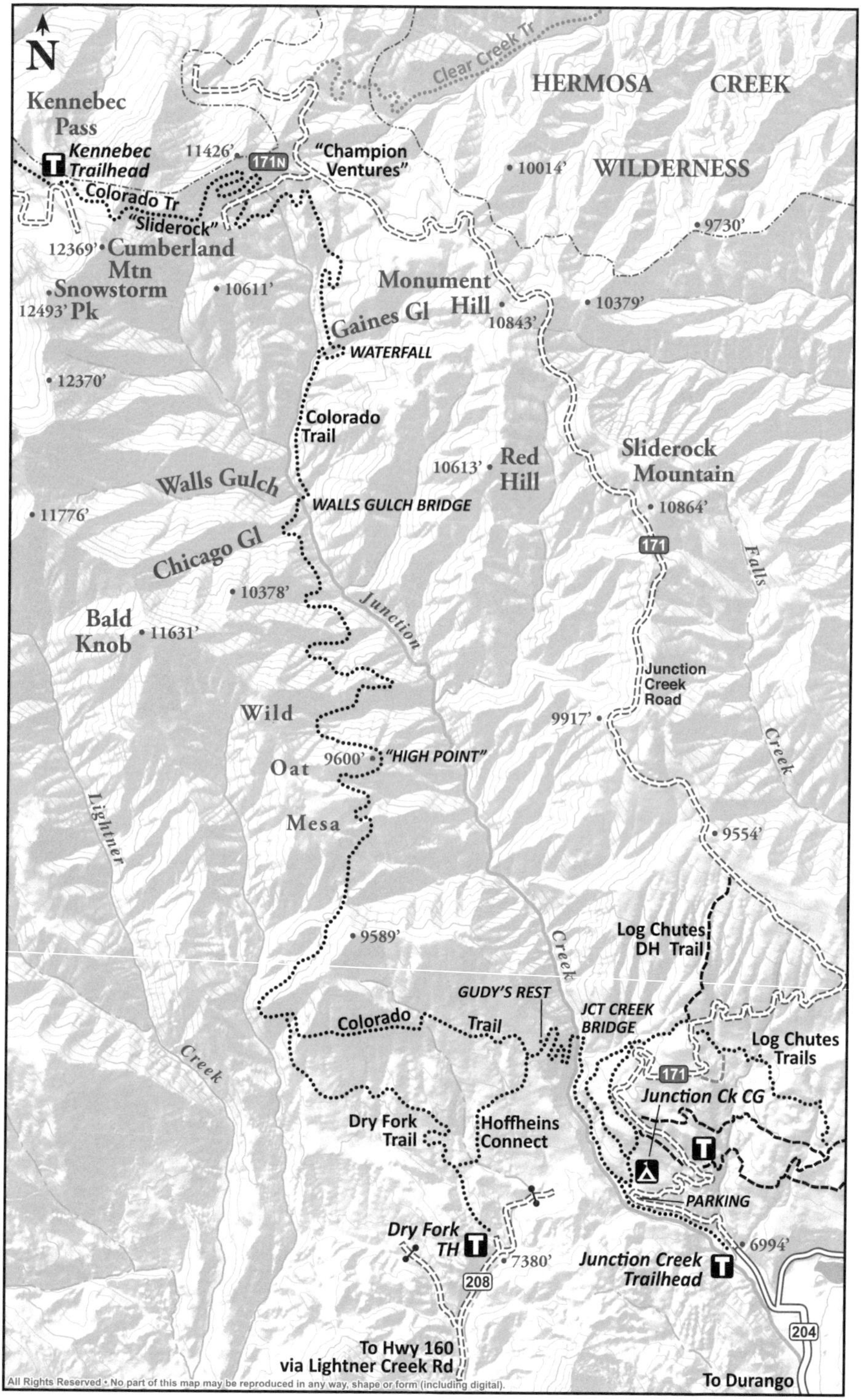

★★★★☆

COLORADO TRAIL, DRY FORK AND HOFFHEIN'S TRAILS

Description: The Colorado Trail (CT) from the Junction Creek Trailhead is a local and visitor favorite! Combined with Hoffhein's Connect and Dry Fork Trails it is a great all singletrack ride, just a few miles from town. The CT rides like higher altitude trails, but is dry a month earlier. The start of this loop is shady and climbs along the creek. The trail then crosses Junction Creek and switchbacks up onto a steep hillside with some moderate exposure, climbing steadily through Ponderosa Pine and fir-spruce forest to Gudy's Rest and Hoffhein's. Next it climbs steeply, with breaks, for one and a half miles, and contours to a long, fast descent on the Dry Fork Trail. To finish the loop, a steady climb on Hoffhein's rejoins the CT, to return to the trailhead. Several ride variations exist on these same trails. Climb to the High Point for a longer out and back addition to the ride, a great early season climb, see option 1 below. Ride the upper section of the loop from the Dry Fork Trailhead, for a shorter ride that skips the exposed sections over Junction Creek and the busiest part of the trail, see option 3. Ride from town to the trailhead on Junction Creek Road (a moderate spin) or on the Ponderosa and Sailing Hawks singletracks, see option 2. All the trails are good in reverse. Be aware of heavy pedestrian, dog, and biker use on the CT from the Junction Creek Trailhead to Gudy's Rest, especially on weekends and holidays.

Distance: 15 mile lollipop loop, 14 miles singletrack, 1 mile of doubletrack
Time: 2 ½ to 3 ½ hours
Difficulty: Advanced imtermediate from Dry Fork Trailhead (option 3). Expert from Junction Creek Trailhead.
Aerobic Effort: High
Elevation: Top: 8,472' **Gain:** 2,313'
Season: May through November
Finding Route: Fairly easy, only a few junctions and these are signed.
Map: Singletrack Maps Durango Trails
Location: Start at the Colorado Trailhead, 3.4 miles out 25th Street/Junction Creek Road/CR 204. Turn west off main onto 25th Street, wind up and through town. Stay left in 2.8 miles and continue 6/10ths mile farther to the CT Trailhead.

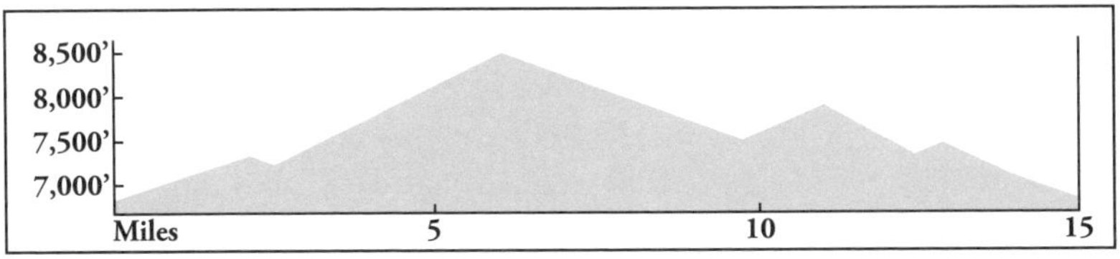

Mileage Log:

0.0 Ride out of the parking area on wide trail.

1.1 Ride straight ahead (left) and down, passing a trailhead on the right.

2.4 Turn left and cross the bridge over Junction Creek and begin climbing.

COLORADO TRAIL, DRY FORK AND HOFFHEIN'S TRAILS

3.8 Pass Gudy's Rest at a nice viewpoint. The trail levels.

4.0 Pass Hoffhein's Connection. Ride straight ahead (right) and begin climbing more steeply. Keep your eyes peeled for downhillers. (Hoffhein's is a fun descent, and skips the steeper climbing to Dry Fork, but doesn't return to Junction Creek. It ends on Dry Fork Road requiring some road riding back to town. See option 2, below.)

5.5 The trail levels and contours through Ponderosa forest.

6.2 Enjoy views of Silver Peak in the La Plata Mountains. Descend.

6.5 Turn left and descend on the Dry Fork Trail, an old doubletrack. Or turn right and continue to the High Point, see option 1 below.

7.4 Turn left onto singletrack.

9.6 Reach the signed bottom of Hoffhein's in a wide, flat area. Turn left, cross a drainage, and start a fairly steady climb. Right leads to Dry Fork Road.

10.8 Back to the CT, turn right and descend.

14.9 Back to the trailhead.

Option 1: Ride to the High Point: At mile 6.5, turn right and climb 3.3 miles to the High Point, or farther. This is a big 3,380' climb from town to 9,425' and generally opens by mid-May. Add one hour.

Option 2: Ride 3.4 miles to the CT from town on Junction Creek Road or on Ponderosa and Sailing Hawks singletracks (see page 59). Access 25th Street/Junction Creek Road from West 2nd Ave. To return to town from the ride, descend either Hoffhein's or Dry Fork Trails and turn right on Dry Fork Road. Stay left at a fork in the road in 8/10ths mile, then turn left on paved Lightner Creek Road after two miles. Ride one mile and take the highway or look for the Lightner Creek/Twin Buttes Trail on the left just before Hwy160. There is a no parking sign and gate, but no trail sign yet. Turn right on gravel before the bridge and ride under the highway, then straight ahead on Roosa Avenue to town.

Option 3: To start at the Dry Fork Trailhead: Drive 3 miles west of Durango on Hwy 160 toward Cortez, and turn right on Lightner Creek Road/CR 207. Drive one mile and turn right on Dry Fork Road/CR 208. In two miles, stay right at a fork, and in 8/10ths mile turn left to the signed trailhead. Ride up the Dry Fork Trail 4 miles, turn right and descend 2 ½ miles on the CT, turn right and down Hoffhein's one mile. Turn left and ride back to the trailhead. It is good in reverse, too. This is an 8.6 mile loop, 7.5 miles of singletrack and 1 mile of doubletrack, and climbs 1,700'. Keep your speed down especially near the trailhead; expect two-way traffic and horses.

★★★★☆

COLORADO TRAIL: SLIDEROCK TO DURANGO

See map page 62

Description: This is a fantastic big ride starting at the Junction Creek Trailhead and climbing nearly to Kennebec Pass, and mostly descending 18 miles on amazing Colorado Trail (CT) singletrack. If you are up for the climbing, it is worth the effort, as the Colorado Trail is one of the best trail rides in the area. Start from Durango with a 2-3 hour ride on Junction Creek Road, climbing moderately a good portion of the way to Monument Hill, with several steeper sections of climbing, and a couple descents for a break. Generally traffic is moderate, but it can be a busy and dusty road on weekends, so get an early start to avoid the traffic. The trail descends steeply from the road with several technical sections, and follows the creek down through wilderness-like terrain in spruce and fir forest. Cross the creek and climb a big mile-long hill out of the creek, and continue to roll the mostly smooth trail in and out of side creeks, contouring and climbing to the high point. From here enjoy miles of great descent. As you get to Dry Fork and Gudy's Rest, expect to see other riders and hikers, even some horseback riders on the fast trail. Weekends can be very busy on the trail. Keep your speed in control, especially around the blind corners. A shuttle to the upper trailhead (mile 18.3) is possible with a high clearance vehicle but takes over an hour to drive to. A 14 mile shuttle up La Plata Canyon from Hesperus to Kennebec Pass is possible, but it has some very difficult 4WD sections. If you don't have high clearance and 4WD, drop riders before the road starts climbing steeply. This adds 9 miles of forest road riding, some of it steep, loose and difficult, to the CT trailhead on Kennebec Pass. Call Hermosa Tours for shuttle information, 877-765-5682. The views and summer flowers up here are spectacular.

Distance: 35.5 mile loop, 17.2 miles of singletrack and 18.3 miles of dirt road; or 17.2 miles singletrack with a shuttle.
Time: 4 ½ - 6 ½ hours, 2 ½ - 4 hours with a shuttle.
Difficulty: Expert
Aerobic Effort: Strenuous
Elevation: Top: 10,450' **Loop: Gain:** 5,811' **With a shuttle: Gain:** 2,451'
Loss: 5,620'
Season: Late May through September or October
Finding Route: Fairly easy, signed and only a few turns.
Map: Singletrack Maps Durango Trails or Latitude 40 Durango Map
Location: Start at the Colorado Trailhead on Junction Creek, 3.4 miles out Junction Creek Road/CR 204. Turn west off main onto 25th Street, wind up and through town. Stay left in 2.8 miles, and continue 6/10ths mile farther to the CT Trailhead.

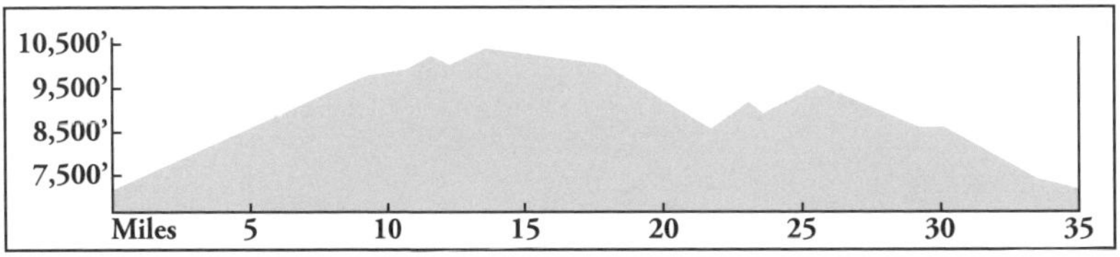

COLORADO TRAIL: SLIDEROCK TO DURANGO

Mileage Log:

0.0 Turn left out of the parking area and ride uphill on dirt Junction Creek Road, FS 171. The road starts out steeply with some washboards, but often is smoother up higher. Switchback past a second CT trailhead and campground on the left.

6.9 Pass the Animas Lookout to the right. Climb steadily. The road narrows. Descend and enjoy the break and views of the La Plata Mountains to the west. Climb again.

15.4 Pass a rocky and steep spur to the left, stay right and climb. Wind around with views to the north of the Needle Mountains. Descend in the dark forest, and climb a little more.

17.5 Turn left on Champion Ventures Road, at a junction in the road in a big flat area. Right leads to the Clear Creek Trailhead. Contour, descend gradually, and climb a little more.

18.3 (approx. mileage) Arrive at the Colorado Trail. Turn left and descend, climb a bit, and start an exciting and partly technical descent down into Fasbinder Gulch.

22.7 Cross a bridge over Junction Creek and start a big climb with a few breaks, and some fun, contouring and shady trail riding through tall forest.

26.6 High Point! Start a fast and smooth downhill.

29.9 After a rocky descent, turn left on the signed Colorado Trail. Dry Fork goes straight ahead. Climb a little, contour and start a fast descent. Expect other users from here on down, keep your speed in control through brushy corners.

32.5 Stay left and pass Hoffhein's Connect Trail. Pass Gudy's Rest and switchback down to cross Junction Creek in the canyon bottom. Turn right and downstream.

34.4 Stay right on the singletrack.

35.5 End at the trailhead.

Colorado Trail/Sliderock | *Dodson Harper*

Colorado Trail/Dry Fork | *Dodson Harper*

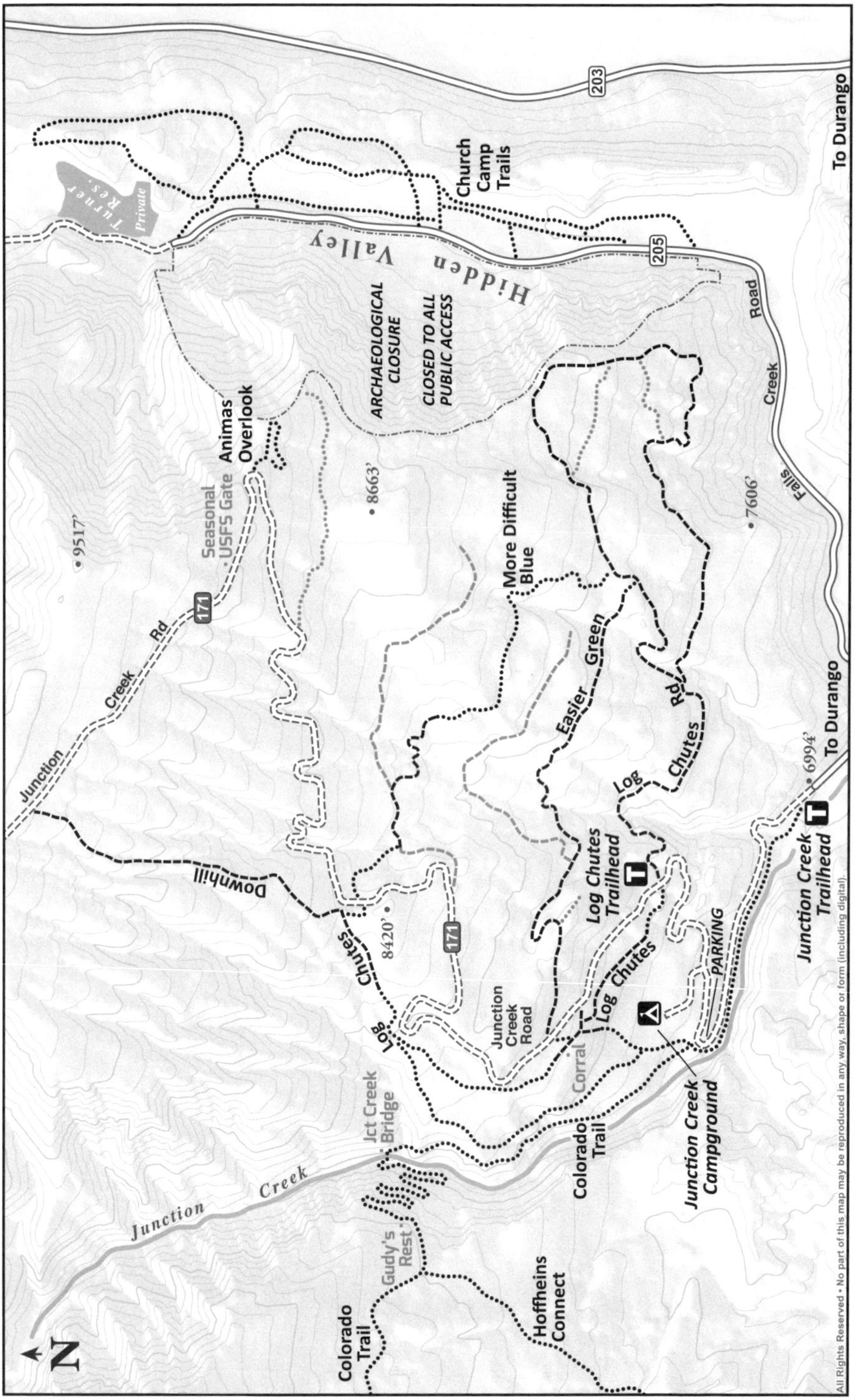
N
Turner Res.
Private
Church Camp Trails
203
Hidden Valley
205
To Durango
ARCHAEOLOGICAL CLOSURE
CLOSED TO ALL PUBLIC ACCESS
Animas Overlook
Seasonal USFS Gate
9517'
Junction Creek Rd
171
8663'
More Difficult Blue
Easier Green
Falls Creek Road
7606'
Log Chutes Rd
To Durango
6994'
Junction Creek Trailhead
Log Chutes Trailhead
Downhill
Log Chutes
8420'
171
Junction Creek Road
PARKING
Log Chutes
Corral
Junction Creek Campground
Jct Creek Bridge
Junction Creek
Colorado Trail
Gudy's Rest
Hoffheins Connect
Colorado Trail
All Rights Reserved • No part of this map may be reproduced in any way, shape or form (including digital).

★★☆☆☆

LOG CHUTES

Description: Log Chutes is a quiet area of trails in the Ponderosa Pine forest, located near the Colorado Trail on Junction Creek Road, 4 ½ miles from Durango. Most of the trails are on old logging roads that are in places narrowing to singletrack, with a few connecters that are true singletrack. Log Chutes has great views, solitude, and is a fun and pleasant ride, but some of the forest here is still recovering from logging activity and not pristine. The upper Log Chutes "blue" or moderate trail is narrow, fun and in places technical on the descent. The lower trail (left at mile 1.7 on the "green" or "easiest" option) is moderate doubletrack; a good trail for folks not used to narrow singletrack. There is an approved downhill trail to the right of the cross country downhill, which is currently not a system trail and not open to mountain biking. Improvements and enhancements are planned in 2015/2016. To get to the downhill trail when it is opened (check with the Forest Service, 970-247-4874) drive or ride 8.2 miles past the CT trailhead on Junction Creek Road to a closed old road on the left, marked with a carsonite brown flexible sign. An alternate start to the descent is 4.8 miles up on the left, or mile 4 of the description below. The end of the new downhill trail will be to the right of the campground. It is slightly cooler at Log Chutes than Horse Gulch or Overend Park, but it can still be hot in the summer.

Distance: Advanced Intermediate Blue Loop: 6.2 mile loop.
Intermediate Green Loop: 4.9 miles. Mostly old logging roads, some sections are narrowing to singletrack.
Time: 1 to 2 ½ hours, depending on route.
Difficulty: Easy intermediate green loop, intermediate with some short expert sections on the blue loop. Proposed downhill trail will likely be expert.
Aerobic Effort: Moderate on the green "easiest" loop, moderately high for short sections on the blue loop.
Elevation: Top: 8,408' **Gain:** 1,074'
Season: May through October
Finding Route: Moderate. Most junctions are signed. A few junctions are overgrown.
Map: Singletrack Maps Durango Trails
Location: From downtown Durango, turn left (west) on 25th Street/Junction Creek Road. Stay left at a fork in the county road at mile 2.8 and drive past the Colorado Trailhead at mile 3.4. Continue 1.1 miles farther up the dirt road and turn right at the signed trailhead. See Sailing Hawks page 59, option, to ride singletrack on the way to the trailhead.

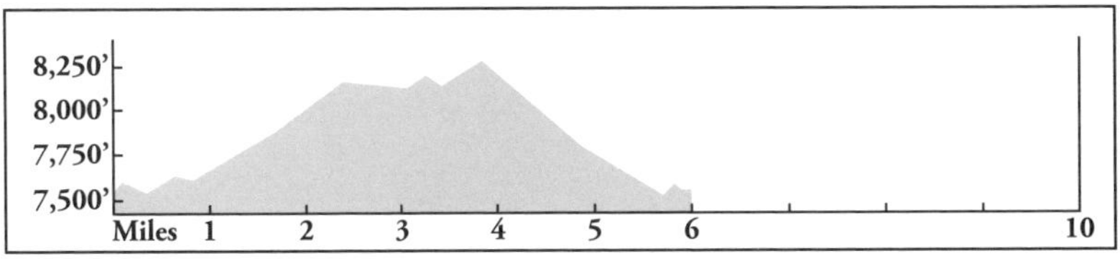

LOG CHUTES

Mileage Log:

0.0 From the parking area climb the old logging road east and through a gate. The road descends, climbs some, and contours.

1.1 At the first major road junction, turn left and climb. There is a gate and small "easiest" sign here.

1.7 Pass a signed "easiest" singletrack on the left and ride to the next left rated blue and "more difficult." (Or, take the lower "easiest" trail if you enjoy more moderate terrain. It soon turns to gradual logging road. This trail rejoins the description at mile 5.1.) Turn left and climb for almost a mile through logging debris and some rocks. Next, descend and contour.

3.3 Merge left and down on a wider doubletrack.

3.6 Turn right onto signed singletrack. This section is narrow and fun.

4.0 Cross Junction Creek Road, and ride almost straight across onto a difficult to see trail in the bushes. As you get a bit farther there is a sign and the trail widens to doubletrack.

4.1 Arrive at a junction. Turn left on an old road and descend steeply. This is where the downhill route comes in. Right away the trail splits, stay left on old doubletrack. The two trails merge quickly.

4.6 Nice viewpoint. In 1/10th mile the trail splits again, go left on somewhat technical singletrack. Right is more downhill with berms and not a system trail, be aware of unfinished sections and hazards.

5.1 Back to doubletrack by a big wood corral. Pass a singletrack on the left (the "easiest" loop coming in.)

5.5 Turn left at a fork in the doubletrack on the edge of a hill, to the trailhead. (Straight leads to Junction Creek Campground.) Turn right almost immediately, which starts narrow but turns into a rough old road. Next contour and follow singletrack on old road.

6.0 Turn left onto a singletrack and climb, cross Junction Creek Road onto singletrack.

6.2 Back to the trailhead.

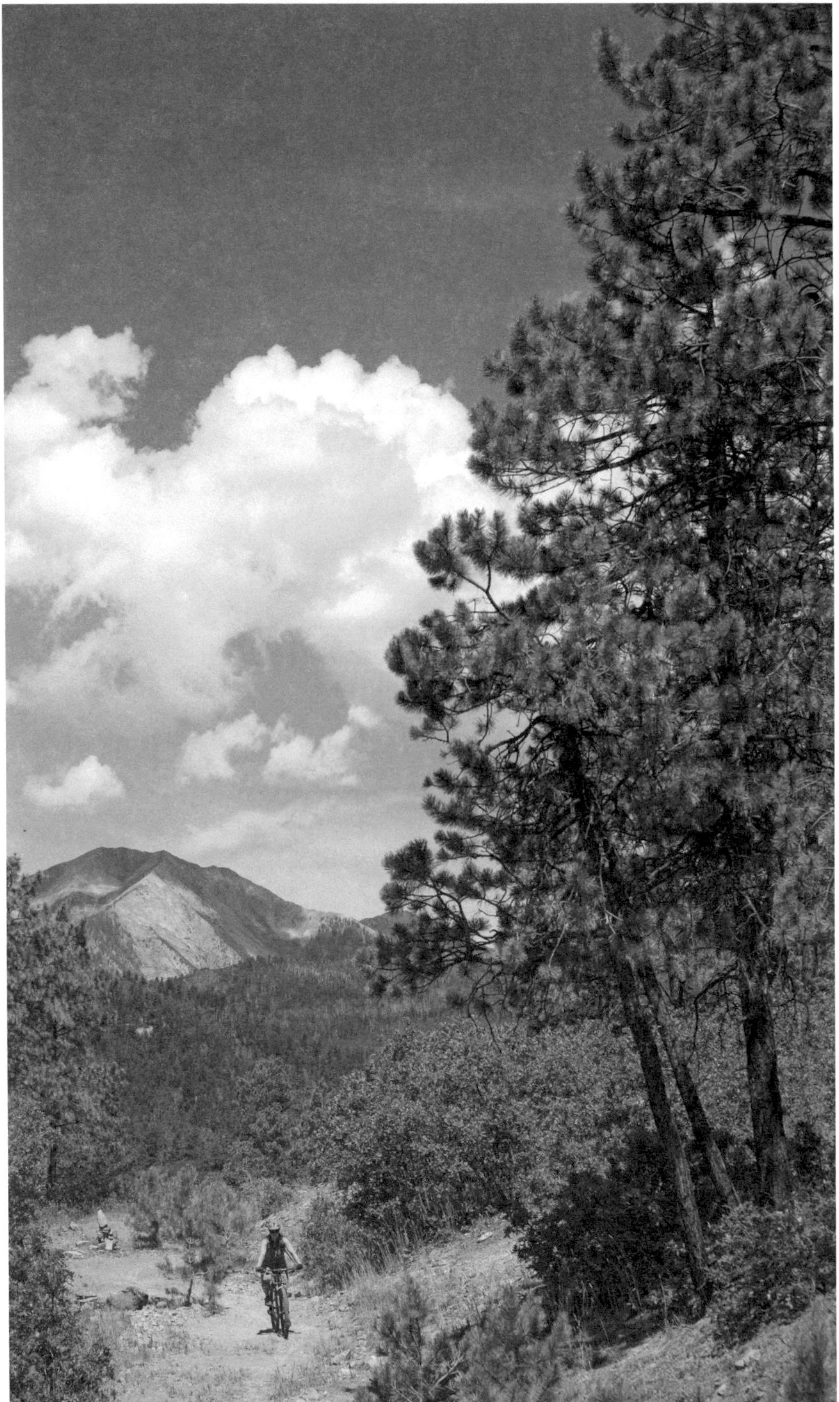

Log Chutes | *Scott DW Smith*

MISSIONARY RIDGE, HAFLIN AND STEVEN'S CREEK TRAILS

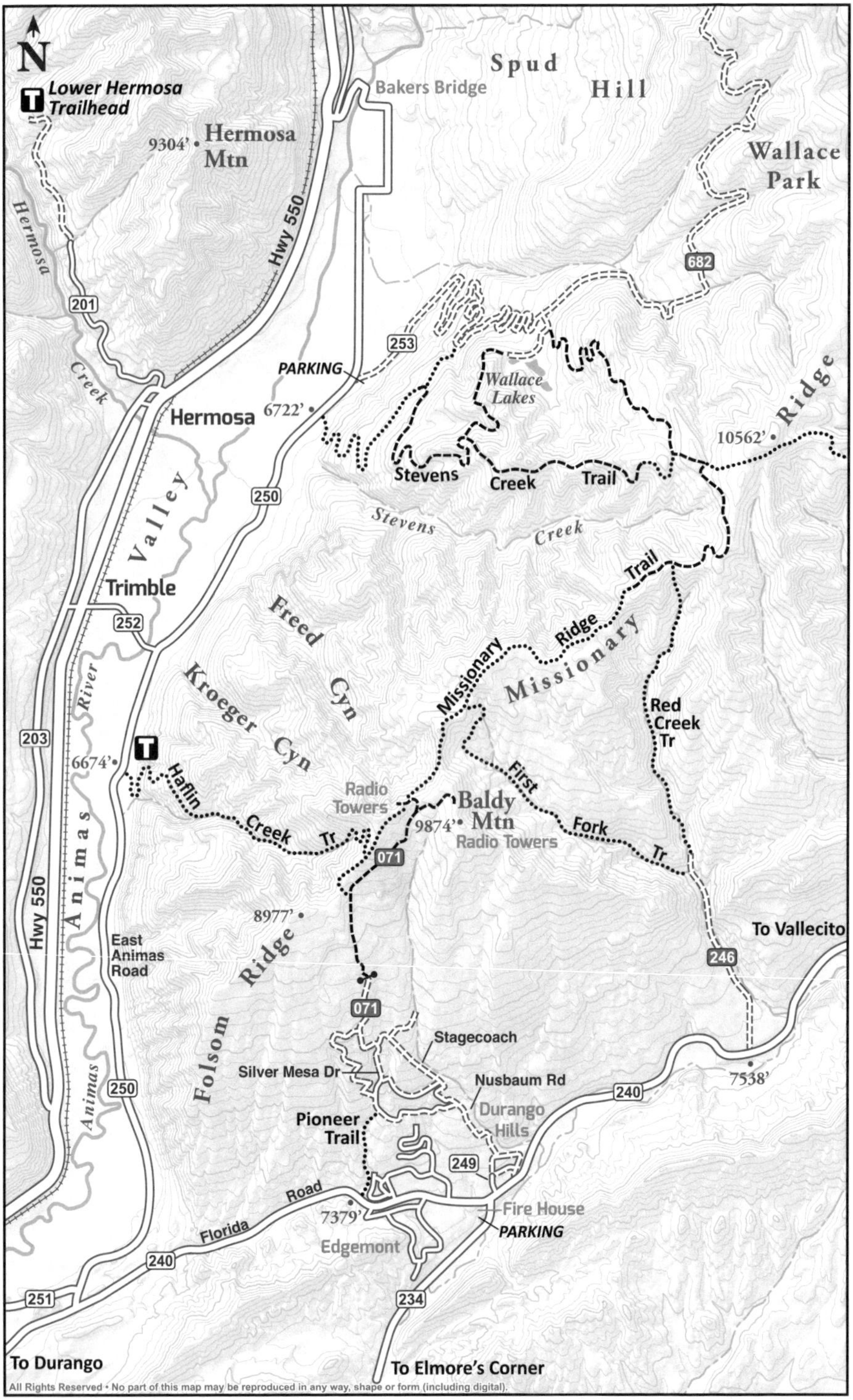

★★★★☆

HAFLIN CREEK TRAIL
Missionary Ridge

Description: The Missionary Ridge to Haflin Creek loop was a favorite local ride before the disastrous forest fires of 2002. The trails have been cleared by the Forest Service and Trails 2000 and are open again, and is an interesting and adventurous place to ride. The landscape and plant life are slowly recovering, but it is like an alien world if you ride it in cloudy weather, with surreal light filtering through the dead, burned trees in the narrow canyon. The Haflin Creek Trail is a rowdy and challenging white-knuckle descent with steep switchbacks, rocky terrain, a few alternative lines amidst hidden stumps and rocks, and several steep and exposed sections overlooking the Animas River Valley. It has a surprisingly moderate rolling mid-section. The bottom of the trail opens up into a Moab-esk red layer with some cliff exposure, rough side-hilling trail, and tight, ledged, switchback goodness. If you don't like exposure and technical riding, you will walk a fair amount, but if you enjoy technical it is a great downhill for expert cross country riders, and especially for bigger travel bikes. If you ride from town, ride up the moderate Pioneer Trail to access the steep subdivision road that leads to the trails, cutting off some of the road. A shuttle is possible to avoid the climb up the strenuous road, see shuttle below. It is usually safe but during wind and snow events several trees in the area may still fall.

Distance: Loop from town: 16.3 miles, 5.2 miles of singletrack, 2.7 miles of dirt road, 8.4 miles of paved road. **With a shuttle:** 5.3 miles, 4.2 singletrack, 1.1 miles of dirt road.
Time: Loop from town: 3 to 3 ½ hours **With a shuttle:** 1 ½ to 2 hours.
Difficulty: Expert with several very difficult sections
Aerobic Effort: High from town, moderate with a shuttle.
Elevation: Loop from town: Top: 9,464' **Gain:** 3,110'
With Shuttle: Top: 9,464' **Gain:** 984' **Loss:** 2,972'
Season: Mid-May through November
Finding Route: Moderate to the trailhead in Durango Hills, then easy.
Map: Latitude 40 Durango Trails or Southwest Colorado Trails.
Location: For the loop, start the ride at the corner of East AnimasRoad/ CR 250 and Florida Road/CR 240, near Bread and San Juan Cycles. Ask one of the businesses in the area to park, or ride from town. Follow the directions to mile 5.5 of Missionary Ridge to Steven's Creek, page 75, to the trailhead, then see description below.
Shuttle: You can leave a shuttle vehicle 5.2 miles out East Animas Road/CR 250 at the signed lower Halflin trailhead to cut off ½ hour of paved road riding or spin the relatively flat road back to town after the ride. To shuttle to the trailhead to start, drive 4.3 miles on CR 240 east from its junction with East Animas Road, to the **first** entrance of Durango Hills subdivision. This is past Edgemont Ranch and just past the junction with CR 234 (by the fire station.) Turn left on paved CR 249 and set your trip odometer to 0. At mile 0.3 turn left on Nusbaum. At mile 1, go

straight on Stagecoach and FS 071. At mile 2, turn left and downhill, passing a spur to the right. Follow FS 071 signs to the top. At mile 2.2, turn right on Silver Mesa, then drive straight on Silver Mesa at 2.6 miles (North Durango is left). At 3.0, reach the trailhead. This cuts off 5.5 miles of riding on paved and dirt road and the Pioneer Trail. Nusbaum to Silver Mesa also leads to the trailhead.

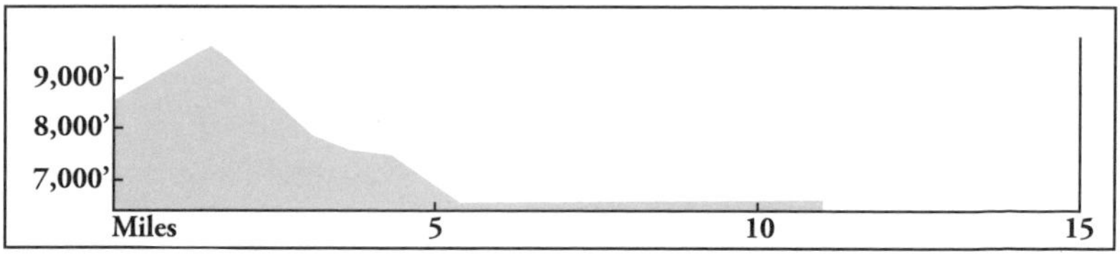

Mileage Log:

0.0 Follow directions page 75 to ride to mile 5.5, or shuttle to the trailhead, see location and shuttle above. Mileage for the shuttle option is in parenthesis.

5.5 **(0.0)** Durango Hills, Missionary Ridge Trailhead. Go right of the gate to a rollover. Climb the forest road.

6.5 **(1.0)** Turn left on the first spur road, just after entering the burn area. Ride 1/10th mile up the spur road and turn right on an unsigned singletrack and climb to the ridge. Across the valley to the west are great views of Silver Mountain in the La Platas.

7.0 **(1.5)** Turn left on the Haflin Creek Trail after a rough climb. There is a hand-made sign here. Contour and descend narrow trail and steep switchbacks. Be careful of down trees that can be head height in the narrow section of the canyon down lower. After one mile, the trail mellows to a meander through the valley.

9.3 **(3.8)** The trail becomes more exposed and climbs a bit. Next are gravelly side hills, technical ledges, and exposed sections.

10.6 **(5.1)** Turn right and descend.

10.8 **(5.3)** Reach the trailhead on East Animas Road. Turn left to town.

16.1 **(10.6)** Stay left and pass CR 251.

16.3 **(10.8)** Junction of Florida and East Animas Roads.

★★★☆☆

MISSIONARY RIDGE AND STEVEN'S CREEK TRAILS

RED CREEK TRAIL

See map page 72

Description: Missionary Ridge was a favorite adventure ride for locals before the forest fires of 2002. The trails have been cleared by the Forest Service and Trails 2000 and are open to ride, and usually safe (except during high winds and storms.) It is an adventurous place to ride. There are sections of smooth singletrack, and rough trail that is still recovering from the fires and lack of use. The trail goes through a big burn area, yet parts of the ride are untouched by the fire and still heavily treed. To ride the loop, start on Florida Road and take the Pioneer Trail to the Durango Hills subdivision. The Pioneer Trail shortens the steep climb through the subdivision. Once through the subdivision, the ride becomes more gradual and pleasant on forest road and singletrack to the radio towers. From here, the singletrack snakes back and forth between the west and east sides of the ridge, sometimes almost totally level. As you get farther out the ridge, there are some hike a bike sections and you will be route finding a bit. Steven's starts as singletrack, but turns to fast doubletrack for several miles, then narrows to rough singletrack near the bottom. The most quality singletrack part of the ride is the Missionary Ridge Trail and you can ride it as an out and back from the Durango Hills Trailhead, skipping Stevens. Shuttle to Wallace Lake for Steven's only, skipping most of the uphill, see option below. Expect a few down trees on all trails in the area. Wear orange in hunting season.

Distance: 30 mile loop, 8 miles of singletrack, 10 miles of dirt road and doubletrack, 12 miles of paved road; or shuttle to cut off between 5.5 to 15 miles of paved and dirt roads.
Time: 5 to 7 hours. Shuttle is 1 to 2 hours shorter.
Difficulty: Expert loop; advanced intermediate out and back from the Durango Hills Trailhead.
Aerobic Effort: Strenuous
Elevation: Top: 10,171' **Gain:** 4,591' **Gain with shuttle:** 2,456'
Season: June through October
Finding Route: Somewhat difficult. Some signs are missing but the route generally follows the ridge. The trail disappears a couple of times. Be sure to take these directions and one of the maps listed below.
Map: Latitude 40 Durango Colorado or Southwest Colorado Trails
Location: For the loop, start the ride at the corner of East Animas Road/CR 250 and Florida Road/CR 240. Ask one of the neighborhood businesses to park, or ride from town. To shuttle to the trailhead, see Haflin Creek Trail, Location, page 73. You can leave a shuttle vehicle 9.6 miles out East Animas Road to cut off another hour of paved road riding. Be sure to park 3/10ths mile past the trailhead at the corner of Missionary Ridge Road/CR 253 to avoid parking on private property.

MISSIONARY RIDGE AND STEVEN'S CREEK TRAILS
RED CREEK TRAIL

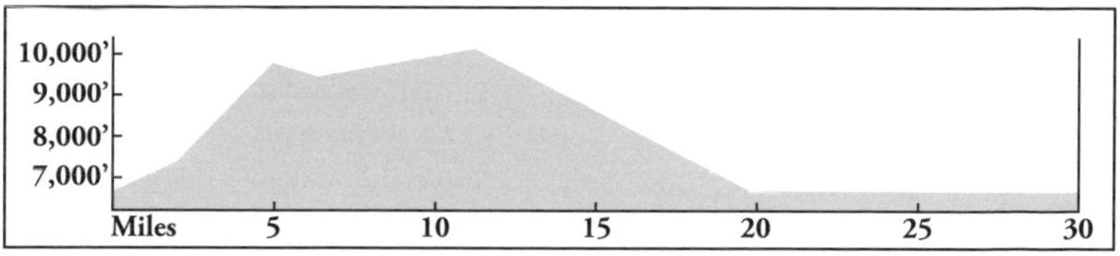

Mileage Log:

0.0 Ride east on Florida Road. Soon start climbing.

2.9 Look for an inconspicuous left turn to private property. Turn left here and in 1/10th mile turn right on the carsonite signed Pioneer Trail. If you pass the giant Edgemont sign on the left side of CR 240, you have missed it. You can also access the trail behind this sign, carry your bike up. Climb the wide path that narrows to singletrack.

3.9 Stay left and climb, passing a spur to a water tower.

4.0 Cross a doubletrack, then turn left on a steep dirt road and climb when the trail ends.

4.4 Continue up Silver Mesa Road, passing a road to the left.

4.7 Continue left on Silver Mesa. Look for the brown FS 071 sign.

5.0 Go straight on Silver Mesa, passing a spur on the left. Look for the FS 071 sign.

5.5 Reach a parking area and locked gate. Go right to a rollover and continue up. If you shuttled, park here.

6.5 Turn left on the first side road, shortly after entering the burn area. In 1/10th mile, turn right on the unsigned singletrack and climb on rough trail.

7.0 Pass the Haflin Creek Trail on the left. Continue climbing for 3/10ths mile, top out and ride down through a meadow.

7.5 Intersect a doubletrack, with towers to the left. Turn right and ride downhill 1/10th mile. When the road gets very close to the ridge, take the somewhat obscure singletrack straight ahead. It was last marked by a cairn and a Missionary Ridge sign that has been propped up. Climb, descend and countour on narrow singletrack along hillsides, in and out of the forest.

8.9 After some switchbacks the trail rolls into a red dirt area. Pass the signed First Fork Trail on the right, see option 2, and a user created trail heading left. Climb straight ahead, and then contour.

11.8 The Red Creek Trail descends steeply right, see option 2.

12.2 The trail rounds the ridge to the right and becomes a doubletrack.

12.7 Merge left onto another doubletrack and descend. Expect to climb over a lot of down trees here.

13.3 Ride through a gate and to a signed junction before a fence, with views of the Needle Mountains. Turn left toward the Stevens Creek Trail. (Right is the continuation of the Missionary Ridge Trail.) There is a left turn that is easy to miss in 3/10ths mile.

13.6 At the gate turn left on singletrack, around the fence. There is a sign in the fence. Descend, contour to a small climb, and descend again.

13.9 The trail disappears; go downhill about 50'. Turn right when the trail reappears and contour.

14.6 The trail merges onto doubletrack.

16.3 Turn left on Steven's at a signed, wide, flat junction. To the right leads to Wallace Lake.

18.3 After the trail narrows, turn sharp left on a switchback. Don't go through the fence.

19.7 The trail splits, go left on true singletrack. Be cautious in one mile, there are sharp switchbacks and neck high wire along the low side of the trail.

20.7 Turn left on East Animas Road. If you shuttled, turn right to the parking spot.

23.4 Stay left on East Animas Road, passing CR 252 to Hwy 550.

29.8 Stay left passing CR 251.

30.0 Back to the junction with CR 240.

Option 1: Steven's Creek shuttle: Drive out East Animas Road/CR 250 for 9.6 miles to Missionary Ridge Road and go right. (Or take Highway 550 north 6 miles and turn right on CR 252/Trimble Lane at the light, cross the river and turn left on East Animas Road. Continue 3 miles to Missionary Ridge Road.) Climb 6 miles to Wallace Lake where there is a big pullout. Ride 1 ½ miles past the lake (south) to Stevens Creek Trail at 16.3 above.

Option 2: First Fork and Red Creek Trails: The First Fork and Red Creek Trails look inviting from the map and up top from Missionary Ridge Trail, but aren't recommended unless you are up for a possibly long hike a bike and route finding. Both can be severely hammered by horse traffic, and very rough. If you do attempt to ride one of these trails there is parking at the corner of CR 234, behind the fire station, 4.3 miles out Florida Road. Ride 1.4 miles back to the Pioneer Trail (on the right) to start the loop. Return from the loop on CR 246 to Florida Road and right to your vehicle. Neither is a good uphill trail.

COLORADO TRAIL/INDIAN RIDGE AND UPPER HERMOSA PARK

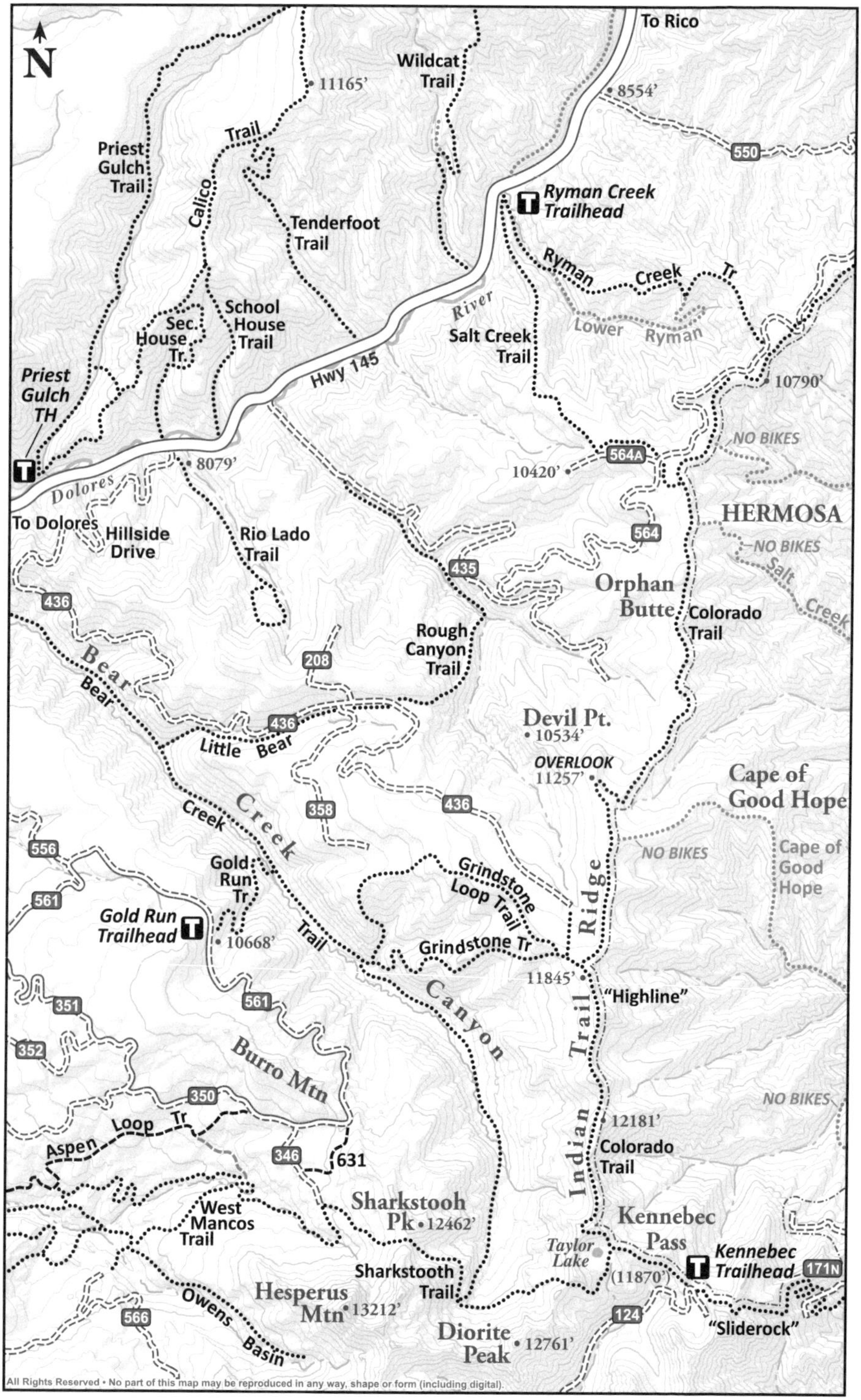

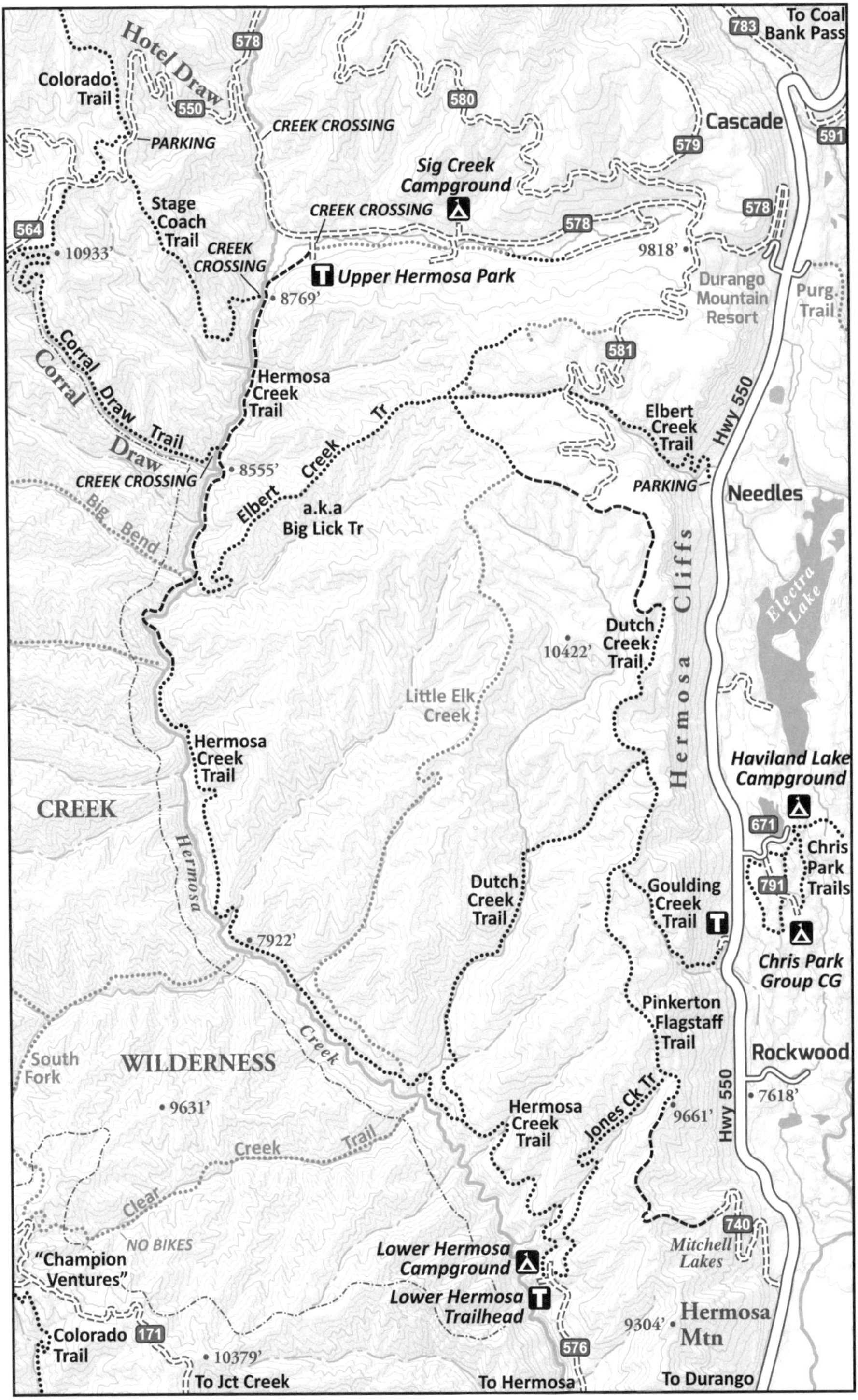
To Coal Bank Pass
783
578
Hotel Draw
550
580
Colorado Trail
PARKING
CREEK CROSSING
Cascade
579
591
Sig Creek Campground
Stage Coach Trail
CREEK CROSSING
578
578
564
10933’
CREEK CROSSING
9818’
Upper Hermosa Park
8769’
Durango Mountain Resort
Purg. Trail
581
Corral Draw Trail
Corral Draw
Hermosa Creek Trail
Elbert Creek Trail
Hwy 550
Elbert Creek Tr
8555’
CREEK CROSSING
a.k.a Big Lick Tr
PARKING
Needles
Big Bend
Hermosa Cliffs
Electra Lake
Dutch Creek Trail
10422’
Little Elk Creek
Hermosa Creek Trail
Haviland Lake Campground
CREEK
671
Chris Park Trails
791
Hermosa
Dutch Creek Trail
Goulding Creek Trail
7922’
Chris Park Group CG
Pinkerton Flagstaff Trail
Creek
Rockwood
South Fork
WILDERNESS
7618’
9631’
Hermosa Creek Trail
Jones Ck Tr
9661’
Hwy 550
Creek Trail
Clear
NO BIKES
740
Mitchell Lakes
“Champion Ventures”
Lower Hermosa Campground
Lower Hermosa Trailhead
Hermosa Mtn
9304’
Colorado Trail
171
10379’
576
To Jct Creek
To Hermosa
To Durango

★★★☆☆

HERMOSA CREEK TRAIL

Upper Hermosa Park, North of Durango *See map pages 78-79*

Description: The Hermosa Creek Trail is a scenic mid-country, forested ride along Hermosa Creek. It is lower altitude than the rides on Coal Bank and Molas Passes, but still a mountain ride. The trail has a moderate amount of climbing overall, but there are still some tough climbs. Perhaps the most fun way to do Hermosa Creek is with a shuttle, but an out and back from the Lower Hermosa Trailhead eliminates getting a vehicle 29 miles to the northern end of the ride. The upper part of the ride starts with 6.5 miles of ATV trail, but don't let this deter you, as it is a good ride with a lot of singletrack. The most pristine part is the central section of the trail, narrow and beautiful, with Ponderosa Pine, fir, spruce and aspen forest, and great views into the creek and of the La Plata Mountains. The 4 miles near the lower trailhead are wide and heavily used. Expect other users and keep your speed in control even though the trail is very fast through here. Hermosa Creek is a hub of many surrounding trails including Stagecoach, Corral, Big Lick, Little Elk, Dutch and Jones Creeks. See these individual rides. Most of these trails are not good climbs from Hermosa, with the exception of Jones Creek. The west side of the trail is now wilderness, including Big Bend, Salt, South Fork and Clear Creek Trails. Wear orange during hunting season, as this area is very popular with hunters. There is a lot of camping near the upper trailhead in Hermosa Park. The Hermosa Trail is good access to Bolam Pass for bike packing routes. Call Hermosa Tours for shuttle information, 877-765-5682.

Distance: 18.8 mile shuttle ride: 12.3 miles of singletrack and 6.5 miles ATV trail.
Time: 3 to 4 ½ hours
Difficulty: Advanced intermediate with several expert sections. Some exposure over steep hillsides, rocky sections, and big climbs.
Aerobic Effort: Moderately high
Elevation: Top: 8,897' **Gain:** 2,180' **Loss:** 3,317'
Season: June through October
Finding Route: Easy, junctions are signed and the route is straightforward.
Map: Singletrack Maps Durango Trails
Location: To leave a shuttle vehicle at the Lower Hermosa Trailhead or ride from that end, drive 8 miles north from Durango on Hwy 550 toward Silverton. Turn left on CR 203, then immediately right on CR 201. The turn off the highway is just before the railroad track crossing. CR 201 becomes FS 576 in one mile. Drive 3.8 miles to the end, turn left and descend to the trailhead. The signed start/end of the trail is at the corner of the trailhead and campground roads. If you are shuttling to the top, return to Hwy 550, turn left and drive north 15.6 miles to Durango Mountain Resort, and turn left. Drive up the paved Purgatory Boulevard and straight ahead onto Hermosa Park Road, FS 578, which is dirt. Stay with Hermosa Park Road, following signs to the Hermosa Creek Trail, 8 more miles. Continue up switchbacks and stay right past Elbert Creek Road at the top of the hill. At the next major junction stay left on FS 578 as Cascade Divide and Relay Roads go right. Continue straight out the valley to Hermosa Creek Trailhead, on the left. Drive across the creek and park by the corrals and bathroom.

HERMOSA CREEK TRAIL

Upper Hermosa Park, North of Durango

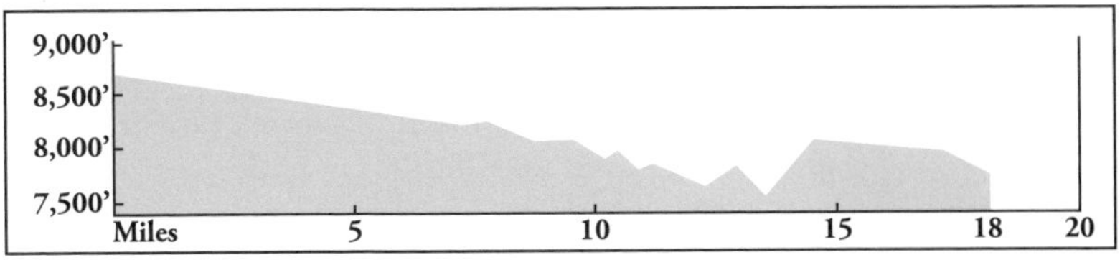

Mileage Log:

0.0 Start riding next to the corral on the signed wide Hermosa Creek Trail.

0.7 Go through a gate and pass the unsigned Stagecoach Trail on the right.

2.9 Pass signed Corral Draw Trail on the right.

4.6 Go right and cross a bridge. Big Lick is straight ahead before the bridge. Next pass the Big Bend Trail on the right in 2/10ths mile.

5.6 Cross a bridge.

6.5 Pass a right to the Salt Creek Trail. The Hermosa Creek Trail turns left and narrows to a singletrack.

11.0 The signed South Fork of the Hermosa Trail goes right.

12.8 Climb a couple big hills and descend a rocky section to the next junction.

13.9 Ride straight past the signed Clear Creek Trail and cross a bridge in 1/10 mile. Start a big climb with a short hike a bike.

14.8 Dutch Creek comes in on the left, no sign. Continue climbing for 1/10 mile, then the trail becomes more rolling and widens.

18.3 Ride straight ahead, passing a spur down to the right, shortly after a "caution: horses" sign. In 1/10th mile ride straight ahead and pass a steep spur on the left and then a spur that goes right and downhill.

18.6 Merge left on the wider main trail and then stay left on the singletrack.

18.7 Pass Jones Creek Trail.

18.8 Lower Hermosa Creek Trailhead.

★★★☆☆

CORRAL DRAW AND THE COLORADO TRAIL

Upper Hermosa Park, North of Durango

See map pages 78-79

Description: Corral Draw is a narrow little trail through the wild mid-country of the Hermosa Creek drainage. It is semi-primitive even though it is open to motorcycles, and next to newly designated wilderness. The last time I was there I saw a great big black bear. It is a moderate length ride when looped with part of the Colorado Trail (CT) and Hotel Draw Road, and like most rides in the area has great views. The loop starts with a moderate road climb and a few miles of singletrack along the ridge on the CT. The Corral Draw Trail cuts long switchbacks through steep open meadows up top, and rolls down fast through the dark timber, then it's back to narrow singletrack, exposed over steep hillsides along the creek. Return to the trailhead on the Hermosa Creek Trail. Camping in the area will allow you to ride several of the Upper Hermosa Creek rides without ever getting in your vehicle, see Colorado Trail: Blackhawk, Hermosa Creek and Elbert Creek to Big Lick. Be careful of the crossing of Hermosa Creek at the bottom of Corral Draw. In the spring and early summer it can be huge and dangerous, and even later in the summer and fall after a lot of rain it can be swift. Check with local bike shops before the ride, and turn back if you have any question about the depth or swiftness of the creek.

Distance: 17.6 mile loop, 6.3 miles of dirt forest road, 8 miles of singletrack, 3.3 miles of ATV trail.
Time: 2 ½ to 3 ½ hours
Difficulty: Expert. Sections of the trail are very narrow and exposed, or rough and overgrown.
Aerobic Effort: Moderately high
Elevation: Top: 10,916' **Gain:** 3,140'
Season: Mid- to late June through October, but the creek may be dangerous until July
Finding Route: Moderate. There are a lot of turns on the CT, but the route is signed with small triangular CT markers. There is a critical and slightly confusing turn at mile 7.3.
Map: Singletrack Maps Durango Trails
Location: Park at the trailhead for Hermosa Creek Trail, 32 miles from Durango. From the last light in Durango drive north on Hwy 550 for 23.6 miles to Durango Mountain Resort (DMR) and turn left into the DMR entrance. Drive up the paved Purgatory Boulevard and straight ahead onto Hermosa Park Road, FS 578, which is dirt. Stay with Hermosa Park Road, following signs to the Hermosa Creek Trail, 8 miles on dirt road. Drive up the switchbacks and stay right past Elbert Creek Road at the top of the hill. Next, stay left as Cascade and Relay Roads go right. Continue straight out the valley to the Hermosa Creek Trailhead, on the left.

CORRAL DRAW AND THE COLORADO TRAIL
Upper Hermosa Park, North of Durango

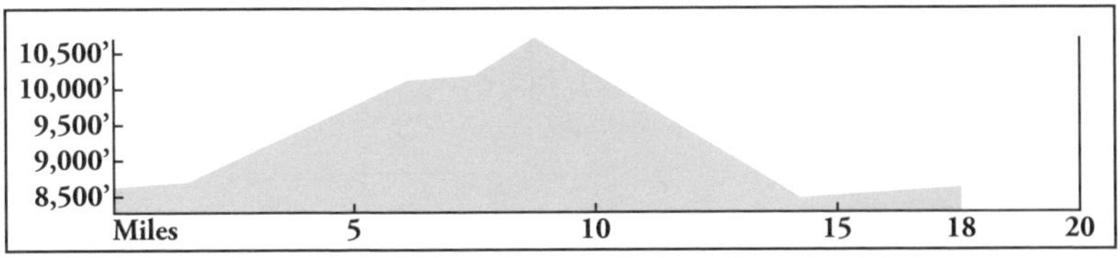

Mileage Log:

0.0 From the trailhead, ride back out to Hermosa Park Road and turn left. Cross Hermosa Creek in 1.5 miles.

2.4 Turn left onto Hotel Draw Road/FS 550.

6.1 Reach the top of Hotel Draw. Look for a sign to the right of the road marking the CT. Turn left on the CT. Ride behind a gate and stay on the CT, a doubletrack turning into singletrack.

7.3 Ride onto a main road, passing an old logging road to the right. The main road forks immediately. Take FS Road 564 to the left. (FS Road 550 continues right and down toward Rico.)

7.5 Turn left on the signed CT singletrack and climb.

8.5 Descend a little and then the trail levels, through conifer forest.

8.9 Turn left on signed Corral Draw Trail and descend the narrow and overgrown trail through meadows and into the forest.

11.8 The trail splits after a trampled area and creek crossing. Stay low (right.) Soon the valley widens, and the trail contours around a slate hillside and descends to Hermosa Creek.

14.3 Cross Hermosa Creek if it is safe, and turn left on the Hermosa Creek Trail. Stay along the creek on ATV trail, passing a couple side trails.

17.4 Back to the trailhead road; ride straight ahead and cross the creek.

17.6 Back to Hermosa Park Road.

Hermosa Creek Trail | *Holly Annala*

★★★★☆

JONES CREEK, PINKERTON FLAGSTAFF AND DUTCH CREEK

Lower Hermosa Creek Trailhead *See map pages 78-79*

Description: This is an adventurous, all singletrack, mid-country loop with a lot of variety. It is a great ride. Much of the ride has amazing aspens for a fall color ride in mid-October. It feels remote and it is likely you won't see many folks out here except at the beginning on the Jones Creek Trail and at the end on the Hermosa Creek Trail. Jones Creek is a mostly smooth and beautiful climb through oak, aspen, Pinyon and Ponderosa Pines. (It is a great 2 hour out and back with a short climb on the Pinkerton Flagstaff to a lookout.) The Pinkerton Flagstaff Trail, although being rerouted and repaired through the years, is rough and rutted in places, and has a few hike a bike sections. It meanders through miles of forest, both conifer and aspen, and has a lot of good singletrack along the ridge and down into Dutch Creek. The descent on the Dutch Creek Trail is really fun; winding and smooth varied with some technical and some rough trail. Hermosa is quite popular; there could be motorcycles, hikers, other bikers, horses, and cows. Be courteous and prepared to stop. Wear orange in hunting season. There is a campground at the start of the ride.

Distance: 18.8 mile loop, all singletrack.

Time: 4 to 6 hours, 2 hours for the out and back.

Difficulty: Expert

Aerobic Effort: Strenuous

Elevation: Top: 10,261' **Gain:** 4,161'

Season: Mid-June through October for the loop, the out and back can be open a month or more earlier.

Finding Route: Fairly easy, signed and not many junctions.

Map: Singletrack Maps Durango Trails

Location: The Lower Hermosa Creek Trailhead. Drive north from Durango 8 miles on Hwy 550 toward Silverton and turn left on CR 203, and immediately right on CR 201. The turn off the highway is just before the railroad track crossing. CR 201 turns into FS 576 in one mile. Drive 3.8 miles to the end, and turn left and descend straight to the trailhead parking, passing the campground to the right.

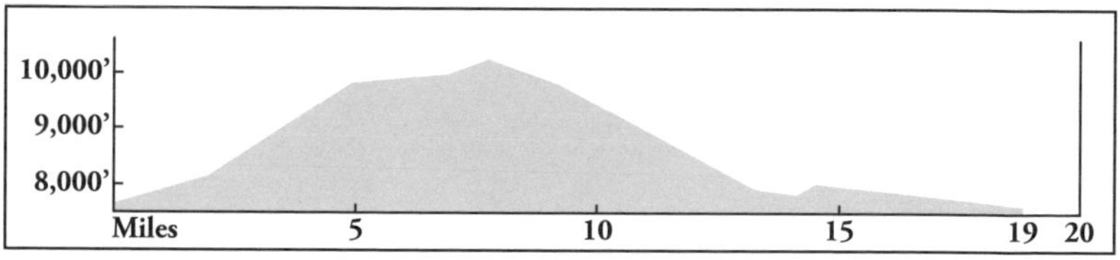

Mileage Log:

0.0 Ride uphill out of the parking area and turn left on the campground road. Turn right immediately on the signed Hermosa Creek Trail and follow it 1/10th mile to a signed right turn to the Jones Creek Trail. Cross the closed section of FS road and start up the Jones Creek Trail, marked with a brown carsonite sign.

4.1 Reach the signed junction with the Pinkerton Flagstaff Trail. Turn left and climb through the aspens, at first moderately. (To do the out and back to the overlook, turn right and climb to the ridge and overlook before returning down Jones Creek Trail. Continuing down Mitchell Lakes Road beyond the lookout is an awful ATV trail, and is not reccommended.)

4.3 Hike a bike section. The trail is rutted, loose and rocky for 6/10ths mile.

4.9 Descend rutted, steep trail through the forest, and then follow moderate singletrack along the ridge. Enjoy views of the La Plata Mountains, Hermosa Creek drainage and Missionary Ridge in open areas.

7.1 Descend a short steep hill, and pass Goulding Creek Trail to the right in 2/10ths mile. (Goulding Creek is steep and ends on Hwy 550.) Continue straight on the Pinkerton Flagstaff Trail, hiking your bike up a short hill.

7.5 After another steep 1/10th mile climb, top out on an open narrow ridge with amazing aspen forest and awesome views of the Needle and Grenadier Mountains to the north.

8.9 After a smooth section of downhill, turn left on the signed Dutch Creek Trail. Dutch Creek starts out rugged and narrow through open meadows and sparse woods. Several technical sections exist right after some full speed, smooth riding. (Dutch also continues straight to Elbert Creek Road).

11.0 Cross Dutch Creek and turn left. Cross it a few more times.

12.0 Steep side hill and some exposure.

13.0 (approx. mileage) Cross Dutch Creek and climb back into the Ponderosa forest.

14.9 Ride through a dip and turn left on the unsigned Hermosa Creek Trail. Climb a few hills, contour, and descend. Keep your speed in control and expect other users.

18.3 Ride straight ahead, passing a spur down to the right.

18.4 Ride straight ahead and pass a steep spur on the left and then a spur that goes right and downhill.

18.6 Merge left on the main wider trail and then stay left on the singletrack.

18.7 Pass Jones Creek Trail.

18.8 Lower Hermosa Creek Trailhead.

★★☆☆☆

ELBERT CREEK AND BIG LICK TRAILS

ELBERT CREEK TO DUTCH, LITTLE ELK OR JONES SHUTTLE

Upper Hermosa Park, North of Durango *See map pages 78-79*

Description: Elbert Creek is a mid-country trail that climbs from the Needles Store (21 miles north of Durango) to above the Hermosa Cliffs, and descends to the Hermosa Creek Trail. It also connects to a few other trails for a different ride if you have a shuttle available. Elbert is a tough climb, challenging but nearly all rideable except when livestock is mixed with heavy snow and rain. Avoid it after heavy precipitation. The top of the trail winds through alpine meadows with amazing views of the Needle Mountains. The descent on Elbert, also known as Big Lick, is very long, on singletrack and very old doubletrack that is narrowing to singletrack. It has some really fun trail and scenic sections, and also several water eroded and rutted sections with possible hike a bike. Much of the ride is through aspen forest, great for a fall color ride, and there are great views of the La Plata Mountains to the west. After descending Elbert/Big Lick, ride the Hermosa Creek Trail, Hermosa Park Road and Elbert Creek Road to return down Elbert Creek Trail. To ride down Little Elk Creek, Dutch Creek, or along the ridge to Pinkerton Flagstaff and Jones Creek Trails to the Hermosa Creek Trail with a shuttle, see option below. A lot of hunters camp and hunt the area, and I suggest avoiding these trails during rifle season, or at least wear hunter orange.

Distance: 27.6 mile lollipop loop: 10.4 miles of singletrack, 6.7 miles ATV trail and old narrowing doubletrack, 10.5 miles of dirt forest road.
Time: 5 -7 hours
Difficulty: Expert
Aerobic Effort: Strenuous
Elevation: Top: 10,451' **Gain:** 4,483'
Season: Mid-June through October
Finding Route: Difficult. Lots of turns, some unsigned, and many livestock and hunting trails that confuse the route. The trail is primitive in places.
Map: Singletrack Maps Durango Trails **and** Latitude 40 Durango Map
Location: Drive 21 miles north of Durango's last traffic light and turn left at the Needles Store. The Elbert Creek trailhead is just south of the Needles Store, next to Hwy 550, near some corrals. Look for inconspicuous trail signs. Park so as not to block anyone's driveway.

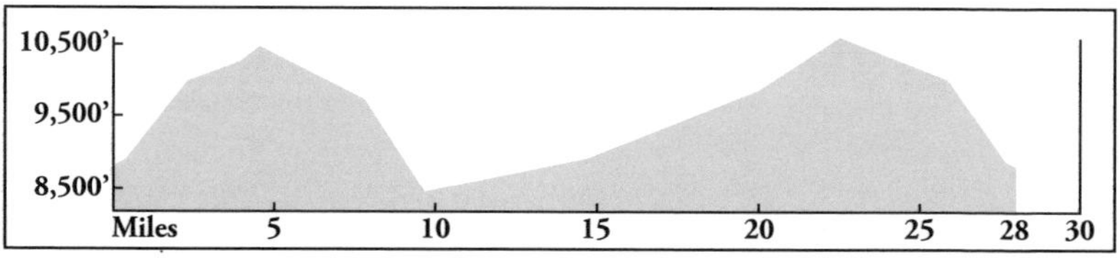

Mileage Log:

0.0 Enter the gate next to the corral and push your bike through another gate

TRAILS UPDATE

DURANGO, CORTEZ, DOLORES AND RICO

For updates on new trails, closed trails, trail conditions and photos go to **Mountain Bike Durango, Cortez, Dolores and Rico Singletrack on Facebook**. This is updated regularly during riding season. A newer website to check is mancostrails.org for Mancos area trails information. This group is working on improving existing trails and creating a new riding area near Mancos. Check Trails2000.org for Durango area updates, and Southwest Colorado Cycling Assoc. on facebook for Dolores, Cortez and Rico updates.

A note on the star ratings in this book: The rating is limited since there are only 5 stars and it is also a subjective rating, and not everyone enjoys what I enjoy. I really like to spend all day out riding in a remote place, so sometimes my judgement is clouded by an adventurous day on a scenic mountain ride. I often overlook hike a bikes, trail in disrepair, and route finding because it is a new and beautiful place. These rides aren't always possible or fun depending on one's time and energy level that day, and what a person likes. Horse Gulch and Twin Buttes are great places to ride and many loops there deserve more stars. Farmington and Aztec offer great riding but got lower ratings because of gas well drilling and difficulty connecting some of the trails. If you don't like to hike a bike, you won't like the Calico or Sharkstooth Trails, but I really think they are special. And on. So please read into the description to find a ride you would like best.

The Telegraph Trails System/Horse Gulch is one of the best places to ride around Durango, with lots of loop options, great trails and scenery. The Sugar Trail is new since this book came out, a great way to connect Skyline to Horse Gulch on moderate trail, or as an up and back from Horse Gulch Road (see page 43). The Smoke Jumper's Trail heads northeast along the ridge at the top of Sugar & Skyline (there is now a low connector to avoid the rocky junction of Hyper Extended Ridge) for a scenic out and back on more advanced trail. Top out at 7,954 and return as there is no legal access yet off the north end. The Medicine Trail (see page 36) is an advanced trail with some drops, freeriders enjoy it. There is a **connector from Cuchillo to Sugar Trail** for more loop options. After descending Cuchillo on the northeast end, swing north and uphill a short distance to a split. Turn right and end across from Sugar (left is the continuation of Cuchillo).

Grandview Ridge Trails: There is a new connector from Sale Barn to Cowboy Trail that avoids the gravel mine and it makes the ride a whole lot nicer now (4 or 5 stars!) Ride up Sale Barn and stay right onto Cowboy at the first signed intersection. Continue on Cowboy with a short stint on Grandview Ridge Road, taking a left over to the Big Canyon area and the continuation of Cowboy, or stay on the road until you reach the Three Springs Trails entrance on the right, by the water tower. There is new singletrack next to the water tower that connects Sidewinder to the gate and Three Springs, replacing the upper section of Grandview Ridge Road.

Three Springs Spur Line Trails: The new Spur Line trails are fun beginner trails and a great place to take kids. From Durango, drive 4 miles south on US Hwy 550/160, and then east (stay left) on Hwy 160 two more miles when the highways split to Three Springs Blvd., and turn left. Turn right onto Wilson Gulch Drive at the first roundabout and turn right at the next roundabout onto a gravel road. Follow signs for about 1/3 mile to the trailhead and parking area on your right. A big map shows the layout of the 5 miles of smooth singletrack. After riding the first section and ending on a dirt road, turn right on singletrack to ride the second loop. You will return to the same spot to finish the first loop.

If you want to ride the more difficult (intermediate with short advanced sections) Three Springs Trails that lead to the water tower, park at the same parking area. Turn right out of the parking area and ride up the gravel road, then turn left on the gravel road behind the housing. Take this past an electric substation, turn right and go through a small gate. In a short distance, turn right onto singletrack and follow it to cross the gas road and continue up singletrack. Stay left through 2 intersections and this will take you to the water tower. A left before crossing the gas well road will take you to the gate that heads to the Grandview Ridge area trails. (Once through the gate, take an at first steep singletrack right or the gas road, and ride up to Sidewinder. Or go left on the road and down the road to Cowboy.) Or, crossing the dirt road just below the water tower, follow the loops around and back across the road again , where a couple lefts will take you back to where you started.

Hermosa Creek Trail, Dutch Creek, Jones: Hermosa Creek Trail and surrounding trails are again open to the public after the 416 Fire. The trails are in good shape thanks to volunteers, but it is very burned and exposed to the sun where it was once shady and cool. Be very careful of falling trees especially during wind and storms. As you get farther out where the trails haven't been cleared yet there could be a lot of downfall. Pinkerton Flagstaff, Corral, Elbert, Big Lick, and West Cross Creek could all be adversely affected by the fire.

West Cross Creek Trail, aka the Stagecoach Trail, has been rebuilt and will be finished in 2019. This 4 mile trail connects the top of Hotel Draw and the Upper Hermosa Trail, and is a great way to finish the Black Hawk section of the CT loop, see page 89. It's a fast and fun mostly singletrack descent (aligned on a very old road grade) for intermediate and advanced riders with fun jumps, steep sections and loose rocks. Riders must ford Hermosa Creek, beware as it can be very high in spring and early summer, and after heavy storms.

Phil's World: Phil's World has a whole new area of riding accessible from the Cash Canyon Trailhead just a few miles from Cortez. This is a nice, quiet trailhead and the trails are fun, mostly intermediate, constructed with love! All are one way with options for shorter or longer loops and fairly well signed. From the parking area, take mostly all lefts and ride Highline, Canal, Ledges and then go right on 6400 Trail to make a good 2-3 hour loop. Add Stinking Springs for a few more miles. It is a bit confusing to get from Stinking Springs back onto Ledges, keep your map handy. To get to the Cash Canyon Trailhead drive 1.5 miles east on Hwy 160 from its' junction with Hwy 145, and turn left on Hwy 29N. Drive 2 miles and turn right on CR L at the Y intersection. The signed trailhead is 1.6 miles on the right. **Poquito Burrito:** This trail has a fair amount of technical riding and some smooth trail, great views. The sign and singletrack are one mile into the Stinking Springs Loop. Look for a map on Southwest Cycling Association's facebook page or pick up a new **Big Loops** map for the whole Cortez area at Kokopelli Bike and Board in Cortez.

Boggy Draw: The McPhee Overlook Trail starts right in Dolores and rolls up and down to House Creek Campground on mostly moderate trail, with a couple stingers and a little exposed feeling at the bottom end. To get to the trailhead turn on B Street at the west end of Dolores and then go left on Central. The parking area and trail are at the end near the lake, about 4/10ths mile. This is a fun and scenic trail constructed with care that skirts the reservoir, a good out and back or as a long lollipop loop with Bean Canyon. It is closed from 12/1 to 5/1 each winter/spring for wildlife, with the lowest section to May Canyon opening 4/16 each spring. Ride **Bean Canyon from Horse Creek Campground** for a nice lollipop loop right from camp. To get to this trailhead, drive out CR 31 until the road becomes FSR 526 and continue straight to FS 538. Turn left and follow this to the campground and stay left to the trailhead. Or try the new **McNeil Trail** from Boggy Trail, or from Italian Canyon for a longer loop. The inner McNeil Trail is smooth and easier, the outer McNeil stays on the rim has some technical sections; it is for more advanced riders. **The Horse Camp Trail** is being worked as this goes to print, and will be completed this summer of 2019. It connects to the northeast corner of The Bean Canyon Loop, crosses FS 526 just east of the junction with House Creek Road 528, and makes a nice loop along a couple canyon rims. See Southwest Colorado Cycling Association facebook page or visit the US Forest Service Public Lands office on Hwy 184 for maps. From Dolores head west toward Cortez and climb the hill on Hwy 145 and turn left on Hwy 184. The office is just uphill and left.

TRAILS UPDATE

DURANGO, CORTEZ, DOLORES AND RICO

Look for the new **Big Loops map at Kokopelli Bike and Board in Cortez.** This simplified new version is a great way to find your way around Cortez and Dolores riding.

Sagehen consists of two loops, upper and lower if you prefer the shorter version. It has great views and slickrock sections along the canyon rim, a steady climb to mile 5 to a nice overlook, nice wildflower meadows in May, and a fun descent. Both loops together take about 3 hours. To reach Sage Hen from Dolores, head west out of town on Hwy 145 and turn right on 184 at the signs for McPhee Reservoir right before the gas station. From here drive 3.9 miles and turn right onto Road 25. When Road 25 dead ends turn right onto the graded road X. Go .7 miles just past the corrals and park next to the closed road FS 500. Ride up this closed road to a sign and posted map of the loop on your right. Both loops are intermediate with advanced intermediate sections.

The northern section of the Calico Trail is closed for repairs from East Fall Creek to the northern trailhead near Meadows Road, on Eagle Peak Road. Access the trail from West Fall Creek Trail, 6 miles up Eagle Peaks Road, see page 150 for directions.

All trails are open in the vicinity of the **Burro Fire**. The fire affected Bear Creek, Gold Run and Grindstone trails so expect downed trees and use extra caution as more trees will be falling.

Farmington has some fun new singletrack in the Road Apple System (see page 172): **Mood Swings** extends past the Anasazi Loop and connects to Kinsey. Ride Anasazi, cross paved Lakewood Drive & follow trail, swing right on a gas road and quick left again on singletrack. Cross paved Hood Mesa Road and go about 100 hundred feet to the left and on to the signed trail. From here follow signs and bike tracks as the singletrack winds north and east to Kinsey Trail/Rigor Mortis, about 3 miles. An option to return is on the newly resurrected **Clarks**, which is not too much farther out Kinsey, just past the yellow posts and cables you ride through, on the left. This trail was somewhat hard to follow when I rode it last. For an alternative route to the **Road Apple**, park at the Foothills TH. Start on Kinsey but ride left to Mood Swings (it is just beyond the private property boundary, 8/10th of a mile in. Head out to the next intersection and back since it is one way.) Ride this trail over to Lakewood Drive and then follow directions on page 176 to complete the loop. Be sure and stop into 505 Cycles in Farmington and visit with the knowledgeable and friendly staff there, 4301 E Main.

Second Avenue Sports moved to a new building at the other end of the block, still on 2nd. **Velorution Cycles** has a new owner and moved to the horse Gulch Trailhead on East 3rd Street.

and onto the singletrack. Stay on the main trail behind the homes. Climb long switchbacks, with some steep and difficult sections mixed in.

1.6 Ride past a cabin and through a meadow, passing a singletrack on the right. This side trail is not open to mountain bikes.

2.0 Ride through an old fence and into alpine meadows. Follow the stream up, staying with the creek as a couple cattle trails turn off the main trail.

2.9 Cross Elbert Creek Road. Turn right on the road and left on the trail. Go through a gate and follow the creek up.

3.4 The trail is braided and another trail follows the far side of the creek. Stay on the south or left side of the creek.

3.5 The trail squeezes next to creek; continue on the left side over some cut logs. There is a crossing to a trail on the right side of the creek, but this goes up another drainage to the top of East Cross Creek Trail (not a good biking trail.)

3.8 Cross the creek to a short, steep climb. Swing right (north) with the trail just before a fence.

4.3 Reach a saddle and the unsigned Butler Trail along the ridge. Ride across the Butler Trail (closed to bikes) and go through a gate to continue on Elbert Creek/Big Lick Trail. After the gate, start downhill and left on the signed Big Lick, and then along a ridge toward the west on a doubletrack narrowing to singletrack, with some climbing.

4.9 After a short steep climb stay left along the ridge on a contouring section through the aspens, passing a closed old road that goes right.

6.3 Stay right as a less used spur heads left. The trail contours and is narrower, with a few steeper descents.

7.2 After a long contour through meadows with sparse aspens and nice views of the Rico Mountains, turn right at a faint split and up a short, steep uphill, and contour again. Ride directly for a small ridge.

7.5 Ride along the narrow ridge with Douglas Fir trees on top. Start a long descent, with steep switchbacks at the bottom.

8.9 Turn right at a switchback when blocked trail goes straight.

9.2 Stay right at another switchback with a spur and ride along exposed hillside.

9.4 T-intersect a singletrack next to the Hermosa Creek. Turn right and ride upstream. Don't cross the bridge ahead, ride straight on the east side of the creek on the Hermosa Creek Trail for several miles, passing Corral Draw and Stagecoach Trails.

ELBERT CREEK AND BIG LICK TRAILS
ELBERT CREEK TO DUTCH, LITTLE ELK OR JONES SHUTTLE
Upper Hermosa Park, North of Durango

14.2 At the end of the trail, ride straight ahead passing the corrals and bathrooms. Cross the creek to Hermosa Park Road and turn right. Continue 5.3 miles on this road. Pass Cascade and Relay Roads on the left near the top.

19.5 Turn right on Elbert Creek Road at the top of the hill. Continue uphill, staying on the main road as it winds through Durango Mountain Resort. Next descend and contour a few small drainages on more gradual road.

24.7 Turn left on The Elbert Creek Trail, on a switchback with a small old sign. Follow your route back down.

27.6 Back to the trailhead and your car.

Elbert Creek to Dutch Creek, Little Elk or Pinkerton Flagstaff and Jones Creek Trails: Leave a shuttle vehicle at the Lower Hermosa Trailhead: See page 80, Location, for directions. Return to Hwy 550, turn left and drive 15.6 miles north on Hwy 550 to Durango Mountain Resort, and turn left. Drive up the paved Purgatory Boulevard and straight ahead onto Hermosa Park Road, FS 578, which is dirt. Drive 2.8 miles up the switchbacks to Elbert Creek Road, FS 581. Turn left and drive 8.4 miles to the end of the road and the trailhead. Dutch to Pinkerton Flagstaff start on the left in the meadow, Little Elk is at the end of the road in the forest on the left. If you choose to ride up Elbert Creek Trail, shuttle to the Needles store, 13 miles north on Hwy 550 from CR 203. Ride to mile 4.3 in the description above, go left and climb on singletrack, before the fence and gate. It is 1.3 miles to Little Elk Trail, and 1 mile on doubletrack beyond that to Dutch Creek Trail, on the right.

With some regret I have taken **The Little Elk Trail** out of the text as it is so difficult to follow in three places. It is not safe to descend toward Hermosa Creek unless you are on the trail, it is very rough, steep and there are cliffs. I suggest riding this trail with someone who knows it.

Elbert Creek Trail | *Holly Annala*

★★★★★

COLORADO TRAIL: BLACKHAWK SECTION
STAGECOACH TRAIL
Upper Hermosa Park, North of Durango *See map pages 92-93*

Description: This is a classic mountain ride on the Colorado Trail (CT) with amazing views, fantastic singletrack, and great descents. It is a local favorite. The loop starts in Upper Hermosa Park with a long steady climb on forest road to Bolam Pass. A series of climbs and a few short descents in high altitude meadows and along ridges lead to the summit of Blackhawk Pass, with awesome views in all directions. The singletrack is varied and fun, challenging but ridable. Next is a long, fast and smooth descent that flows through alpine meadows and dark forest, and in and out of drainages. Descend Hotel Draw Road, the Stagecoach Trail, or the 6 mile longer alternative Corral Draw, see options below. A short spin on the Hermosa Creek Trail and you're back to the trailhead. Be careful of the crossing of Hermosa Creek at the bottom of Corral Draw and Stagecoach Trails. In the spring and early summer, it can be huge and dangerous, and even after a lot of rain later in the summer and fall it can be quite swift. Turn back if you have any question about the depth or swiftness of the creek. Upper Hermosa Park has plenty of camping so you can ride several rides in the area without getting into your car. See Hermosa Trail, Corral Draw and Elbert Creek to Big Lick.

Distance: 24.1 mile loop, 9.6 miles of singletrack, 14.9 miles of dirt road. With Corral Draw: 30.4 mile loop, 16.4 miles singletrack, 8.4 miles dirt road and 4.5miles of ATV trail and doubletrack
Time: 4 to 6 hours
Difficulty: Expert
Aerobic Effort: High
Elevation: Top: 11,989' **Gain:** 4,806'
Season: July through October
Finding Route: Moderate, the CT and roads are signed. Stagecoach is not signed.
Map: Singletrack Maps Durango Trails. It is the only map that shows Stagecoach Trail.
Location: Park at the Upper Hermosa Park Trailhead, 32 miles from Durango. See page 82, location, for directions.

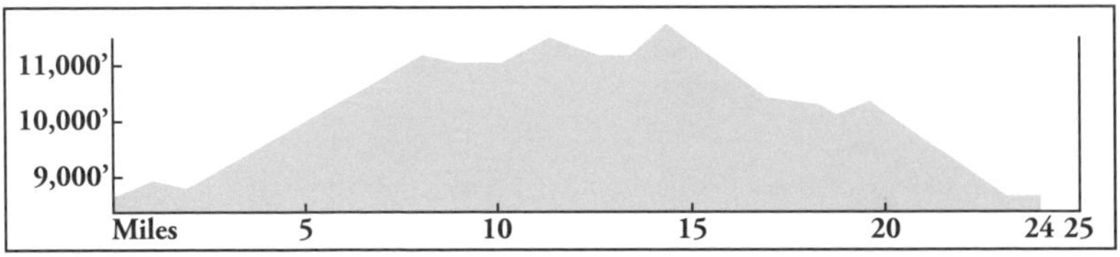

Mileage Log:

0.0 Turn left on Hermosa Park Road from the trailhead. Cross Hermosa Creek in 1.5 miles.

2.4 Stay right and pass Hotel Draw Road/FS 550 on the left. Continue on mostly moderate grade for over 4 miles. After a couple of switchbacks, climb steeply.

COLORADO TRAIL: BLACKHAWK SECTION
STAGECOACH TRAIL
Upper Hermosa Park, North of Durango

7.8 Pass a historic mine and buildings. Stay left and climb a bit more.

8.2 Turn left on a spur road to a campsite when the road levels, just before the lake. Ride straight onto the signed CT singletrack and climb.

9.1 Top of the first climb. Descend and contour around Hermosa Peak.

9.8 Turn left on an old road and descend, then climb.

11.2 Turn right on the signed CT singletrack and continue climbing.

12.1 Reach the summit of Section Point. Enjoy amazing views of Lizard Head and the Rico Mountains. Descend a switchback to the left, passing the faint Circle Trail on the corner, and contour around the hillside on smooth singletrack. Start a big and challenging but all rideable climb.

15.0 Summit of Blackhawk Pass and a great lunch spot unless thunderstorms are chasing you. Get ready for miles of awesome descent.

18.9 Intersect FS 550 at the top of Hotel Draw. Go left and down on the road, or see options below.

22.6 Turn right on FS 578.

25.0 Back to the trailhead.

Corral Draw: At mile 18.9, stay on the CT 2.8 more miles. Turn left and descend Corral Draw 5.4 to Hermosa Creek Trail, turn left and return to the trailhead, 3.3 miles on ATV track. See page 82 for details.

Stagecoach Trail: This is full speed descent, and a great alternative to riding down Hotel Draw Road. It is an old doubletrack that is narrowing to singletrack, and quite steep in places. The Stagecoach Trail is currently not a system trail, not maintained and not currently open to mountain bikes, but hopefully will be adopted into the system soon. Check with the forest service for an update. If you do ride it, be cautious of water erosion and deep ruts. Be aware that the crossing of Hermosa Creek at the bottom can be quite dangerous in early summer, turn back if you have any doubts about crossing.

18.9 At the top of Hotel Draw Road, turn right and climb the road for 6/10ths mile. Don't take the continuation of the CT here as it bypasses the start of the trail.

19.5 At the top of the hill, turn left onto the unsigned Stagecoach Trail. FS 550 continues right and downhill. There are a couple steep mounds closing this old road to motorized, but no sign. Climb a little as you ride out on a ridge. In ½ mile, start the descent.

COLORADO TRAIL: BLACKHAWK SECTION
STAGECOACH TRAIL
Upper Hermosa Park, North of Durango

22.8 Turn sharp right and head down a very steep and rutted singletrack section. Ride out into a meadow. Cross Hermosa Creek and climb a steep hill to the Hermosa Creek Trail and turn left.

24.0 Ride left onto the trailhead road, bathroom and parking to the right. Continue across the East Fork of Hermosa Creek to your vehicle.

To ride Stagecoach Trail only: Access from Hotel Draw. Park as above and ride to mile 2.4, and turn left and climb Hotel Draw Road 3.7 miles to the top (mile 18.9, above.) Stay left on the road for another 6/10ths mile to the Stagecoach Trail. Follow the directions above from here.

Colorado Trail/Blackhawk Pass | *Dodson Harper*

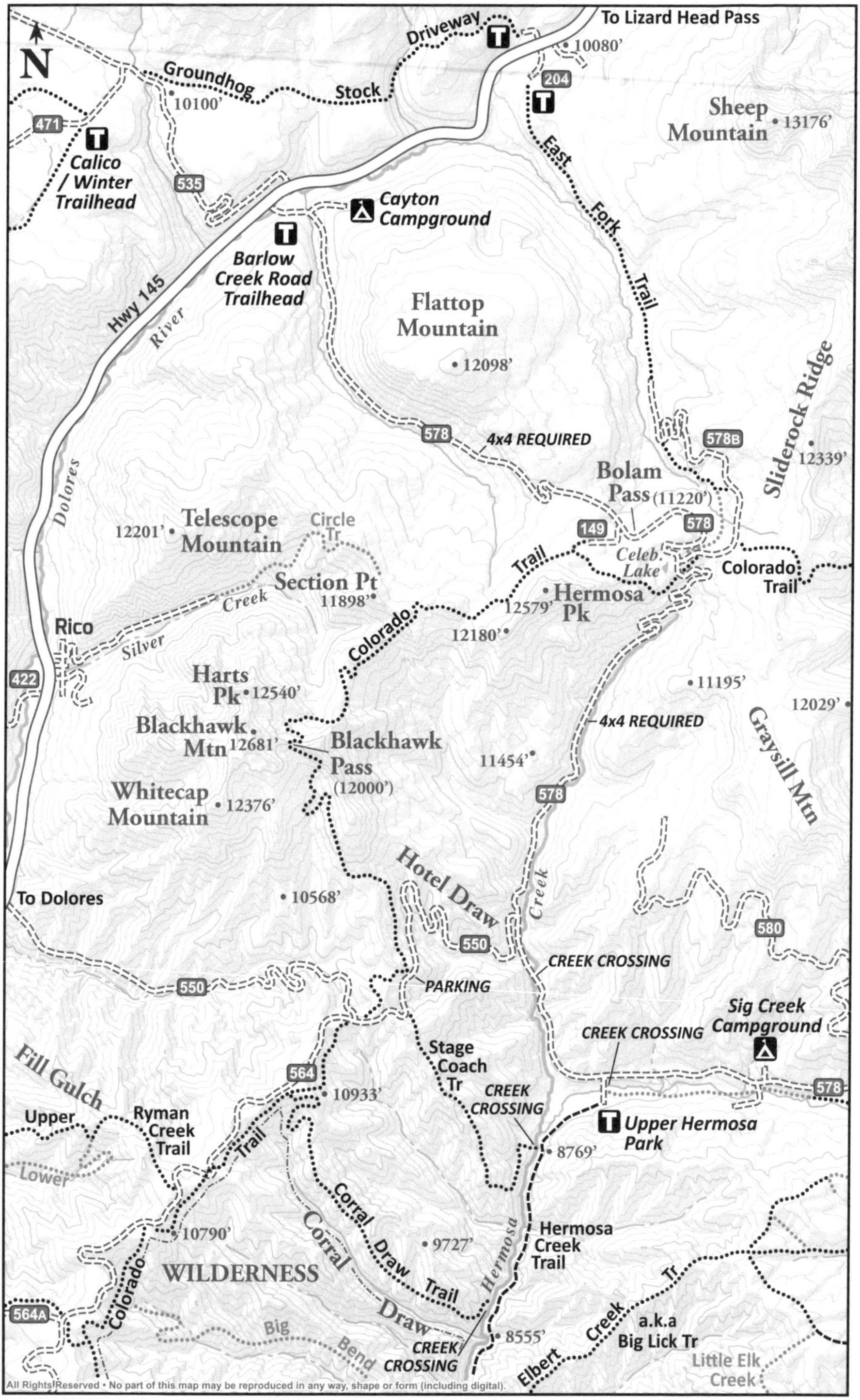
To Lizard Head Pass
N
Driveway
10080'
Groundhog
Stock
10100'
204
471
Sheep Mountain
13176'
Calico / Winter Trailhead
East Fork Trail
535
Cayton Campground
Barlow Creek Road Trailhead
Hwy 145
River
Flattop Mountain
12098'
Slickrock Ridge
578
4x4 REQUIRED
578B
12339'
Bolam Pass (11220')
Dolores
Telescope Mountain
12201'
Circle Tr
149
578
Celeb. Lake
Colorado Trail
Section Pt
11898'
Creek
Trail
Hermosa Pk
12579'
Rico
Silver
Colorado
12180'
422
Harts Pk
12540'
11195'
12029'
Graysill Mtn
Blackhawk Mtn
12681'
Blackhawk Pass (12000')
4x4 REQUIRED
11454'
Whitecap Mountain
12376'
578
Hotel Draw
Creek
To Dolores
10568'
550
580
CREEK CROSSING
550
PARKING
Sig Creek Campground
CREEK CROSSING
Fill Gulch
Stage Coach Tr
564
10933'
CREEK CROSSING
578
Upper
Ryman Creek Trail
Trail
Upper Hermosa Park
8769'
Lower
Corral Draw Trail
Corral Draw
10790'
9727'
Hermosa
Hermosa Creek Trail
WILDERNESS
Colorado
564A
Big
Bend
CREEK CROSSING
8555'
Elbert Creek Tr
a.k.a Big Lick Tr
Little Elk Creek

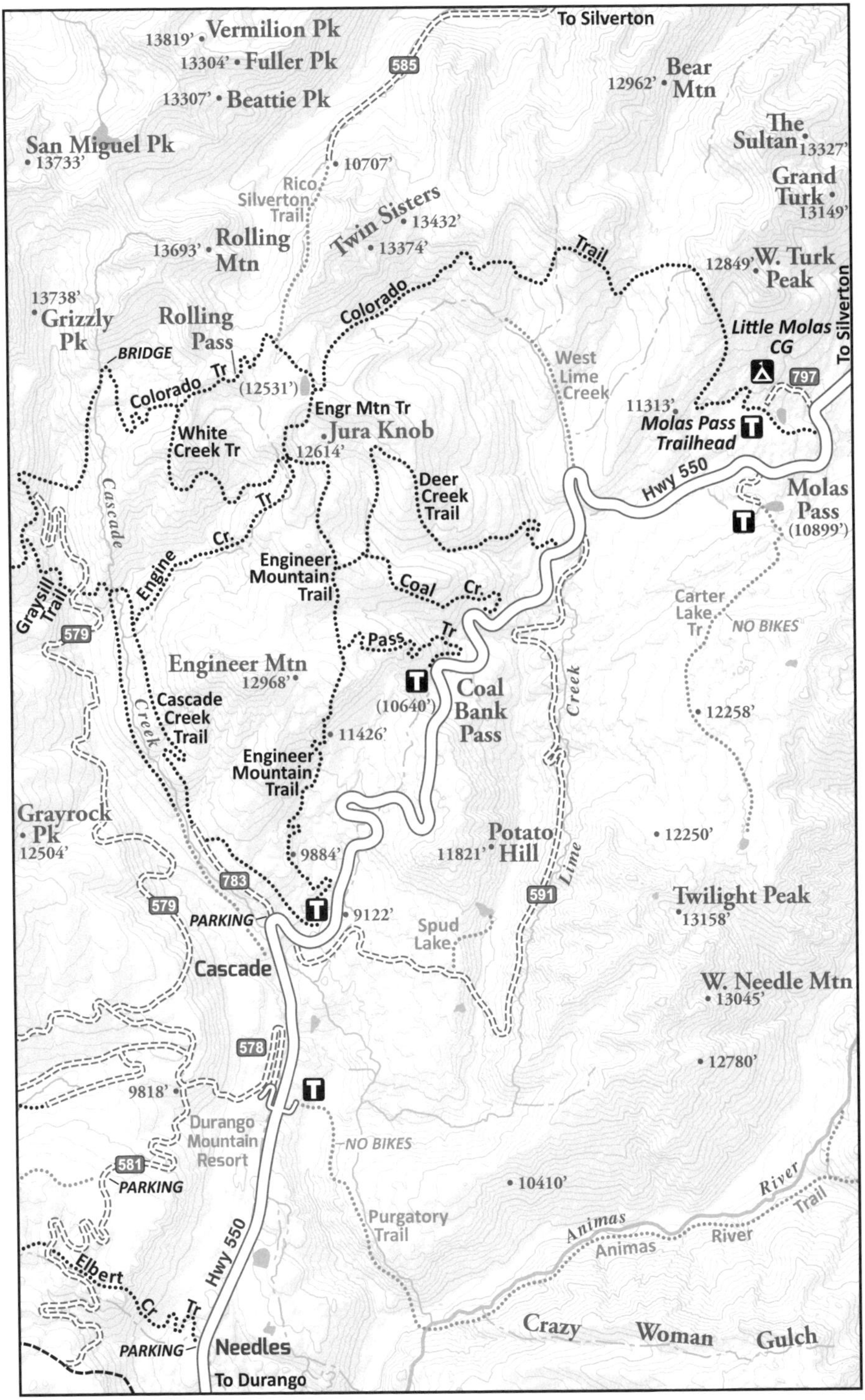
To Silverton
13819' • Vermilion Pk
13304' • Fuller Pk
13307' • Beattie Pk
585
Bear Mtn 12962'
The Sultan 13327'
Grand Turk 13149'
San Miguel Pk 13733'
10707'
Rico Silverton Trail
Twin Sisters 13432'
13374'
13693' Rolling Mtn
Colorado Trail
12849' W. Turk Peak
13738' Grizzly Pk
Rolling Pass
Little Molas CG
To Silverton
BRIDGE
Colorado Tr
(12531')
West Lime Creek
797
11313'
Molas Pass Trailhead
Engr Mtn Tr
Jura Knob
12614'
White Creek Tr
Deer Creek Trail
Hwy 550
Molas Pass (10899')
Cascade
Engine Cr. Tr
Engineer Mountain Trail
Coal Cr.
Graysill Trail
579
Carter Lake Tr
NO BIKES
Pass Tr
Engineer Mtn 12968'
(10640')
Coal Bank Pass
Cascade Creek Trail
Creek
12258'
11426'
Engineer Mountain Trail
Grayrock Pk 12504'
Potato Hill 11821'
12250'
9884'
Lime
783
591
Twilight Peak 13158'
579
PARKING
9122'
Spud Lake
Cascade
W. Needle Mtn 13045'
578
12780'
9818'
Durango Mountain Resort
NO BIKES
581
PARKING
10410'
Purgatory Trail
Animas River Trail
Animas River
Hwy 550
Elbert Cr. Tr
Crazy Woman Gulch
PARKING
Needles
To Durango

★★★☆☆

PASS TRAIL TO ENGINEER MOUNTAIN TRAIL

Coal Bank Pass, North of Durango *See map pages 92-93*

Description: This is a really fun, moderate length alpine loop with an awesome, fast descent. It has the high altitude singletrack experience with amazing views and great singletrack and is only two hours long with a shuttle. The ride starts on Coal Bank Pass with a climb on the Pass Trail, through old growth forest and high alpine meadows. There are a few short technical sections of limestone and big tree roots that you may have to walk, but overall the climb is moderate. The descent on the Engineer Mountain Trail is long, crossing meadows and winding through dark timber and aspen forest. It rolls next to cliffs overlooking the upper Animas Valley on good singletrack with quite a few switchbacks. Closing the loop involves a shuttle or riding 4.5 miles on Hwy 550. Start the ride early morning in thunderstorm season. The Engineer Mountain Trail can have a lot of cows in the late summer and fall in some years, making the trail quite mucky. Check with the Forest Service, 970-247-4874. See page 110 for details on riding the Engineer Mountain Trail from Molas Pass, a longer and more difficult option. The Engineer Mountain Trail is also a good but challenging ascent to access other trails in the area, see page 99.

Distance: 7.8 mile shuttle ride, all singletrack. **Loop:** Add 4.5 miles paved road.
Time: 2 hours, add 1 hour if you ride the highway instead of shuttling.
Difficulty: Advanced intermediate with several expert sections.
Aerobic Effort: Moderately high overall, high for short distances. High altitude.
Elevation: Top: 11,664' **Gain:** 1,060' **Loss:** 2,551'
Season: Late June or early July through early October
Finding Route: Easy. Deer Creek is difficult to follow.
Map: Singletrack Maps Durango Trails
Location: This ride requires a shuttle or a 4.5 mile ride up the highway. To get to the bottom of the ride where you will leave one car, drive 26.7 miles north of the last light in Durango on Highway 550 to an unmarked turn on the left to the Engineer Mountain Trailhead. This is 3 miles after passing Durango Mountain Resort and less than one mile after the big highway switchback over Cascade Creek. Continue another 4.5 miles to the top of Coal Bank Pass with bikes and riders. Just past the rest stop and pass is an unmarked dirt road on the left to the Pass Trailhead.

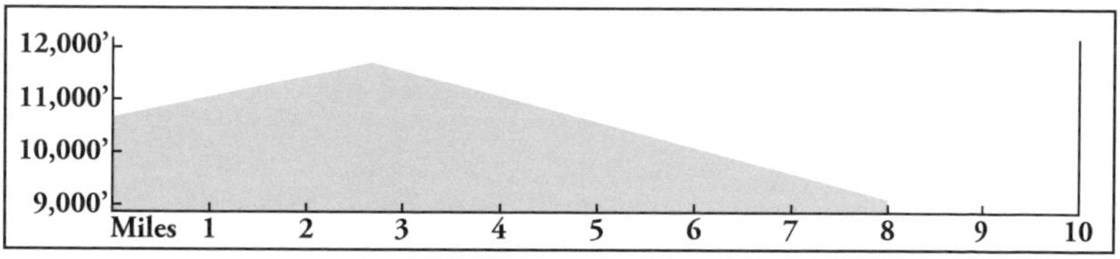

Mileage Log:

0.0 Take the signed Pass Trail out of the parking area. Twilight Peak looms across the valley. Pass a couple of spur trails, stay on the main trail.

PASS TRAIL TO ENGINEER MOUNTAIN TRAIL
Coal Bank Pass, North of Durango

2.4 Turn left and climb on the signed Engineer Mountain Trail through alpine meadows and along the flank of Engineer Mountain.

2.9 Start the descent. Roll into the forest around good switchbacks on mostly fast trail. Down lower enter meadows and aspen forest, where the trail becomes more rutted and rough. There are great views of the West Needle Mountains across the valley.

7.8 Ride next to a small pond; stay left when the Cascade Trail goes right and end in the parking area.

PASS TRAIL TO COAL CREEK
★★★★☆

DEER CREEK

Coal Bank Pass, North of Durango

See map page 92-93

Description: This is a moderate length and really fun loop in the high alpine area north of Durango, just below the Colorado Trail. It climbs and descends through meadows and big old growth forest. It has the high altitude singletrack experience with amazing views, great singletrack, and awesome flowers in late June and in July while only being a two or three hour ride. On the climb up the Pass Trail, there are several short technical sections of limestone steps and big tree roots that you may have to walk, but overall the trail is a moderate climb. Up higher on the Engineer Mountain and Coal Creek Trails are a couple of rutted sections of hike a bike. The descent is really fun! It has steep and rutted sections with amazing views up higher, faint cairned sections, smooth contouring sections, and short steep switchbacks intermixed with gradual singletrack, all through amazing spruce, fir, pine, and aspen forest. Close the loop with a one mile ride on Hwy 550. Start early morning in thunderstorm season to get back before the lightning and rain (July and August.) There are quite a few hikers here, be courteous. Coal and Deer Creeks are not good uphill trails.

Distance: 7.6 mile loop
Time: 1 ¾ to 2 ½ hours
Difficulty: Expert
Aerobic Effort: Moderately high. High altitude.
Elevation: Top: 11,875' **Gain:** 1,885'
Season: Late June or early July through early October
Finding Route: Moderate. Signed at junctions. The start of the Coal Creek Trail is faint for ½ mile and difficult to follow, with only cairns for markers.
Map: Singletrack Maps Durango Trails or Latitude 40 Durango Trails
Location: The Pass Creek Trailhead is located on Coal Bank Pass, 30.2 miles north of Durango from the last stoplight on Hwy 550. Just after the pass and rest pullout, turn left on an unmarked dirt road to the trailhead.

PASS TRAIL TO COAL CREEK

DEER CREEK

Coal Bank Pass, North of Durango

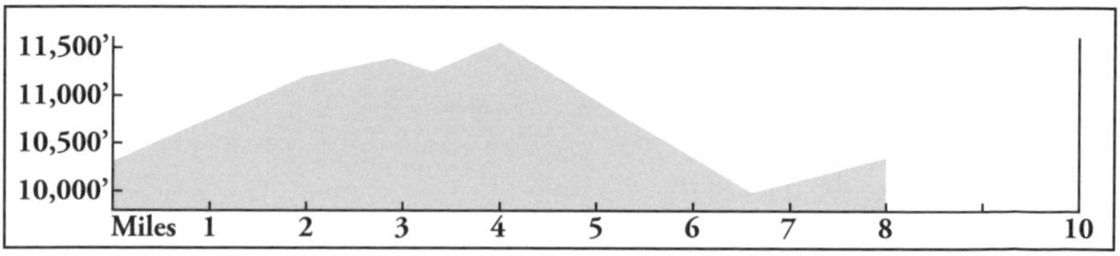

Mileage Log:

0.0 Take the signed Pass Trail out of the parking area. Twilight Peak towers across the valley from the trail. Stay on the main trail passing a couple spurs.

2.4 Turn right on the Engineer Mountain Trail and climb.

3.3 After a braided and more difficult climb through an meadow, turn right at the signed Y intersection to Coal and Deer Creek Trails. Climb rutted trail, with 3/10ths mile hike a bike.

3.8 The trail levels and starts downhill. Look for a tiny Coal Creek Trail sign on the right near some big flat rocks and a cairn. The main Coal Creek Trail is just after the sign. Enjoy amazing views of the Silverton area, the Needles, and the Grenadiers. Turn right and start a steep and rutted descent through high alpine meadows. (Or to ride Deer Creek, continue left. See option below.)

4.1 The trail disappears at a small saddle. Turn right across a red dirt area and look for cairns. The trail switchbacks down three turns and goes left and contours, becoming visible again. Don't descend to the creek. The next section contours ½ mile and then descends steeply through the forest.

6.3 After a short exposed section ride carefully onto the highway shoulder. Turn right and ride up the highway.

7.5 Turn right onto the dirt road to the trailhead. End at the parking area.

The Deer Creek Trail is very primitive and quite difficult to follow but explores an interesting drainage. It is rutted, rough, and overgrown with several hike a bike sections. It takes about 1 more hour to ride than Coal Creek. Ride as above to mile 3.8 and turn left. Start down, then contour across the meadow and climb rutted trail. At mile 4.3, top out and pass a pond and swampy area on the left. When the trail starts to descend, turn right out of the drainage and onto the bench to the right, and turn left on the grassy trail marked with a few cairns. Soon the trail is easier to follow as it descends into a deep rut through tall willows. Cross the drainage to the left, descend and contour, and descend steeply to cross a main creek at 5.0. Turn right and descend along the creek. 5.6: Contour left away from the creek and descend through a big meadow. 6.5: Start a series of climbs. 7.5: Top out, contour and descend steep loose switchbacks. 8.4: Turn right on Hwy 550. 11.1: Right and back to parking.

★★★★☆

PASS TRAIL AND WHITE CREEK TO GRAYSILL TRAIL

PASS TRAIL TO ENGINE CREEK TRAIL

Coal Bank Pass, North of Durango *See map pages 92-93*

Description: This is an incredible big ride in the alpine area of Coal Bank Pass, with great singletrack and amazing views. The Graysill Trail, a steep and fun trail that switchbacks down from the Colorado Trail (CT), is one of my favorites! It descends on the flanks of the massive Graysill Mountain, with Grayrock Peak and Engineer Mountain looming nearby. The Pass Trail is a fun and relatively moderate way to access the higher trails of this area, good singletrack winding up through the meadows and woods to the foot of Engineer Mountain and the Engineer Mountain Trail (EMT). A right turn on the Engineer Mountain Trail takes you up rough singletrack, across the big basin of Engine Creek, to the little-ridden White Creek Trail. The White Creek Trail is similar to the CT, but lower. It winds its way around and into the Cascade Creek drainage, mostly above treeline, and descends to meet the CT. A fast descent into and a big climb out of Cascade Creek on the CT leads to the Graysill Trail. Smooth switchbacks and steep and technical trail wind you back down to the Cascade Creek Trail for a few more miles of singletrack. Riding the loop via the Pass Trail and EMT is similar in difficulty to the CT to Graysill Loop, see page 108, but allows riders to connect the loop with a 4 ½ mile ride on Hwy 550 (instead 11.5 miles on the highway to the CT/Molas Pass trailhead.) Another shorter option is to descend the Engine Creek Trail from mile 5.1, see option below. This area is prone to a lot of rain and thunderstorms, get an early start and plan your ride for a dry day.

Distance: 19.8 mile shuttle ride, 19.3 miles of singletrack, ½ mile dirt road. For a loop, add 4 ½ miles of pavement.
Time: 3 ½ to 5 hours
Difficulty: Expert
Aerobic Effort: Strenuous
Elevation: Top: 11,802' **Gain:** 2,804' **Loss:** 4,714'
Season: July through September or early October, depending on early season snows.
Finding Route: Moderate with one obscure junction, and the trail disappears after crossing Cascade Creek, requiring some route finding.
Map: Singletrack Maps Durango Trails
Location: This ride requires a shuttle or a 4 ½ mile ride up the highway. Leave a shuttle vehicle at the Engineer Mountain Trailhead, 26.7 miles north of Durango, on the left. The turn to the trailhead is unsigned and easy to miss. It is 3 miles past Durango Mountain Resort, and 8/10ths past Cascade Creek and the big switchback over it on Hwy 550. Continue to the top of Coal Bank Pass with bikes and riders. Just after Coal Bank Pass, turn left on a dirt road to the Pass Trail trailhead.

PASS TRAIL AND WHITE CREEK TO GRAYSILL TRAIL

PASS TRAIL TO ENGINE CREEK TRAIL

Coal Bank Pass, North of Durango

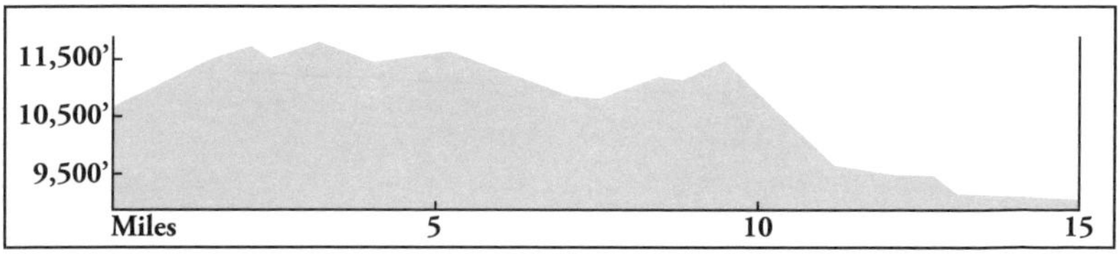

Mileage Log:

0.0 Take the signed Pass Trail and climb moderately, and then more steeply in the dark forest. There are several short technical sections of limestone steps and big tree roots that you may have to walk but overall the climb is moderate and mostly rideable.

2.4 Turn right on the Engineer Mountain Trail.

3.3 After a climb on braided trail through a meadow, turn left on the Engineer Mountain Trail toward White and Engine Creek Trails. Deer and Coal Creek Trails are right.

5.1 Arrive at a 4-way junction with a falling down sign. A sharp left leads to Engine Creek (see option below.) Straight ahead and right the EMT continues up steeply to the CT (not a good uphill.) Take White Creek Trail straight ahead and left, cross a creek and climb.

8.0 Cross a creek and turn left on the CT.

9.1 Cross a big fork of Cascade Creek at the bottom of the descent.

9.6 Cross Cascade Creek on a bridge. Start a technical climb with some hike a bike.

12.0 Keep right at a trail junction and climb. Left goes down to Cascade Divide Road.

12.6 After an abrupt V creek crossing and entering a big high altitude meadow, turn left on the somewhat obscure Graysill Trail. Look for a small sign in a tree.

13.9 Cross Cascade Divide Road and look for the trail to the left.

14.7 Unsigned trail junction. Go left and cross Cascade Creek for more ridable trail that is technically easier but has more climbing, unless the creek is high. Climb the bank on the other side and walk downstream to find the trail. Once you find the trail, pass a spur to the right in 3/10ths mile and ride straight ahead. If the creek is high and dangerous, stay right and cross the creek down lower where it is wider and easier. When the trail gets close to the creek a couple miles (approx.) downstream, look for the unsigned crossing to the doubletrack on the other side. Be aware a primitive trail continues to Cascade Village. This side of the creek is technical with some hike a bike.

PASS TRAIL AND WHITE CREEK TO GRAYSILL TRAIL
PASS TRAIL TO ENGINE CREEK TRAIL
Coal Bank Pass, North of Durango

15.3 Pass Engine Creek Trail on the left. Descend and cross a bridge by a waterfall. The trail climbs and descends a few sections.

17.2 The trail widens to old road.

17.7 Ride through a gate and head down the road and turn left on the easy-to-miss singletrack in 2/10ths miles. Climb, contour, and descend.

19.8 Ride across the dam of a small pond and end at the Cascade and Engineer Mountain Trailhead.

Pass Creek to Engine Creek Trail: Another great trail to ride in the area after climbing the Pass Trail is Engine Creek. Despite the rough nature of sections of the trail, there aren't many trails that are like Engine Creek. The character of the creek drainage and the steep and technical descent on singletrack are unique. It has a horse outfitted hunting camp down low, so the lower singletrack is often very rough and braided, especially in the fall after heavy rain or snow during hunting season. See below for details on Engine Creek.

★★★☆☆

ENGINEER MOUNTAIN TRAIL TO ENGINE CREEK
ENGINEER MOUNTAIN TO COLORADO, WHITE AND GRAYSILL TRAILS
Coal Bank Pass, North of Durango *See map pages 92-93*

Description: This is a great way to combine these incredible high altitude trails into a loop without highway riding or a shuttle. The Engineer Mountain Trail is a big two plus hour climb to Engine Creek, almost all rideable by strong climbers except for some rutted sections. Up higher it winds around the flanks of the massive rock faces of Engineer Mountain. Engine Creek is a unique and rowdy experts-only descent with a lot of character. It rolls next to the scenic creek much of the way down, with a few bigger drops and steep sections, and exposure to the creek to keep it fun and exciting. It is often very rough at the bottom due to horse use and precipitation in hunting season, but if you haven't done it you should give it a go anyway for the rest of the experience. Another awesome and longer option is to climb the Engineer Mountain Trail, contour on the White Creek Trail to the Colorado Trail (CT,) and descend the Graysill Trail to Cascade Creek. See option below. The Engineer Mountain Trail is a also great downhill, ride it as an out and back or access it from the Pass Trail or CT, see pages 94 and 110. All these trails are non-motorized. Start very early in thunderstorm season. Cattle can be grazing here some years and with rain can make a muddy mess. Contact the Forest Service for current information, 970-247-4874.

ENGINEER MOUNTAIN TRAIL TO ENGINE CREEK

ENGINEER MOUNTAIN TO COLORADO, WHITE AND GRAYSILL TRAILS

Coal Bank Pass, North of Durango

Distance: 16.1 mile loop, 15.5 miles singetrack, ½ mile doubletrack.
Time: 4 to 5 ½ hours
Difficulty: Expert with a few short very difficult sections on the descent of Engine Creek.
Aerobic Effort: Strenuous
Elevation: Top: 11,800' **Gain:** 3,150'
Season: Late June or early July through early October
Finding Route: Moderate
Map: Singletrack Maps Durango Trails
Location: Drive 26.7 miles north of the last light in Durango on Hwy 550 and turn left on the unmarked dirt road to the Engineer Mountain Trailhead. This is 3 miles past Durango Mountain Resort and 8/10ths mile after crossing Cascade Creek on the big highway switchback.

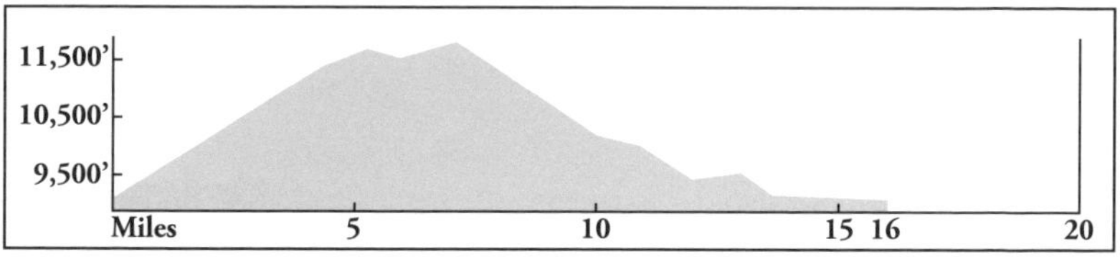

Mileage Log:

0.0 Ride onto the signed singletrack, pass a pond, and stay right on the Engineer Mountain Trail. To the left is the return route of this loop, the Cascade Trail. The beginning of the climb has some steep sections with little warm up and is quite challenging. Once the trail enters the dark conifer forest, it is lower angle with switchbacks, and more forgiving.

4.9 Enter high alpine meadows on the flanks of Engineer Mountain.

5.4 Ride straight past the signed Pass Trail on the right and a trail to Engineer Mountain on the left. Contour and soak up great views of the Silverton area and the Needle Mountains.

6.5 After a braided climb in a meadow, turn left at the Y intersection toward White and Engine Creek Trails, on the Engineer Mountain Trail. Deer and Coal Creek Trails are to the right. Climb over a saddle, contour, and finally descend, being cautious of some sudden exposure after one steep, rutted switchback.

8.3 Arrive at a 4-way intersection with a broken sign. Engine Creek Trail descends sharply to the left, White Creek Trail is straight ahead and slightly left (see option below) and Engineer Mountain Trail goes straight ahead and then climbs steeply to the right to the CT (not recommended as a climb.) Turn left on the Engine Creek Trail and start down steeply, then roll moderately across a wide bench and into the forest. Soon the trail gets steeper again.

9.1 At the junction of two creeks, cross and climb a short steep hill, and descend along the drainage with big exposure and some drops.

10.2 Ride through a meadow, then back into the woods on undulating terrain. Cross several creeks and negotiate the rough section.

11.6 Turn left on the Cascade Creek Trail. Cross a bridge with a great waterfall. Climb and descend, staying on the main trail above the creek.

13.7 Pass a right turn to the creek. The trail widens to an old road. Pass a cabin.

14.0 Squeeze through the gate and descend the road. In 2/10ths mile turn left on the singletrack that is easy-to-miss, marked with a user sign. Climb, contour, and descend.

16.1 Turn right to the parking area near the pond.

Engineer Mountain to Colorado, White Creek, Graysill and Cascade Trails: At mile 8.3 above, ride the White Creek Trail to the Colorado Trail (CT) and turn left. White Creek is smooth singletrack with very little elevation gain or drop. Stay on the CT for 4.6 miles to descend Graysill and Cascade Trails. This is a 23 mile all singletrack loop, no shuttle needed. See page 97, Pass Trail and White Creek to Graysill Trails, for details.

Colorado Trail to Graysill | *Bill Koons*

★★★★★

THE COLORADO TRAIL

Molas Pass to Durango *See map pages 92-93 and 78-79*

Description: This section of the Colorado Trail (CT) is the ultimate in high altitude riding, with miles of amazing singletrack, great views, and wilderness-like alpine terrain. The ride starts high on Molas Pass at 10,900', and contours above the Animas River and Lime Creek drainages, with amazing views of the Needle and Grenadier Mountains. It snakes through the San Juans and into the La Plata Mountains. It is perfect for a three day overnight trip. Some hearty souls ride it in one very long day, but to really enjoy the beauty, two to four days are needed. There are lots of options for camping along the way, either with a support vehicle, or for bike packing, near water and shelter. The CT is a nice out and back ride from Molas Pass as well, or there are plenty of loop options for day rides with sections of the CT, see pages 97,108,110,140 (options),142. The CT maintains high altitude through this entire section, so good fitness and some acclimatization is a must. The trail has many smooth sections, but also a lot of technical riding, so riding skills are important also. This area gets a lot of thunderstorms and rain in July and August; be prepared with good rain gear and get an early start each day.

Day 1: The ride starts on Molas Pass, 38 miles north of Durango and 7 miles south of Silverton on Hwy 550. Climb and contour 10 miles to Rolling Pass on singletrack. After a long, fast descent into Cascade Creek and a big, challenging climb to Bolam Pass, riders arrive at the first good opportunity for vehicle supported camping at mile 18.4, see below for details. From Bolam Pass and Celebration Lake the CT climbs around Hermosa Peak to Blackhawk Pass for a beautiful descent that ends on Hotel Draw Road. Hotel Draw is the second good vehicle access area with lots of camping for your first or second night.

Day 2: From Hotel Draw the CT winds along the top of a broad, forested ridge, on and off the road, utilizing a few sections of old logging roads and also some quality singletrack. Next, climb great trail up to Indian Ridge, where the views and ridge top riding are incredible. There is some hike a bike, and some really amazing scree riding. Often thunderstorms will chase you from the ridge. After descending to Taylor Lake, cross Kennebec Pass Road, climb once more and descend steeply into Junction Creek. Junction Creek Road presents a final night of vehicle support camping opportunity.

Day 3: After crossing Junction Creek Road, continue on semi-primitive trail down steep, rocky and rutted, but awesome trail down into Fasbinder Gulch and across Junction Creek. One last killer of a climb and miles of mostly smooth contouring trail and seemingly endless downhill swoop into Durango.

Alternate Routes from Rico and Dolores area: Ride up East Fork Trail (Lizard Head Pass) to Bolam Pass, head south on the CT, continue to Grindstone or Sharkstooth Trail and descend Bear Creek Trail. Barlow Creek Road is steep, high clearance, and requires 4WD for the support vehicle. Scotch Creek Road is steep in places, high clearance, and 4WD is recommended. There is also camping near the top of Hillside Drive, a mostly smooth road until the last few miles, and is 2WD high clearance unless it rains. An alternative loop in reverse is to ride up Hillside Drive, turn left on the CT and continue to East Fork and down. Cross Hwy 145 and ride the Groundhog Stock and Calico Trails to the end on Highway 145.

Distance: 70.5 miles point to point, 65 miles of singletrack and 5 ½ miles of doubletrack, closed to motorized.
Time: Approximately 14 to 22 hours over several days for riders with good fitness and riding skills, and acclimated to altitude. The first two days are the longest.
Difficulty: Expert
Aerobic Effort: Very high to strenuous. Parts of the CT in this section are more moderate but still high altitude. The last day has a lot of downhill; but has one long, challenging climb.
Elevation: Top: 12,507' **Gain:** 12,108' **Loss:** 15,779'
Season: July through mid-September or early October. The last 17 miles from Junction Creek are usually dry by the end of May for a day ride, see page 65.
Finding Route: Easy to moderate overall, with a few areas of more difficult. There are many turns but the CT is fairly well marked. Look for the small triangular CT markers along the route. Once you arrive at Hotel Draw (mile 30,) the route finding is more difficult with many spur roads and trails, until about mile 40.
Map: Singletrack Maps Durango Trails or Latitude 40 Durango Trails
Location: Leave a shuttle vehicle at the Colorado Trailhead, 3.4 miles out 25th Street/Junction Creek Road from Durango. See page 63, Location, for detailed directions. Start the ride at Molas Pass, 38 miles north on Hwy 550 from Durango. Drive 2/10ths mile past Molas Pass and turn left on Little Molas Lake Campground road and drive to the trailhead at the end. Hermosa Tours does shuttles, 877-765-5682. If you start on Hwy 550 at the rest area, add 1.1 miles to the ride information, below. The signed CT starts 1/10th mile past the rest area, on the left.

Camping, vehicle access information:
Little Molas Lake Campground: Free camping before your trip at the trailhead. If it is full, there is pay camping about one mile north on Hwy 550 at Molas Lake.

Cascade Divide Road: Cascade Divide Road comes very close to the CT at mile 15.7, with a few camping options up rough road, access from Hermosa Park Road. This makes the first day short.

Bolam Pass Road: The road to Bolam Pass requires a high clearance vehicle and 4WD is recommended for the very steep section and possible washouts to the camping at or near Celebration Lake. There is a big creek crossing at the bottom of the road near Hermosa Park. On the back side of Bolam on Barlow Creek Road there are more camping spots but they require a little extra climbing to get to. The CT to Bolam Pass Road is about 4 to 6 hours.

Barlow Creek Road and FS 149: Camping near the CT at mile 20.8. Rough road but few other campers. Drive from Rico, or over Bolam Pass.

Hotel Draw: Hotel Draw is an easier access than Bolam Pass Road (often possible with 2WD,) but may require 4WD with heavy rain or if the road is damaged. There is a big creek crossing at the bottom of the road near Hermosa Park. There are plenty of vehicle campsites along the road near the trail. If you don't have an appropriate vehicle, it is possible for riders to descend the road to a 2WD accessed camping spot, although it will require a big climb back up in the morning. This is 6 to 10 hours from Molas Pass, 3-4 hours from Bolam Pass.

La Plata Canyon Road/Kennebec Pass: This is a possible campsite but not the best. One section of the road is very difficult 4WD, and the top is a busy trailhead area with little room for a camp. The top of Junction Creek Road is better.

Junction Creek Road: Drive 16-18 miles up high clearance road to many campsites, within a couple miles of easy riding of the trail. Most campsites are before arriving at the CT (riders will turn left on the road.)

Bike packing: There is a lot of water and camping opportunity along the first 28 miles of trail to just beyond Blackhawk Pass. The top of Hotel Draw and FS 564 have no water sources, and on to Taylor Lakes (Kennebec Pass) water is very limited near the trail. Junction Creek Road has no water. Once you descend from Junction Creek Road, there are several streams until the trail climbs out of the creek. It is often dry beyond here until the Junction Creek crossing, near Durango.

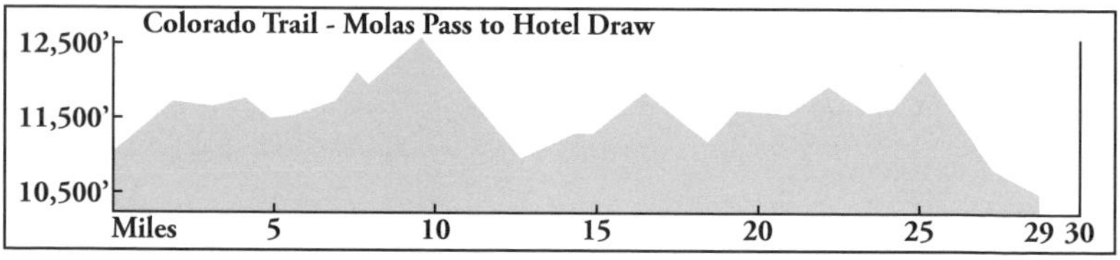

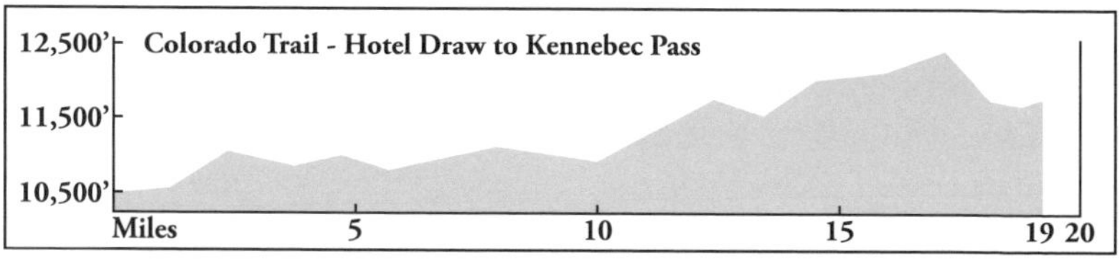

THE COLORADO TRAIL
Molas Pass to Durango

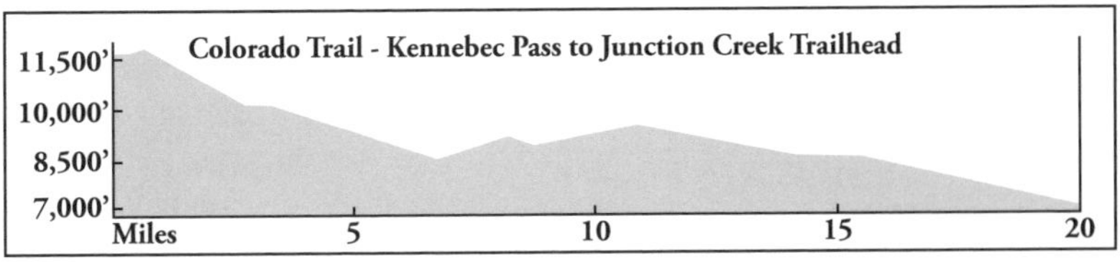

Mileage Log:

0.0 From the Little Molas Lake Campground trailhead, start a mostly moderate two mile climb on the signed CT singletrack. The trail is easy to follow for the next 18 miles with very few junctions.

2.0 The trail levels, then climbs, descends and contours the upper meadows of the big West Lime Creek basin, crossing many creeks along the way.

7.0 Start a big climb toward Rolling Pass.

9.2 Turn right at the signed junction on the CT and climb. Left is the Engineer Mountain Trail. Pass the unsigned and faint Rico-Silverton Trail into the south fork of Mineral Creek on the right in 7/10ths mile, just below a big switchback.

10.1 Summit Rolling Pass. Start a fast, rocky and switchbacking descent into the Cascade drainage. Roll into the forest down lower.

11.7 Turn sharp right around a tree with a Colorado Trail sign in it, staying with the CT. White Creek Trail is straight ahead off the switchback.

12.8 Cross a big fork of Cascade Creek at the bottom of the descent. In ½ mile, cross Cascade Creek on a bridge. Start a technical climb with some hike a bike.

15.7 Keep right at a junction, and climb again for nearly two miles with a few breaks. Left goes to Cascade Divide Road.

16.3 Pass the easy-to-miss Graysill Trail on the left. It has a small sign.

17.4 Summit of the climb. Views of the San Miguel and Rico Mountains, and Lizard Head in front of you. Contour north and west, and descend a doubletrack left.

18.4 Turn left down Bolam Pass Road. Right leads to the East Fork Trail, see page 161.

19.0 Turn left on the signed CT singletrack and descend to Celebration Lake.

19.2 Roll straight ahead onto a campsite road next to the lake and onto the signed CT singletrack and climb. (Left at the lake is Bolam Pass Road to Hermosa Park Road, right leads over the pass to Barlow Creek Road.)

20.8 Turn left onto a doubletrack, FS 149. Right leads to Barlow Creek Road. Descend and then climb.

22.2 Turn right onto signed CT singletrack and climb.

23.1 Ride over the pass at Section Point, overlooking the Rico Mountains. Descend to a sharp switchback and stay left. (The faint Circle Trail goes straight off the switchback and toward Rico. There is route finding and hike a bike to get to it.) Descend, contour, and climb onto a ridge-top trail. Continue into meadows, climbing steadily and then steeply toward Blackhawk Pass.

26.0 Blackhawk Pass. Enjoy amazing views in all directions. Start a long, fast descent. As you near Hotel Draw the trail widens to an old logging road.

30.0 Reach Hotel Draw Road. Stay right on the CT and pass a gated spur road on the left. The trail follows an old logging road that is slowly turning to singletrack.

31.2 Turn right onto FS Road 550, and turn left immediately at a fork onto FS Road 564. FS 550, Scotch Creek Road, turns right to Rico. If you start descending road, you are going the wrong way!

31.3 Turn left onto singletrack and climb more, contouring along the southeast side of the ridge. The CT goes on and off FSR 564 for the next several miles, staying near the ridge with little descending.

32.7 Stay right, passing the Corral Draw Trail and continue climbing.

33.9 Back to the road, turn left. There are several vehicle support campsites along here. This is 7 to 10 hours from Molas Pass on the CT.

34.0 Turn left onto the signed singletrack.

34.1 Cross the road, climb, and cross the road again in 1/10th mile, staying with the singletrack. Climb past a closed road sign. Contour and descend in meadow.

34.9 Turn left onto the road, go around the hill, and in less than 1/10th mile turn left on the singletrack.

35.6 Turn left onto the road, then left on the singletrack in a short distance.

36.0 Swing left passing a big camping area.

36.4 Stay right, passing the signed Big Bend Trail (now in wilderness) on the left.

36.9 Pop out of trees next to road, stay left and climb.

37.1 Pass the signed Salt Creek Trail to the right in the flats.

37.8 Pass the Salt Creek Trail (now in wilderness) into Hermosa on the left.

40.2 (approx. mileage) Start climbing a big hill, up long switchbacks.

41.7 (approx. mileage) Pass an overlook to the right; soon the trail levels.

43.2 Pass signed Unmaintained Trail 547 (Cape of Good Hope) on the left.

44.4 Turn left and climb into the open, staying on the CT/Highline Trail. The Hillside Connection/Grindstone Trail turns right. Climb onto Indian Ridge.

48.1 Stay left, passing a signed spur on the right to Taylor Lake, and descend a steep section of trail with a short hike a bike for most riders.

48.6 Turn left on the CT at a signed junction near Taylor Lake. The Sharkstooth Trail goes right.

49.8 Turn right in a parking area at the top of Kennebec Pass Road, then immediately left onto the signed singletrack and climb to the pass.

50.4 Summit of the pass. Stay left in 1/10th mile and descend narrow hillside trail on scree and switchbacks, with some exposure.

52.2 Cross Junction Creek Road. The trail continues just to the left. Descend the somewhat tricky narrow trail, climb shortly, and descend more to Junction Creek. Watch out for slippery roots and wood water bars.

56.6 Cross a bridge and start a long climb, then continue intermittent climbing and contouring for a couple more miles.

60.5 High point! Enjoy the views and start a fast descent on a very old doubletrack. Be aware of more riders and hikers using the trail from this point on. Shortly after a rocky section, look for a fork in the trail.

63.8 Turn left at the junction on the CT. The Dry Fork Trail continues straight. Climb a short distance, then contour through Ponderosa Pine forest. Next descend a steep, rutted and fast section. Be very careful of other users.

66.4 Pass Hoffhein's Connection to the right. Continue straight (left) on the CT and pass Gudy's Rest. Descend long switchbacks to Junction Creek.

68.0 Cross a bridge, turn right and climb and descend along Junction Creek.

69.4 Turn right and continue past a trailhead, closer to the creek now.

70.5 End at the Junction Creek Trailhead.

Colorado Trail/Hotel Draw

★★★★★

GRAYSILL TRAIL AND THE COLORADO TRAIL

Molas Pass, North of Durango *See map pages 92-93*

Description: This is an incredible big ride in the alpine area of Molas Pass, with great singletrack and amazing views. The Colorado Trail (CT) from Molas is a classic high country trail, not to be missed! It has miles of great trail that contour the big high alpine basins of West Lime and Cascade Creeks, a crossing of the high Rolling Pass, fast descents and big climbs. The Graysill Trail, a steep and fun trail that switchbacks down from the CT, is one of my favorites. It descends on the flanks of the massive Graysill Mountain, with Grayrock Peak and Engineer Mountain looming nearby. This area is prone to a lot of rain and thunderstorms, so get an early start and plan your ride for a dry day. If you don't have a shuttle vehicle and aren't comfortable hitchhiking or riding 11.5 miles up to Molas Pass after the ride, start from Coal Bank Pass and ride Pass, White Creek and Graysill Trails. This route involves a much shorter ride on Hwy 550 to connect the loop, see page 97. Or ride up the Engineer Mountain Trail to White Creek, Colorado and Graysill Trails, with no shuttle or highway riding involved, see page 101. Graysill is not a good uphill trail, as it has lots of hike a bike.

Distance: 24.5 shuttle ride, 24 miles singletrack ½ mile dirt road.
Time: 4 ½ to 6 hours
Difficulty: Expert
Aerobic Effort: Strenuous
Elevation: Top: 12,510' **Gain:** 4,116' **Loss:** 5,930'
Season: July through September or early October
Finding Route: Moderate, except for one obscure junction at the start of the Graysill Trail, and the trail disappears after crossing Cascade Creek, requiring some route finding.
Map: Singletrack Maps Durango Trails
Location: Leave a shuttle vehicle at the Engineer Mountain Trailhead, 26.7 miles north of Durango, on the left. The turn to the trailhead is unsigned and easy to miss. It is 3 miles past Durango Mountain Resort, and 8/10ths past Cascade Creek and the big switchback over it on Hwy 550. Drive a second car with bikes and riders 11.7 miles farther, just past the top of Molas Pass, and turn left onto Little Molas Lake Campground road. Drive to the end to the CT Trailhead. If you park at the rest area on the summit of Molas Pass on Highway 550, ride toward Silverton 1/10th mile on the highway, turn left on the CT and ride 1.1 miles to the Little Molas Lake trailhead.

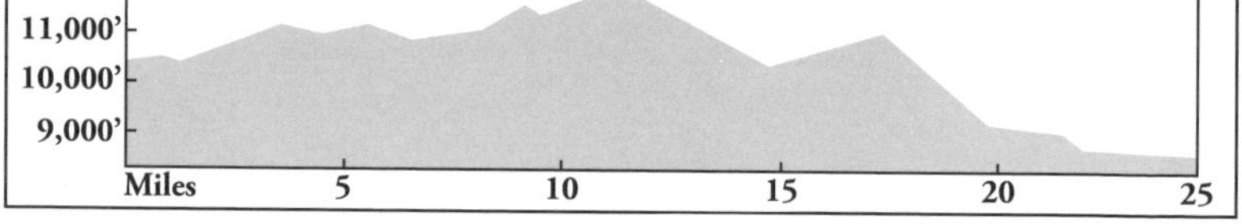

GRAYSILL TRAIL AND THE COLORADO TRAIL

Molas Pass, North of Durango

Mileage Log:

0.0 From the Little Molas Lake Campground trailhead, follow the directions for the Colorado Trail, Molas to Durango section, to mile 15.7, see page 104, then follow the directions here.

15.7 Keep right at a trail junction and climb again. Left goes down to Cascade Divide Road.

16.3 Just after an abrupt V creek crossing and entering a high altitude meadow, look for a small Graysill sign in a tree and hard to see singletrack on the left. Turn left and start an exciting descent of sharp switchbacks.

17.6 Cross Cascade Divide Road. Look for the trail to the left. This starts the technical section.

18.4 Unsigned trail junction. Go left and cross Cascade Creek for better trail that is technically easier and has more climbing, unless the creek is high. Climb the bank on the other side and walk downstream just a bit to find the trail. Once you find the trail, pass a spur to the right in 3/10ths mile. If the creek is high and dangerous, stay right and cross the creek down lower. When the trail gets close to the creek a couple miles (approx.) downstream, look for the unsigned crossing to the doubletrack on the other side. Be aware a primitive trail continues to Cascade Village. This side of the creek is technical with some hike a bike.

19.0 Pass Engine Creek Trail on the left. Descend and cross a bridge by a waterfall. The trail climbs and descends a few sections.

21.9 The trail widens to old road.

22.4 Ride through a gate and head down the road and turn left on the easy-to-miss singletrack in 2/10ths miles.

24.5 Ride across the dam of a small pond and end at the Cascade and Engineer Mountain Trailhead.

White Creek Trail | *Holly Annala*

★★★☆☆

COLORADO TRAIL TO ENGINEER MOUNTAIN TRAIL

COLORADO TRAIL TO WHITE AND ENGINE CREEK TRAILS

Molas Pass, North of Durango *See map pages 92-93*

Description: This is an adventurous ride with nine amazing miles of singletrack riding on the Colorado Trail (CT) that contours high basins and mountainsides with great views. It has a couple big climbs at high altitude. The descent on the Engineer Mountain Trail (EMT) from the CT is a very steep, rutted and difficult up top with hike a bike likely. Next the trail crosses expansive high alpine meadows with great views, contouring and climbing rough trail with some hike a bike, and thankfully some moderate contouring and descending singletrack. Down lower roll through dark timber and aspen forest for 5 miles on mostly rideable, moderate trail with good switchbacks and a few rutted sections. In some years there can be quite a few cows on the lower section in late summer and early fall, making the ride a mess with rain. Check with the Forest Service, 970-247-4874. For a much easier ride on the EMT start on the Pass Trail, see page 94.

Distance: 18.7 miles, all singletrack
Time: 3 ½ to 5 hours
Difficulty: Expert with a few short very difficult sections on the descent, near the top.
Aerobic Effort: Strenuous
Elevation: Top: 11,900' **Gain:** 3,440' **Loss:** 4,260'
Season: July through September or early October. Horses can wreak havoc with the mid-section of the EMT if there is a lot of precipitation during hunting season.
Finding Route: Fairly easy
Map: Singletrack Maps Durango Trails or Latitude 40 Durango
Location: This ride requires a shuttle unless you want to hitchhike or ride 11.5 miles up Hwy 550. Leave one car at the bottom, 26.7 miles north of the last light in Durango on Hwy 550. This is three miles past Durango Mountain Resort and less than one mile after crossing Cascade Creek on a big highway switchback. The unmarked turn to the trailhead is on the left. Continue to the top of Molas Pass 11.5 miles with bikes and riders. Once you reach Molas Pass, you can either park on the highway at the rest area on the right, or continue just over the pass and turn left onto Little Molas Lake Campground road. Drive to the end and park at the trailhead. From the rest area, the signed CT is 1/10th mile on the left toward Silverton, and the Little Molas Trailhead is one mile farther on the singletrack.

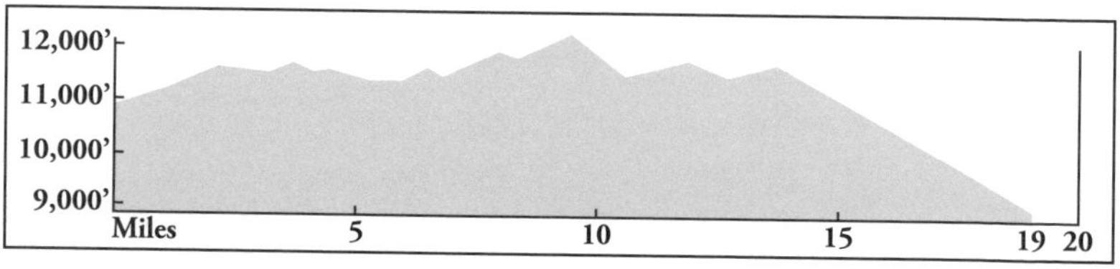

COLORADO TRAIL TO ENGINEER MOUNTAIN TRAIL
COLORADO TRAIL TO WHITE AND ENGINE CREEK TRAILS
Molas Pass, North of Durango

Mileage Log:

0.0 Follow directions for the CT from Molas Pass to mile 9.2, page 104.

9.2 At the signed intersection with the Engineer Mountain Trail, ride straight ahead and climb through tight willows and across a wide basin. (The CT continues right and up.)

9.6 Start the descent on rutted, then technical and steep trail. There can be huge ponds on the trail after significant rain.

10.5 Intersection with a broken sign. White Creek Trail is to the right, Engine Creek Trail is straight and down, and EMT continues to the left. Take the EMT and begin climbing and contouring around the basin, with some hike a bike. (Engine Creek is a fun descent from here also, see page 99).

12.3 Arrive at the signed junction with Deer and Coal Creeks. Turn right and descend the braided trail through a meadow, then climb.

13.3 Ride straight ahead, crossing the Pass Creek Trail and an unsigned trail to the right up to Engineer Mountain. Climb one more hill.

13.8 Descend through the dark timber, and meadows and aspen forest down lower.

18.7 Ride straight ahead next to the pond to the parking area, passing the Cascade Creek Trail on the right.

Colorado Trail to White and Engine Creek Trails: This is a twist on several great trails in the alpine area north of Durango, with excellent views and track. The ride starts with the Colorado Trail (CT) from Molas Pass and climbs to 12,500' on Rolling Pass, descends fast trail into the Cascade drainage, explores the contouring White Creek Trail and descends technical and steep Engine Creek Trail. This is a 22 mile expert ride, nearly all singletrack, and takes 4-5 hours. It requires a shuttle, see page 110, Location, for directions. From the trailhead follow the directions for the CT from Molas Pass, to mile 11.7, see page 104 for details. Ride straight ahead (left) onto the White Creek Trail as the CT takes a sharp right around a tree. Cross a creek and a meadow strewn with boulders, and climb into the forest. After one mile, the trail contours around a big basin above treeline, and descends to cross Engine Creek. Turn right at the next junction on Engine Creek Trail; the Engineer Mountain Trail coming in from the left and continuing straight ahead. Turn left on the Cascade Creek Trail after an exciting descent on the Engine Creek Trail. See page 99 for details on Engine and Cascade Creek Trails.

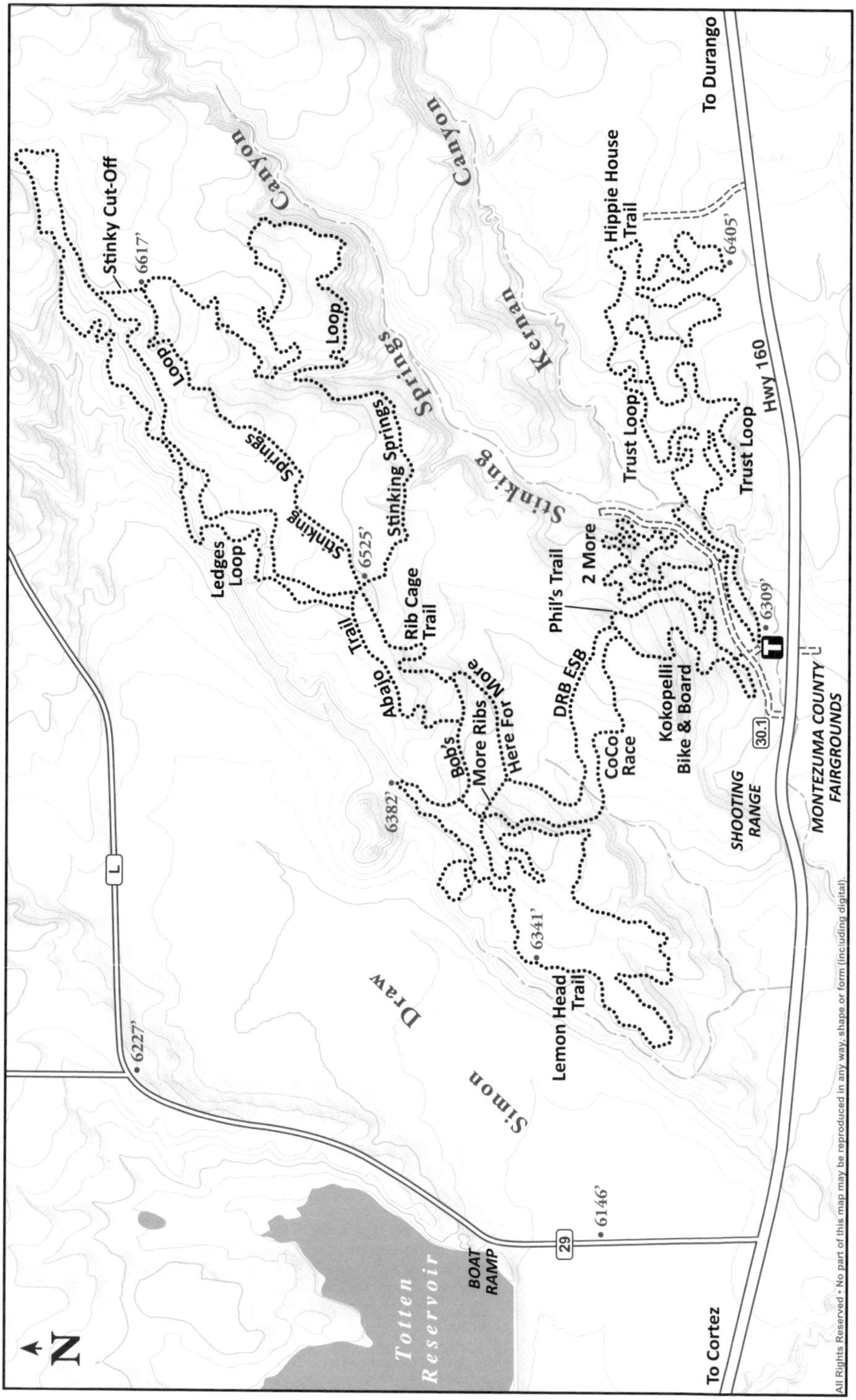
To Durango
Hippie House Trail
Canyon
Canyon
Kerman
Stinky Cut-Off
6617'
Loop
Loop
Springs
Stinking Springs
Springs
Stinking
Stinking
6405'
Hwy 160
Trust Loop
Trust Loop
Ledges Loop
6525'
Rib Cage Trail
Phil's Trail
2 More
6309'
Abajo Trail
More
Here For
More Ribs
Bob's
DRB ESB
CoCo Race
Kokopelli Bike & Board
30.1
MONTEZUMA COUNTY FAIRGROUNDS
SHOOTING RANGE
6382'
6341'
Lemon Head Trail
L
Draw
Simon
6227'
6146'
29
BOAT RAMP
Totten Reservoir
N
To Cortez

★★★★☆

PHIL'S WORLD

See map page 112

Description: Phil's World is a gem of a trail system. The trails wind and swoop through Pinyon-juniper forest and bank through arroyos; and the system has great views of Mesa Verde, the Sleeping Ute Mountain and Cortez. There are many stacked trails, making possible several different long or short loops. The climbs are short or moderate, so Phil's World is a welcome break from strenuous high country riding. The riding is fast if you want it to be and the trails are one direction only, alleviating congestion and keeping contact with other groups at a minimum. Phil's World is popular, especially in the spring and fall since it is dry sooner than everything else around it. It is rideable year-round except for 2 or 3 months in the winter. It can be very hot in the summer. Call Kokopelli Bike and Board for conditions. The Southwest Colorado Cycling Association (previously Kokopelli Bike Club) is working on expanding the trail system, visit their website for updates.
Location: From Durango, drive 39 miles west on Hwy 160 from the intersection of Highways 160 and 550 in Durango. Turn right across from the Montezuma County Fairgrounds on County Road 30.1, just after a guardrail and a small green sign, on a bumpy rocky road. Drive 2/10ths mile to parking on the right.

List of Phil's World Trails:
Kokopelli Bike and Board: Beginner, 1.1 miles. Short and easy.
Coco Race: Intermediate, 1.2 miles. Moderate with a couple of technical sections.
Lemon Head Trail/Elbow: Advanced intermediate with expert sections, 3.5 miles.
Abajo: Intermediate, 7/10ths mile. Nice views and some climbing, rolling trail.
Ledges: Advanced intermediate, 4.9 miles. The longest trail and the longest climb, more rocky and rough than the rest of the trails. It goes through a big burned area. Some fun sections, but not as fun as the Stinking Springs Loop if you need to choose.
Stinking Springs: Advanced intermediate with a few expert sections, 5.3 miles. Super fun longer loop, lots of character. Some short technical sections as it traverses a sandstone ledge overlooking Stinking Springs Canyon and swooping, flowing descents that Phil's is known for. Ride the whole loop!
Rib Cage: Advanced intermediate, 9/10ths mile. Big arroyo drops, fast flow and fast momentum climbs. These will make you giggle.
Here For More: Intermediate, 1 mile. Swoop and flow, easier than Rib Cage.
2 More: Intermediate 1 mile. Climb and descend with a few fun technical moves. Connecter to Trust Loop/ Hippie House.
Trust Loop/Hippie House: Beginner/easy intermediate, up to 6.1 miles. Smooth, fast, fun and nice views. Great beginner loop.

BEGINNER PHIL'S LOOP
Trust Loop/Hippie House Trail

Distance: 6.1 miles, all singletrack
Time: 1 hour
Difficulty: Beginner/easy intermediate

PHIL'S WORLD

Aerobic Effort: Moderate
Elevation: Top: 6,453' **Gain:** 320'
Season: March or April through December
Finding Route: Easy
Map: Singletrack Maps Phil's World

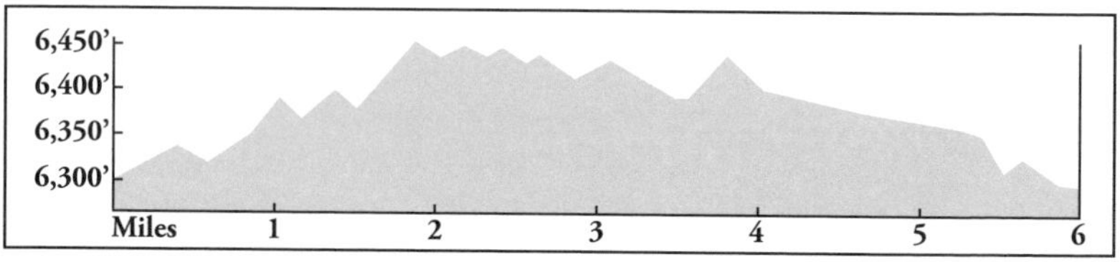

Mileage Log:

0.0 Ride out of the parking area to the east, on the signed Trust Loop/Hippie House Trail.

0.3 Stay right passing the incoming trail from 2 More.

1.6 Stay left and continue the loop, or the quick way back is to the right.

4.2 Ride straight ahead at the intersection from mile 1.6.

6.1 Back to the trailhead.

Optional Beginner 5 mile Loop: Ride the intermediate loop below to mile 2.3, go right on Bob's, right on Here for More and back to the trailhead.

PHIL'S INTERMEDIATE AND ADVANCED LOOPS

These start north out of the parking area with the same basic loop, with options to lengthen or shorten the loop. **Intermediate loop: Ride Kokopelli, Coco Race, Bob's, Here for More, 2 More, Trust/Hippie House. Advanced intermediate loop: Add Lemon Head, Abajo, Stinking Springs and/or Ledges.**

Distance: Up to 28 miles of singletrack.
Time: Intermediate loop: 2-3 hours **Advanced Intermediate Loop:** 3-5 hours
Difficulty: Intermediate to advanced intermediate with a couple short expert sections.
Aerobic Effort: Moderate, moderately high for the whole loop.
Elevation: Top: Between 6,425 and 6,633 depending on loop. **Gain:** Up to 1,854' for all loops, total.
Season: March or April through December
Finding Route: Fairly easy, well signed but many junctions. Last time I was here a lot of the signs were torn or worn off.
Map: Singletrack Maps Phil's World

PHIL'S WORLD

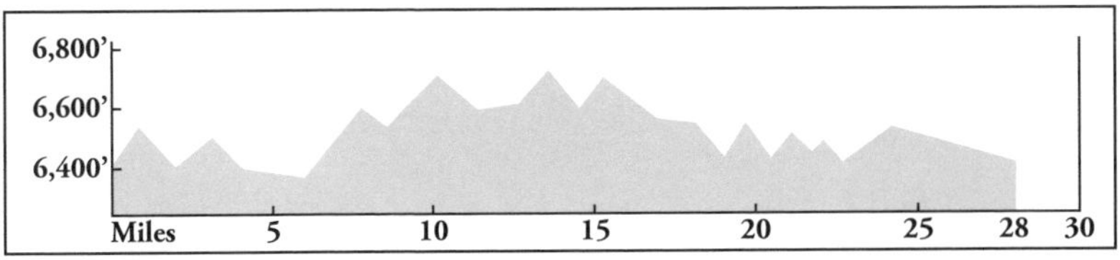

Mileage Log:

0.0 From the parking area take the singletrack and ride across the road, through the fence. At the pay station, leave a donation, then go left.

1.1 Turn left, right goes back to the trailhead. The trail gets more interesting with some small sandstone cliffs and a couple technical sections.

2.3 Turn left and climb a short steep hill to Lemon Head and wind around the edge of the cliff. Roll fast smooth sections and a bit of technical on The Elbow section. (Or turn right on Bob's to skip this section.)

6.5 Merge left with Bob's, then cross a road in1/10th mile.

6.7 Turn left at the signed intersection onto Abajo. Climb.

7.4 Go right to Stinking Springs, or left to add Ledges, see option 1 below.

7.5 Left on Stinking Springs. Climb and enjoy rolling downhills, some technical riding, great views and generally fun singletrack.

12.8 Merge onto Ribcage. This is a real hoot.

13.9 Junction at the top of a hill. If you want another Ribcage, go right and ride up Abajo and do it again. Or go left and continue the fun on Here for More.

14.9 Turn left toward the trailhead.

15.4 Turn left for 2 More and climb, then descend some techy sections and some smooth fast trail. (Right leads directly back to the trailhead.) Cross the main road.

16.4 Intersect the Trust/Hippie House Loop. Turn left for some really smooth fun trail. Or go right back to the trailhead.

17.6 Stay left at a junction to complete the loop. Right is faster back to the trailhead.

20.2 Back to the junction at 17.6, ride straight ahead (left) to parking area and soak up great views of Mesa Verde ridge from the sage meadows.

22.2 Back to the trailhead.

Option 1: To add the Ledges Loop, turn left and climb a cobbled hill at mile 7.4. At mile 10.6 you have the option of cutting straight over to Stinking Springs loop via the Stinky Cutoff, but you miss some really fun trail this way. I recommend going straight (right) on Ledges loop at 10.6, then left at 12.2 on Abajo and left at 12.3 on Stinking Springs (both are signed) and do the whole Stinking Springs Loop. Ledges adds just short of 5 miles to your loop.

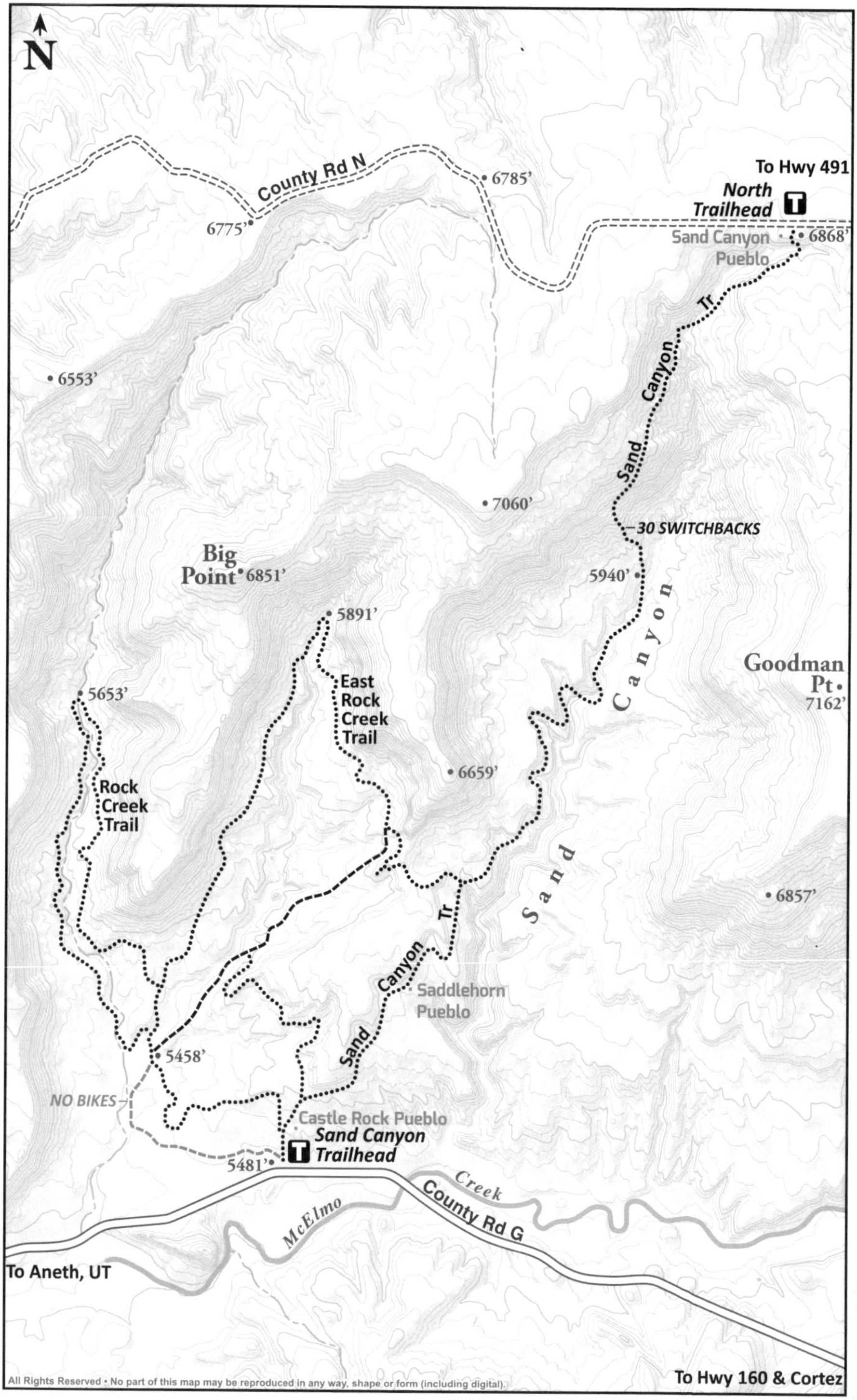
N
County Rd N
6785'
6775'
To Hwy 491
North Trailhead
Sand Canyon Pueblo
6868'
6553'
Sand Canyon Tr
7060'
30 SWITCHBACKS
Big Point
6851'
5940'
5891'
Sand Canyon
Goodman Pt
7162'
5653'
East Rock Creek Trail
6659'
Rock Creek Trail
6857'
Sand Canyon Tr
Saddlehorn Pueblo
5458'
NO BIKES
Castle Rock Pueblo
Sand Canyon Trailhead
5481'
Creek
County Rd G
McElmo
To Aneth, UT
To Hwy 160 & Cortez

★★★★☆

SAND CANYON TRAIL

Description: The Sand Canyon Trail is a unique riding experience in desert red rock country. The singletrack (much of it built with mountain biking in mind) winds through interesting desert canyons, crosses big expanses of slickrock, and passes by Native American Indian ruins! Several side trails beckon a look on foot to other ruins, as bikes aren't allowed off trail. The longer loop described here is moderate in length and rocky and technical in many places. The shorter, inner loop is easier, see option below. Additional distance can be added by continuing up the main Sand Canyon Trail for an out and back, or by riding both short and long loops. The trails and loops are fun either direction, but I recommend them in a clockwise direction. The riding here is open nearly all year but can be quite hot in the summer. There is a nice campground and fantastic ruins at nearby Hovenweep National Monument. There is BLM dispersed camping available fairly close, but you may encounter late night 4-wheelers. Continue out CR G for both options.

Distance: 10.8 miles, all singletrack
Time: 2-3 hours
Difficulty: Advanced intermediate with expert sections. The shorter loop has some advanced sections in the first 1.3 miles on the slickrock, but after that it is much easier (intermediate) without the expert technical riding.
Aerobic Effort: Moderate
Elevation: Top: 5,593' **Gain:** 1,038'
Season: March through December
Finding Route: Moderate, a few places require keeping track of cairns. New signs and maps make it much easier.
Map: Mountain Bike Map for Cortez, Dolores, Mancos and Rico
Location: Drive 2.8 miles south from Cortez on Hwy 160 West/491 South past where Hwy 491 splits from Hwy 160 and the road curves south. At the stoplight, go right on County Road G, marked by a big brown Hovenweep National Monument sign. Drive 12.3 miles on this curvy road to a parking area on the right on top of slickrock, marked by a Canyon of the Ancients sign. This is about 1 hour and 15 minutes from Durango, and 60 miles.

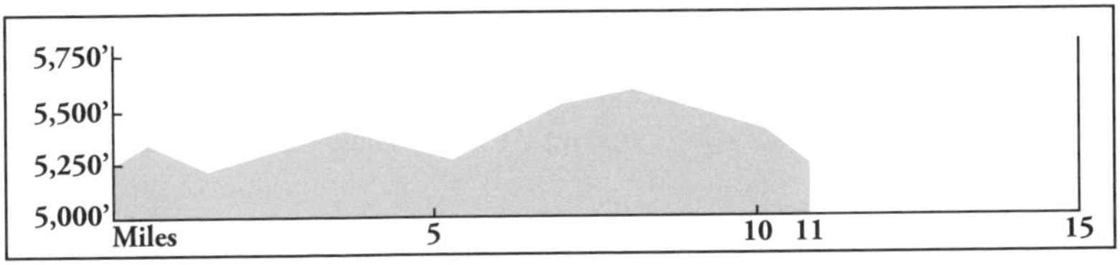

Mileage Log:

0.0 Start up the slickrock past the sign for the monument, passing next to a sandstone butte on the right. Continue on singletrack 2/10ths mile, passing a spur trail on the right, and ride over broken rock and more slickrock. At a sign/map before the top of the slickrock, look a few hundred feet to the left for a cairn with a blue diamond and bike symbol on it. Turn left toward the cairn, and then uphill to the singletrack at the cairn. The trail follows sections of singletrack between large slickrock expanses that are marked with cairns and lined with sticks at some corners. This is fun and technical riding.

0.7 Look for cairns to the right as the trail climbs the slickrock.

1.3 Merge right on old road and go past a trail map/sign, then left on singletrack with a green marker. Go downhill and through a wash. Straight (right) is the east side of the East Rock Trail. See option below for the shorter, easier loop.

1.4 Turn left at another sign on singletrack, and look for a yellow marker. This is the Rock Creek (AKA West Rock) Trail.

5.6 T-intersection with the East Rock Creek Trail. Turn left and uphill, the trail has a green diamond marker in a tree. Go around the head of the canyon on technical and rocky trail. A natural bridge is at the top of the canyon in the cliffs.

8.4 Intersection; go left on a connector to the Sand Canyon Trail. (Or right and down on the continuation of East Rock Trail. Go left at next signed intersection (approx. one mile down) for a smooth trail with ruins back to top of the slickrock, to mile 10.5.)

8.6 After a smooth section along the canyon rim, turn left. Right is a viewpoint trail.

9.1 After descending a couple steep switchbacks, turn right on the Sand Canyon Trail. Keep your speed down and be courteous to the many hikers here.

10.5 Reach the top of the slickrock and a cairn. Go straight ahead toward the signs and cairns. (To the right is a cairn with a white diamond reflector, this is the connector to East Rock Trail, and a good trail either direction. It has several interesting cliffs and ruins.)

10.6 Pass the trail you went out on, or do another lap. See option below.

10.8 Trailhead.

Additonal or Easier Loop: Ride the loop as above, out the slickrock section, to mile 1.3. Ride straight ahead, passing a singletrack to the left and climb old doubletrack, the east side of the East Rock Trail. At the next signed junction in less than a mile, turn right onto another old road and hike a bike up a short steep section. The smooth singletrack winds around cliffs and ruins one mile to the Sand Canyon Trail. Turn right at a map/sign, and ride down to the trailhead. This loop is fine in reverse as well. It is about 3 ½ miles and takes less than 1 hour.

Sand Canyon Trail | *Holly Annala*

Sand Canyon Trail | *Holly Annala*

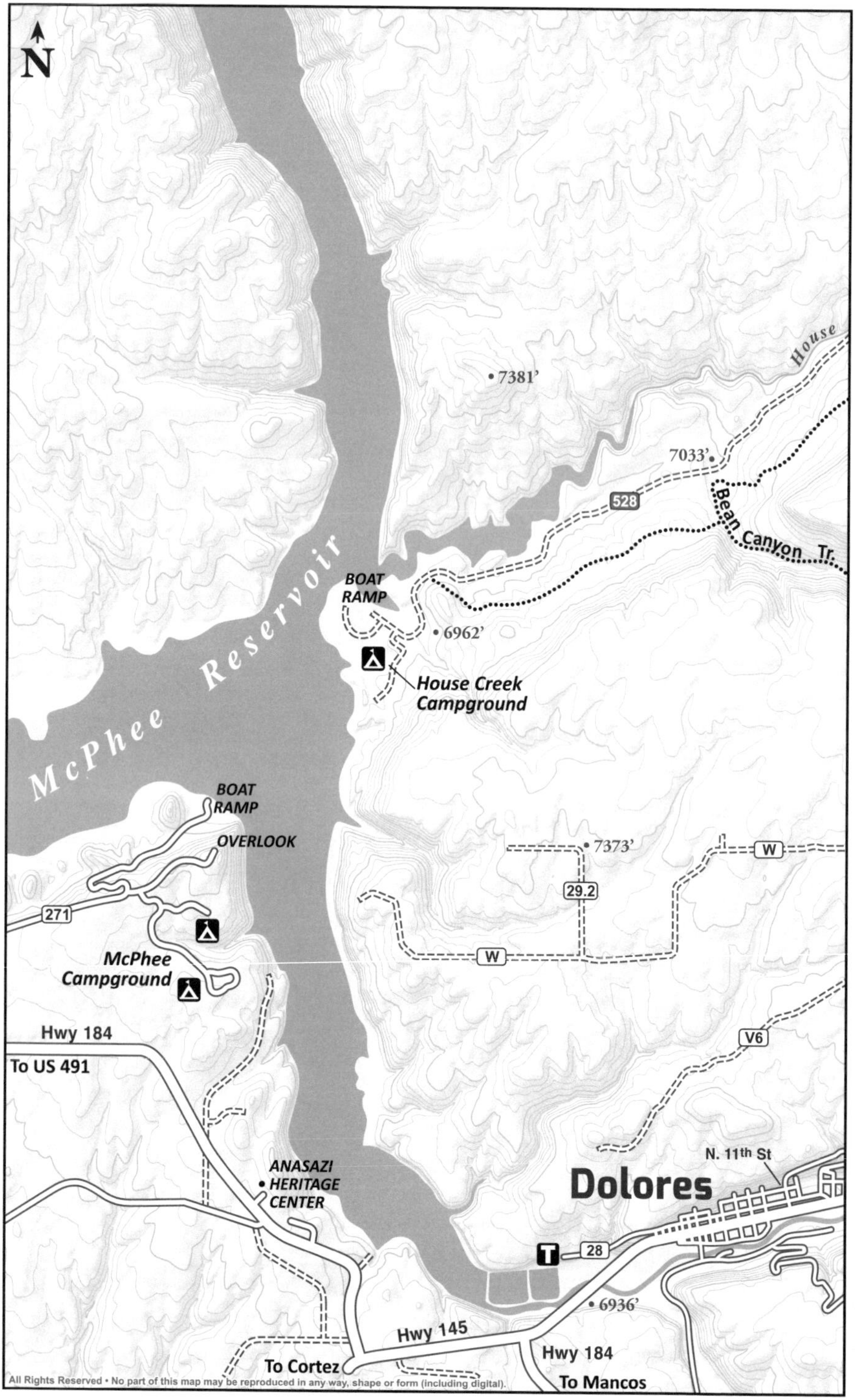
N
House
7381'
7033'
528
Bean Canyon Tr.
McPhee Reservoir
BOAT RAMP
6962'
House Creek Campground
BOAT RAMP
OVERLOOK
7373'
W
29.2
W
271
McPhee Campground
V6
Hwy 184
To US 491
N. 11th St
Dolores
ANASAZI HERITAGE CENTER
28
6936'
Hwy 145
Hwy 184
To Cortez
To Mancos

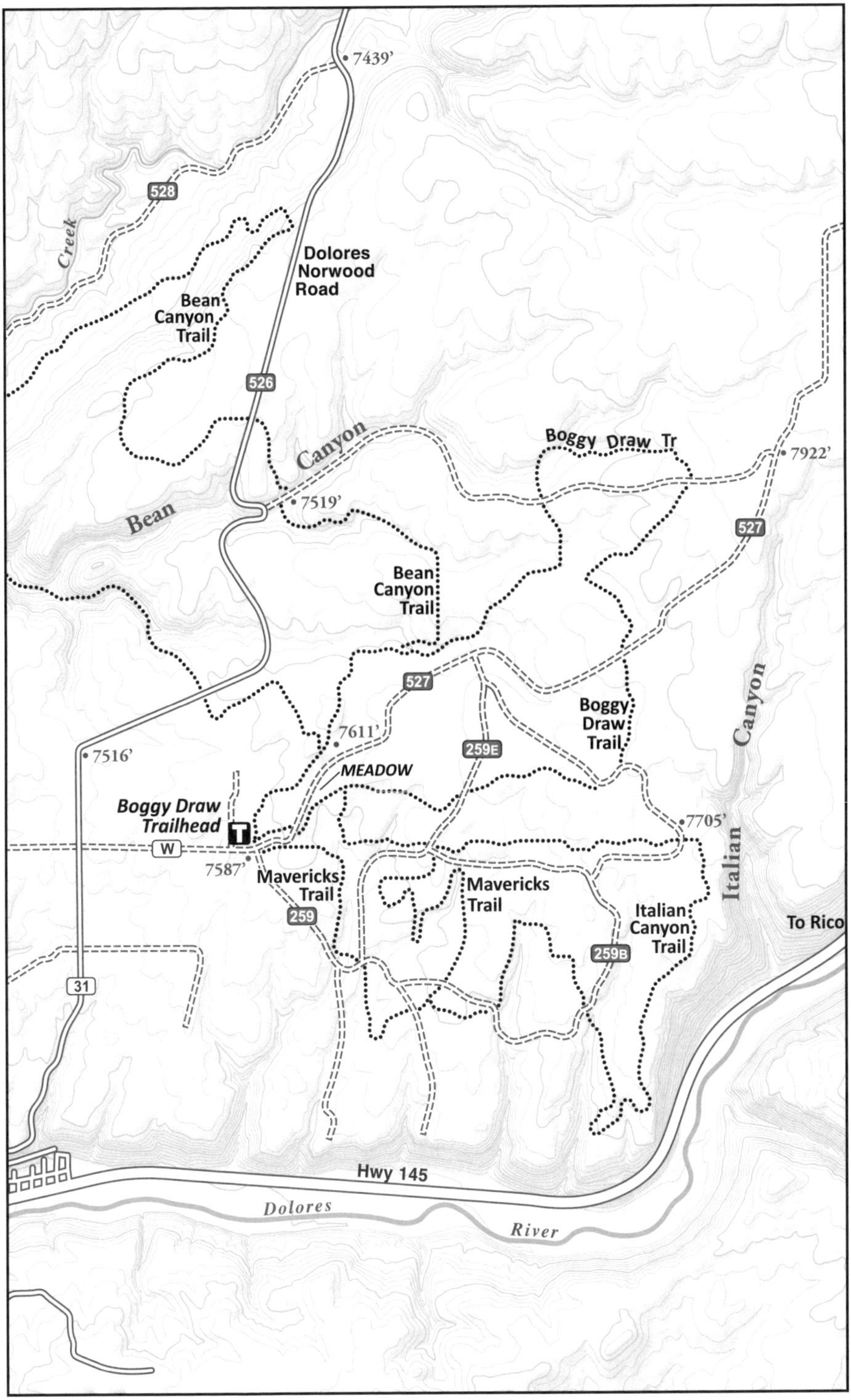
7439'
528
Creek
Dolores
Norwood
Road
Bean
Canyon
Trail
526
Canyon
Bean
7519'
Boggy Draw Tr
7922'
527
Bean
Canyon
Trail
527
Boggy
Draw
Trail
Canyon
7611'
7516'
259E
MEADOW
Boggy Draw
Trailhead
7705'
W
7587'
Mavericks
Trail
Mavericks
Trail
Italian
Italian
Canyon
Trail
To Rico
259
259B
31
Hwy 145
Dolores
River

BOGGY DRAW TRAIL SYSTEM

Overview, Getting to Boggy Draw *See map pages 120-121*

Description: The Boggy Draw Trail System is an uncrowded, non-motorized system of winding singletracks that roll moderately across a big expanse of Ponderosa Pine forest and onto lower benches of sage, scrub oak, and Pinyon-juniper trees. Nothing here is strenuous and there are only a few technical sections, so beginner and intermediate riders have several moderate options. Maverick and Boggy Draw Trails are the easiest, Italian and Bean Canyon have a little more climbing, descending and technical riding. By combining all the loops (recommended in a counter-clockwise direction) a long ride is possible for more advanced riders. The trails are fast singletrack built especially for mountain biking. Most of the trail system is easy to follow and signed. Take along the Mountain Bike Map for Cortez, Dolores, Mancos and Rico. The lower benches of Maverick and Bean Canyon have nice flowers in May and some amazing flowering bushes that make the whole area fragrant. There is lots of wildlife; I've seen elk, turkeys and a bear here, and plenty of songbirds. There is good primitive camping at Boggy Draw that is easy to get to, just pull off the main dirt road on numerous side roads. There is the House Creek Campground on FS Road 528 (off CR 31/ FS 526 from Dolores) and a new, two mile moderate trail leads to the Bean Canyon Loop from the campground. A new trail is being planned from the town of Dolores to the House Creek Campground, starting at the west end of town. The trailhead is located 4/10ths of a mile from Hwy 145 where it enters town from the south, on CR 28, next to the cemetery. At this point it is a short out and back, but in a few years it will be complete.

Getting to Boggy Draw: From Durango drive 26 miles west on Hwy 160 to Mancos, and turn right on Hwy 184. Drive 17 miles and turn right on Hwy 145, and continue 1.6 miles through Dolores to the north end of town and turn left on North 11th Street. There is a big brown sign for McPhee Reservoir at the turn. Drive to the end of 11th Street, go right and up the hill onto CR 31. Top out and continue to the top of next hill and turn right on W Road, 2.2 miles from Main Street. There is a brown BLM sign for the Boggy Draw Trailhead here. Continue 1 mile to the trailhead and parking area. Driving from Cortez, turn left off Hwy 160 East onto Hwy 145 (just east of Cortez) and go straight to Dolores. To get to the House Creek Campground, follow the directions above as if you are going to Boggy Draw, but continue past W Road on CR 31 and pass the FS boundary where the road becomes FS 526. Drive 4.5 miles past the boundary on FS 526 to FS 528 and turn left, and continue 5.6 miles to the campground. The signed McPhee Overlook Trail is on the left, just before a cattleguard, ½ mile before the campground.

★★★☆☆

MAVERICK AND ITALIAN CANYON LOOPS

Boggy DrawTrail System *See map pages 120-121*

Description: The Maverick and Italian Canyon loop is a moderate ride with great views of the Sleeping Ute, the La Plata and San Juan Mountains, and the Dolores River valley. It has fast winding singletrack through Ponderosa forest and scrub oak woodlands. There are sagebrush meadows with great flowers in the spring and early summer. For a beginner loop, see Maverick option below. This loop can be combined with the Boggy Draw and Bean Canyon loops to make a longer loop.

Distance: 9.1 miles, all singletrack
Time: 1 ½ to 2 hours
Difficulty: Intermediate, see Maverick below for a beginner option.
Aerobic Effort: Moderate
Elevation: Top: 7,509' **Gain:** 760'
Season: May through November
Finding Route: Easy except for one confusing junction. Well signed.
Map: Mountain Bike Map for Cortez, Dolores, Mancos and Rico
Location: See Getting to Boggy Draw, page 122. The Maverick Trail is to the south of the trailhead, across another cattleguard, on the left.

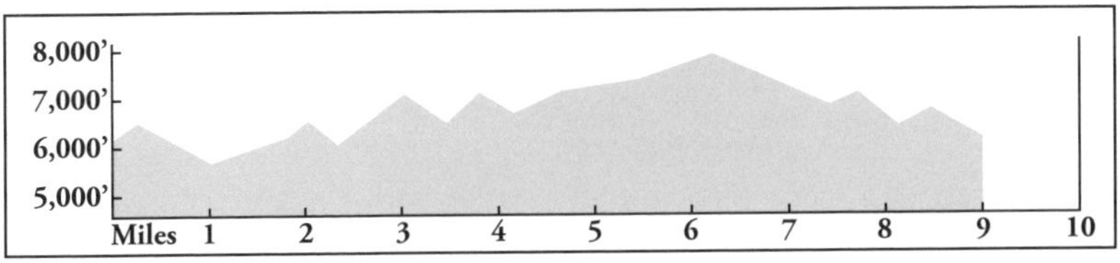

Mileage Log:

0.0 From the trailhead parking, look for the signed Maverick Trail singletrack, across a cattleguard. Ride across the slickrock and onto smooth singletrack.

1.1 Cross two forks of a doubletrack.

1.8 Cross a doubletrack.

1.9 Turn right at the signed intersection onto the Italian Canyon Trail. (Maverick goes to the left, see option below.) Roll through Ponderosa forest.

2.4 Cross a doubletrack and enter a small canyon. Climb for ½ mile into the forest.

3.5 Cross a doubletrack and climb a steeper hill for 2/10ths mile, then ride across a scrub oak mesa with great views. Descend and then contour around the rim overlooking the Dolores River.

6.0 Overlook.

6.3 Descend along a fence. Caution! In ½ mile the trail is very close to the fence!

7.7 End the Italian Canyon Trail at a confusing junction with a 3-way road junction and a T-intersection with the Maverick singletrack. Turn right on the

MAVERICK AND ITALIAN CANYON LOOPS
Boggy DrawTrail System

Maverick singletrack, go over a cattleguard, then left on the singletrack. (Left on Maverick would take you back to the junction with the start of Italian canyon, mile 1.9)

8.1 Steep down next to fence, caution! Next climb a short, steep hill.

8.6 Intersection with the Boggy Draw Trail. Go left to the parking area. Cross a doubletrack and ride across a dam on singletrack. Cross another doubletrack.

9.0 Ride onto the main road, turn right and descend to the trailhead.

Maverick Trail, beginner loop option: Follow the directions above to mile 1.9 and go straight (left) on Maverick. At 2.7 miles cross the pond's berm and head left. At 4.4 miles, ride straight ahead to follow Maverick and go left after the fence. At 5.3 turn left back to the parking area, Boggy Draw trail goes right. This is 5.8 miles long and takes 1 to 1 ½ hours.

BEAN CANYON LOOP
★★★★☆

Boggy DrawTrail System

See map pages 120-121

Description: The Bean Canyon loop winds and rolls through Ponderosa Pine and Pinyon-juniper forest on singletrack built especially for mountain bikes. I like Bean Canyon best of all the trails out here for interest and variety. The Bean Canyon loop has a longer descent than the other Boggy Draw loops, rolls across sage flats on the lower section, and has a longer climb out. It is mostly smooth rock-less terrain, but has a few short technical sections. In May there are some great flowers on the lower half. This loop is fine in either direction but clockwise involves a short hike a bike, whereas counter clockwise as described here, does not. A moderate two mile trail now leads to the lower part of the Bean Canyon Trail from the House Creek Campground, The McPhee Overlook Trail. The trailhead is located on FS 528, ½ mile before the campground, right before a cattleguard, on the left. Eventually this trail will continue past the campground and end in the west end of Dolores, 4/10ths mile from Hwy 145 where it enters town from the south on CR 28.

Distance: 13.5 mile loop, 12.5 miles of singletrack, 1 mile doubletrack.
Time: 1 ¾ to 2 ½ hours
Difficulty: Intermediate with a few short advanced sections.
Aerobic Effort: Moderate
Elevation: Top: 7,710' **Gain:** 1,099'
Season: May through November. Bean Canyon is closed west of the Dunton/ Norwood Road December 1 through March 1 for wildlife.
Finding Route: Moderate, signed but many junctions. The flow of the trail is fairly easy to follow at road crossings, just look ahead.
Map: Mountain Bike Map for Cortez, Dolores, Mancos and Rico.
Location: See Getting to Boggy Draw, page 122.

BEAN CANYON LOOP

Boggy DrawTrail System

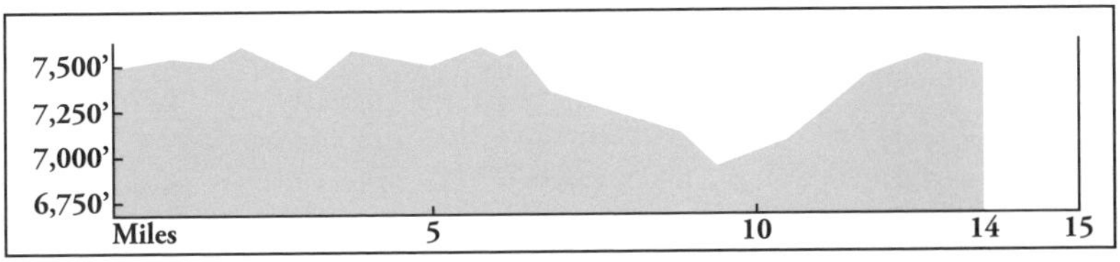

Mileage Log:

0.0 From the trailhead, take the Boggy Draw Trail 199 north out of the parking area, near the kiosk. The trail starts out flat and smooth, then climbs shortly.

0.5 Ride under the powerlines and cross two doubletracks. In 2/10ths mile, the trail splits. Continue straight ahead on The Boggy Draw Trail.
The Bean Canyon return route is on the left (no sign.)

1.5 Turn left on the signed Bean Canyon Trail after crossing a cattleguard.

1.7 Swing left and climb gradually along a fence. After a short descent leave the fenceline.

2.4 Merge onto a road and right onto the singletrack. Poles mark both trails.

3.3 In a meadow, cross a dirt spur road off the paved road to your left, and continue on the singletrack. Climb more steeply.

3.8 Cross the paved road, FS 526. The singletrack is a little left after crossing.

5.8 Nice viewpoint on a rock ledge. McPhee Reservoir is to the southwest, and Lone Cone and the San Miguel Mountains are to the northeast.
Ride along the rocky rim and straight onto the singletrack in 1/10th mile.

6.3 Steep downhill. In 1/10th mile stay left and continue downhill.

6.8 Turn left off an old road section for more smooth, signed singletrack.

9.4 After a descent and a draw crossing, turn left and climb. Pass the signed right turn to House Creek Campground before the climb.

11.6 At the top of a steeper climb, pass a pond on the left and cross a doubletrack. In 2/10ths mile cross a paved road.

12.7 Cross a powerline road. In 1/10th mile, turn right and return the same way you started the loop.

13.1 Cross the powerline road.

13.5 Back to the trailhead.

★★★☆☆

BOGGY DRAW TRAIL

Boggy DrawTrail System

See map pages 120-121

Description: The Boggy Draw loop is mostly smooth, easy riding and fast winding trail through Ponderosa forest, on singletrack built especially for mountain biking. The majority of the loop is moderate, and by using a road to bypass the upper section of the loop it is a good beginner/easier intermediate loop. The upper section of the loop continues a little higher in the forest and wildlife is often seen here. Make a longer loop by riding Italian Canyon before the Boggy Draw Trail, or continuing to ride Bean Canyon after Boggy.

Distance: 8.1 mile loop, 7.5 miles of singletrack, 6/10ths mile of doubletrack and dirt road.
Difficulty: Beginner, with an intermediate section that can be avoided at mile 4.0.
Aerobic Effort: Moderate
Time: 1 ½ -2 hours
Elevation: Top: 7,874' **Gain:** 440'
Season: May through November. The Boggy Draw Trail stays wet a little longer in the spring than Maverick, Italian, and Bean.
Finding Route: Easy, well signed but quite a few turns.
Map: Mountain Bike map for Cortez, Dolores, Mancos and Rico
Location: See Getting to Boggy Draw, page 122.

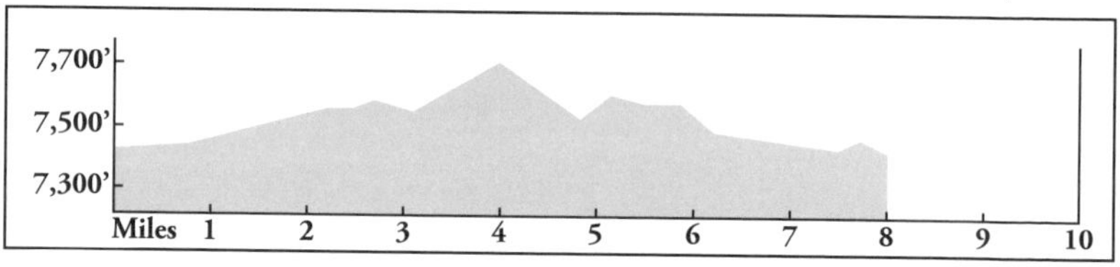

Mileage Log:

0.0 Start up the main road, CR W, past the parking area.

0.2 Turn right on the signed Boggy Draw singletrack. Cross a campground road, go over a dam and cross another doubletrack.

0.6 Ride straight (stay left) on Boggy Draw Trail, right is Maverick.

1.2 Merge left on road for 1/10th mile, then right on singletrack.

2.2 Cross a doubletrack and pass another doubletrack on the right.

2.7 Cross the main road.

3.3 Turn left on the doubletrack.

3.6 Ride straight onto singletrack.

4.0 Cross a more major dirt road. Beginners can go left here and ride approximately 8/10ths of a mile on the road, looking for the singletrack, and left again on the trail to avoid the more difficult part of the trail.

4.5 Go through the gate and left. Be careful of the fence, it is close to the trail.

5.1 Cross the road. Beginner riders turn left on the trail here.

6.1 Merge left onto a road and right on hidden singletrack, before the pond.

6.6 Ride straight ahead, passing the Bean Canyon Trail, or add this 10 mile loop by turning right.

7.5 Turn left on the Boggy Draw Trail to the trailhead, passing the return from Bean Canyon.

7.7 Cross the campsite and powerline roads. Stay on the singletrack.

8.1 End at the parking area.

Hippie House Trail/Phil's World | *Holly Annala*

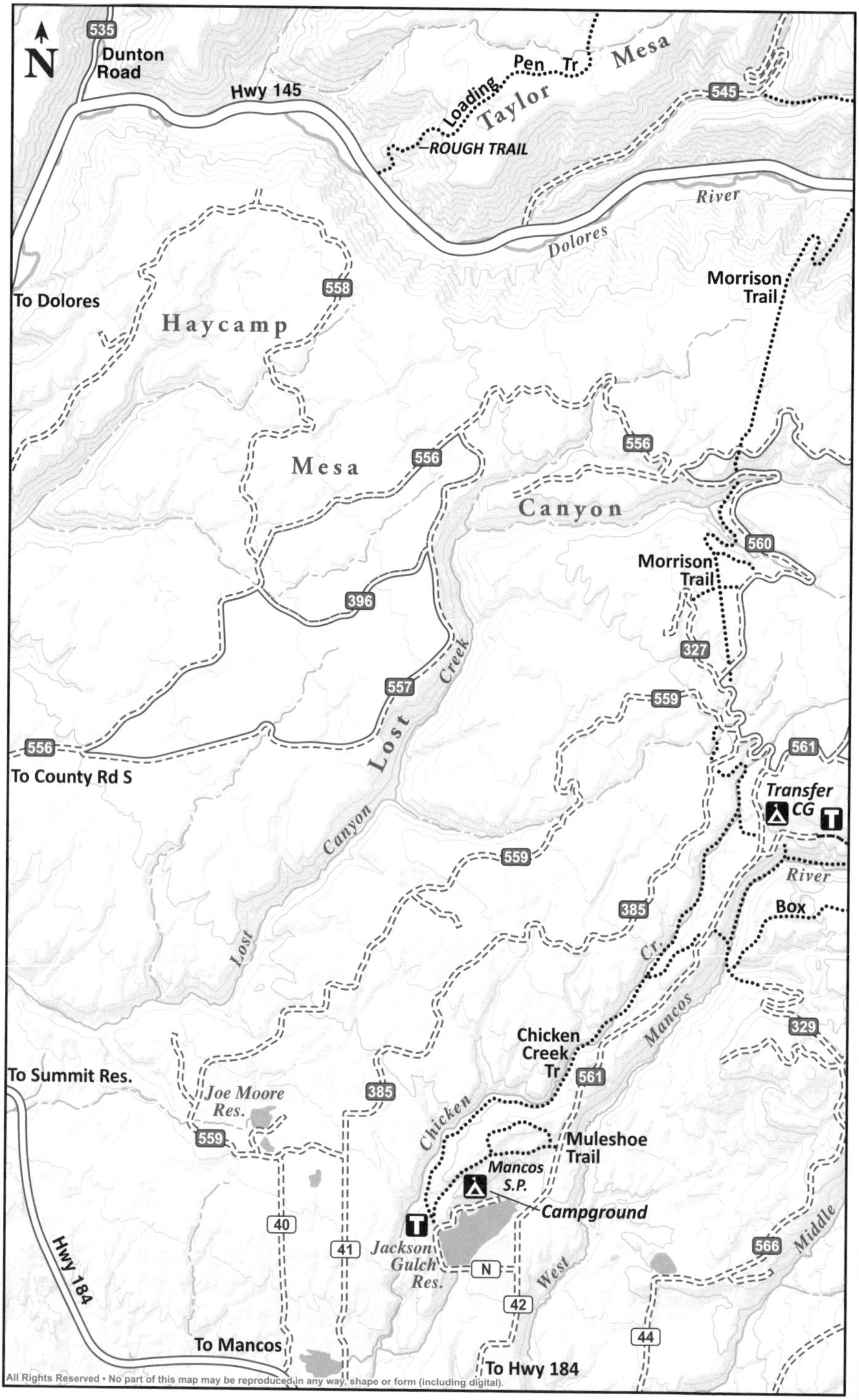
N
535
Dunton Road
Hwy 145
Loading Pen Tr
Taylor Mesa
ROUGH TRAIL
545
River
Dolores
To Dolores
558
Haycamp Mesa
Morrison Trail
556
556
Canyon
560
Morrison Trail
396
327
557
Lost Creek Canyon
559
556
To County Rd S
561
Transfer CG
559
River
385
Box
Cr.
Lost
Mancos
329
Chicken Creek Tr
To Summit Res.
Joe Moore Res.
385
561
559
Chicken
Muleshoe Trail
Mancos S.P.
Campground
40
41
Jackson Gulch Res.
N
42
West
566
Middle
Hwy 184
To Mancos
44
To Hwy 184
All Rights Reserved • No part of this map may be reproduced in any way, shape or form (including digital).

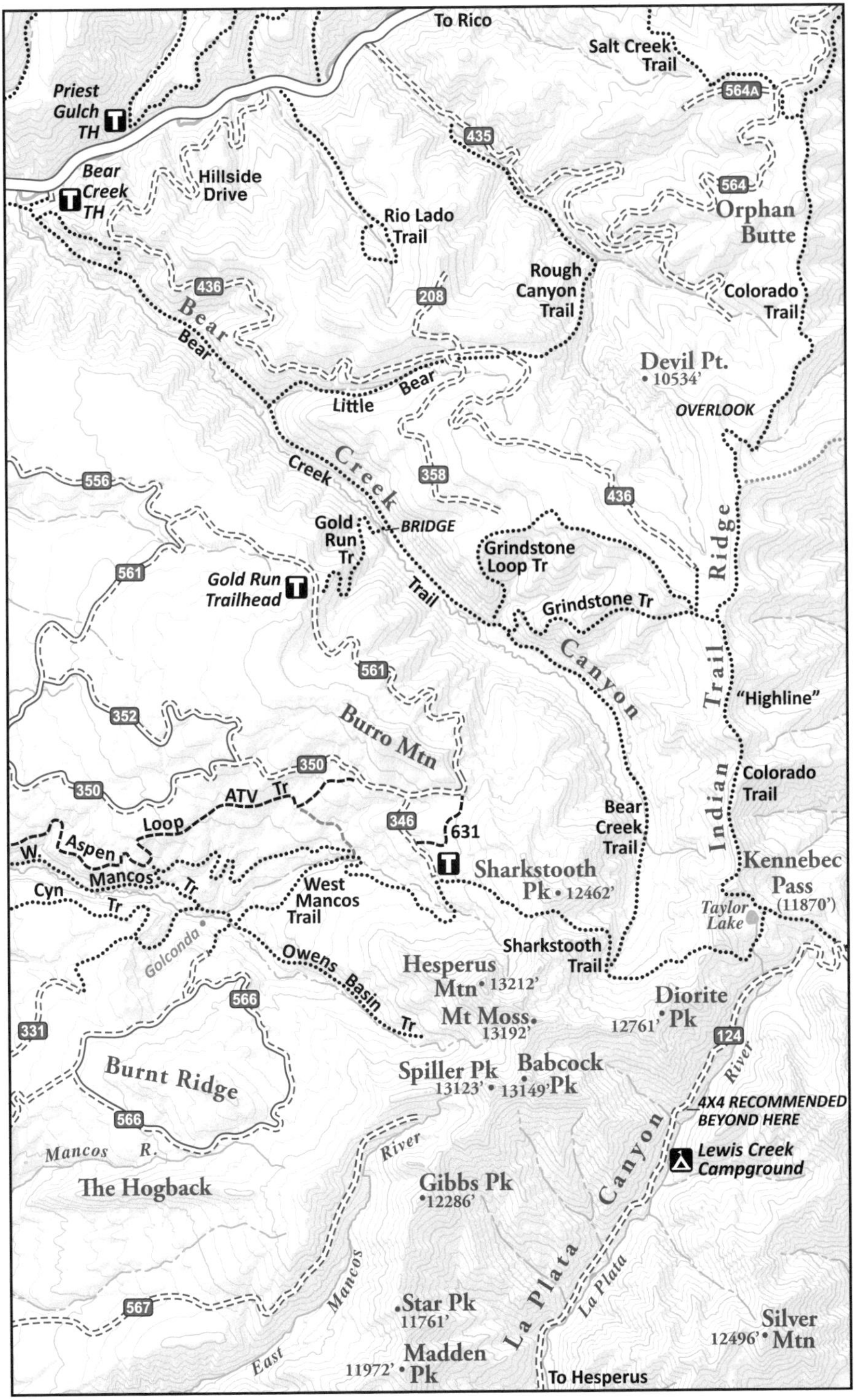
To Rico
Salt Creek Trail
564A
Priest Gulch TH
435
Bear Creek TH
Hillside Drive
564
Orphan Butte
Rio Lado Trail
Rough Canyon Trail
Colorado Trail
436
208
Bear
Bear
Devil Pt.
10534'
Little Bear
OVERLOOK
Creek
Creek
556
358
436
Ridge
Gold Run Tr
BRIDGE
Grindstone Loop Tr
561
Gold Run Trailhead
Trail
Grindstone Tr
Canyon
561
Trail
"Highline"
352
Burro Mtn
350
Colorado Trail
350
ATV Tr
Loop
Bear Creek Trail
Indian
346
631
W. Aspen
Mancos Tr
Sharkstooth Pk
12462'
Kennebec Pass
(11870')
Cyn Tr
West Mancos Trail
Taylor Lake
Golconda
Sharkstooth Trail
Hesperus Mtn
13212'
Owens Basin Tr
Diorite Pk
12761'
566
Mt Moss
13192'
331
124
River
Spiller Pk
13123'
Babcock Pk
13149'
Burnt Ridge
4X4 RECOMMENDED BEYOND HERE
566
Lewis Creek Campground
Mancos R.
River
The Hogback
Gibbs Pk
12286'
Canyon
La Plata
La Plata
Mancos
567
Star Pk
11761'
Silver Mtn
12496'
East
Madden Pk
11972'
To Hesperus

★★☆☆☆

CHICKEN CREEK TRAIL

See map pages 128-129

Description: Chicken Creek is a fun, moderate length ride in the Mancos State Park/ Transfer Campground area between the La Plata Mountains, Mancos and Dolores. The ride isn't well known with mountain bikers, but is a nice loop on a shady creek with lots of aspens, a good color ride for the fall. Most of the climbing is on dirt road, and the trail is mostly downhill. The trail is at times very rough and can have quite a few down trees (especially in spring or after wind and snow events,) and there are often cattle here in summer. Expect some hike a bike. Check with Kokopelli Bike Shop in Cortez, 970-565-4408, for current conditions. There are several other rides in the area, including Sharkstooth, Morrison and Bear Creek Trails, see page 132 and 136 for details. The West Mancos Trail on the other side of FS 561 from Chicken Creek was rough and unrideable due to down trees when I was there last. There are plenty of camping opportunities on the forest, including the Transfer Campground right across from the Chicken Creek Trail, 9.6 miles out CR 42/FS 561. The road can be really dusty at times; ride the loop early in the morning or weekdays during busy times to avoid the traffic.

Distance: 14.6 miles, 8 miles of singletrack, 6.6 miles graded dirt road.
Time: 3-4 hours
Difficulty: Advanced intermediate with expert sections
Aerobic Effort: Moderate
Elevation: Top: 8,940' **Gain:** 1,607'
Season: June through October
Finding Route: Mostly easy. A few unmarked turns but the route is straightforward.
Map: Mountain Bike Map for Cortez, Dolores, Mancos and Rico
Location: From Durango, drive 26.3 miles west toward Cortez on Hwy 160, and turn right in Mancos at the light onto Hwy 184. Drive 3/10ths mile and go right toward Mancos State Park on CR 42/West Mancos Road. Pass CR N to Mancos State Park on the left in 4 miles (alternative pay camping and parking for the ride, the singletrack ends at the park.) Continue on CR 42 to the Forest Service (FS) boundary and sign at mile 5.4, and park just past the boundary. The road is now FS 561. Alternatively, camp in the Transfer Campground (4.2 miles past the FS boundary) and ride the trail first, then ride up the road to camp.

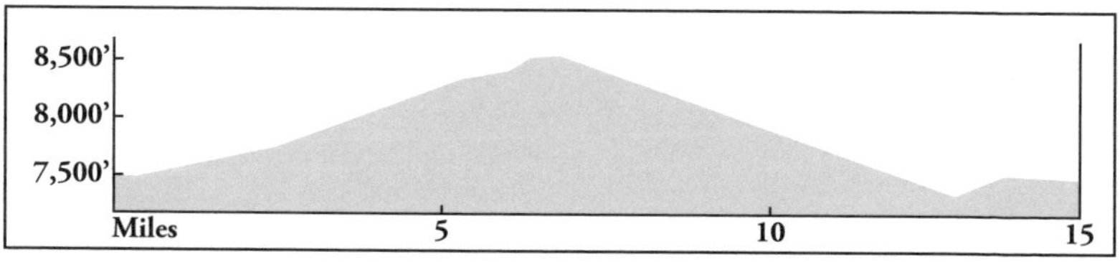

Mileage Log:

0.0 Start riding up FS 561 from the FS boundary.

3.1 Pass the Rim Trail on the left, just past a cattleguard.

CHICKEN CREEK TRAIL

4.2 Stay left on FS 561 and pass the Transfer Campground.

4.4 Just past a corral and parking area, turn left at the signed Chicken Creek Trailhead. Ride across the flats and then descend into the aspens.

4.9 Turn left on signed singletrack in the creek bottom. The Morrison Trail goes right.

6.4 Ride straight ahead, passing the Rim Trail on the left. Go through a gate in 2/10ths mile.

7.4 Go through another gate. There are quite a few creek crossings through here.

8.1 Ride straight on signed Chicken Creek Trail 615, just past an old stove. A spur trail goes left.

8.4 Cross a creek and climb a switchback out of the creek to dark forest. This section is more difficult with steep climbs and rough trail.

9.7 Descend and cross the creek. Go through a gate.

9.8 Ride straight (left) down the creek as the Chicken Creek Connector turns right at Dean's Sawmill Site.

10.5 Big climb left of the creek.

11.0 At an unsigned junction, go left through a silver gate on singletrack and climb. Straight along the fence is a dead end.

11.3 Pass a sharp left turn.

11.6 Pass another sharp left turn.

11.8 Reach the Chicken Creek Trailhead and parking next to lake. Ride out of the parking area and turn right on the road. In about 1/10th mile, go left onto singletrack along the lake, heading toward the dam. A few other trails surround the lake.

12.3 Turn left at the end of the trail and go across dam and out through the park.

13.1 Turn left on CR 42.

14.5 Back to the FS boundary.

★★★☆☆

MORRISON AND GOLD RUN TO BEAR CREEK

See map pages 128-129

Description: This is a big loop that starts 12.5 miles south of Rico and 23 miles north of Dolores, at the Bear Creek Trailhead. The Morrison Trail starts the loop with switchbacks up through giant aspens on good singletrack, with a few steep sections. This is a great trail. The upper section is quite flat. A steady climb for 7.1 miles on FS 556 and FS 561 up Haycamp Mesa through aspen forest and conifers leads to the technical and scenic Gold Run Trail descent. In the fall the trail glows with yellow leaves! Finish the ride on the fun and moderate Bear Creek Trail to end the loop. For an epic day, continue riding 6 miles farther on road to the Sharkstooth Trailhead, and descend Bear Creek from the top, see page134. Bear Creek and Morrison Trails are good out and back rides as well. This area can have a lot of down trees after big storms and in the spring, check with the Forest Service, 970-882-7296, or Kokopelli Bikes in Cortez, 970-565-4408.

Distance: 20.6 mile loop, 12.6 miles singletrack, 8 miles dirt road, logging road, and ATV track
Time: 4 ½ - 6 ½ hours
Difficulty: Expert
Aerobic Effort: Very high
Elevation: Top: 10,240' **Gain:** 3,039'
Season: Late June through October
Finding Route: Moderate, most junctions are signed and the route is straightforward. The upper part of the Morrison trail is somewhat difficult to follow due to current logging operations.
Map: Mountain Bike Map for Cortez, Dolores, Mancos and Rico or Latitude 40 Southwest Colorado Trails
Location: To get to the Bear Creek Trailhead, drive 22.9 miles north of Dolores from 11th Street (the turn to Boggy Draw) on Hwy 145 to the trailhead on the right, or 12.5 miles south of Rico.

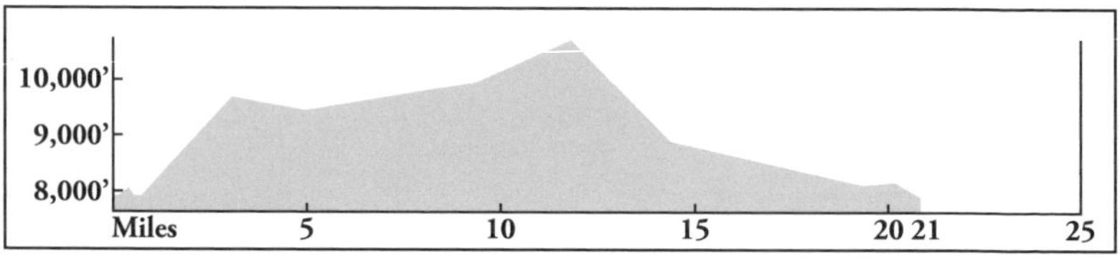

Mileage Log:

0.0 From the parking area, cross the bridge and turn right on the Bear Creek Trail. Climb steeply, and then the trail levels.

0.3 Turn right on the signed Morrison Trail and descend back to the Dolores River. Ride through a field and gates, then between fences and through another gate, to the other side of the valley.

0.7 The signed Morrison Trail swings left and starts climbing a steady grade. This is a beautiful section of trail.

2.6 (approx. mileage) Swing left onto an old road.

2.7 Turn left onto singletrack and switchback up to the mesa top.

3.0 (approx. mileage) The trail levels. Follow signs across an old road.

3.5 Ride straight across a meadow.

4.0 Ride straight ahead through a logging area, about 3/10ths mile. Next follow the singletrack to the left.

4.5 Ride through gates and onto ATV trail.

5.0 Turn left on FS 556.

9.8 Turn left on FS 561.

12.1 Turn left onto the Gold Run Trail at the trailhead. Descend moderate, then technical trail.

14.0 Cross a bridge and turn left on the Bear Creek Trail.

16.1 Cross Little Bear Creek and continue straight ahead and climb, passing the Little Bear Creek Trail on the right.

18.6 Ride straight past the Little Bear Creek Pack Trail, to the right, and climb.

19.9 Stay right, climb a short steep hill on the main trail. In 1/10th mile at a signed junction, pass a trail to the right. Soon start descending switchbacks.

20.3 Stay right and pass the signed Morrison Trail.

20.6 Cross the bridge to the parking area.

Bear Creek Trail | *Rob Mahedy*

★★★★★

MORRISON, SHARKSTOOTH AND BEAR CREEK

See map pages 128-129

Description: This epic ride has lots of great singletrack, amazing high altitude riding and views, and a long ride on forest road in the middle. The Morrison Trail is an excellent singletrack that climbs through massive aspen groves. The top of the trail is a straight old road section partially through current logging areas. Next, climb moderate forest road for 13 miles to Sharkstooth Trail. Sharkstooth is an amazing trail that climbs high above timberline and into the heart of the La Plata Mountains on some smooth and rideable pine needle covered trail and some very difficult rocky trail. A challenging, then rollicking descent of 13.7 miles on the Bear Creek Trail leads back to the trailhead. There are several sections of hike a bike over scree fields and rough trail.

Distance: 35.2 mile loop, 22.1 miles singletrack, 13.1 miles graded dirt road, logging road and ATV trail.
Time: 7-9 hours
Difficulty: Expert/Epic with several extremely difficult sections
Aerobic Effort: Strenuous
Elevation: Top: 11,945' **Gain:** 5,532'
Season: July through September or early October
Finding Route: Moderate, the route is straightforward. A couple turns are not signed. The Sharkstooth Trail is faint near the top of Bear Creek Trail.
Map: Mountain Bike Map for Cortez, Dolores, Mancos and Rico or Latitude 40 Southwest Colorado Trails
Location: To get to the signed Bear Creek Trailhead, drive 22.9 miles north of Dolores from 11th Street (the turn to Boggy Draw) on Hwy 145 to the trailhead on the right, or 12.5 miles south of Rico.

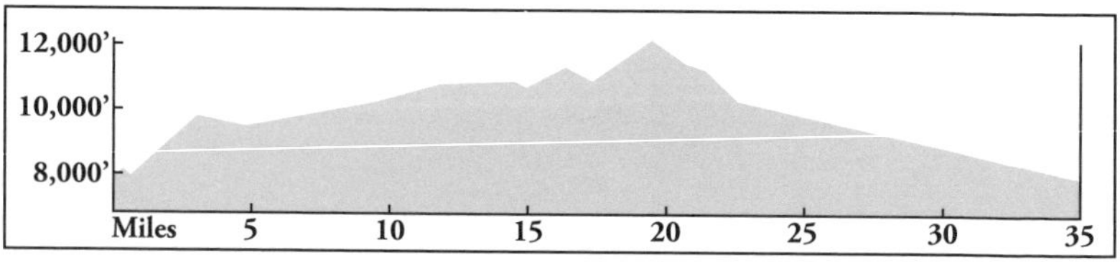

Mileage Log:

0.0 Follow the directions on page 132 for Morrison and Gold Run to Bear Creek, to mile 12.1, but continue straight past the Gold Run Trailhead. The road gradually becomes more narrow and primitive.

16.6 Arrive at a many way intersection. Go straight ahead on an unsigned ATV trail. (Right is the main road, FS 350, which will arrive in the same place but in a more roundabout fashion; left is a closed logging road.) In 2/10ths mile stay right on the main ATV trail marked with brown carsonite signs.

17.6 Turn left on FS Road 346.

MORRISON, SHARKSTOOTH AND BEAR CREEK

18.1 Arrive at the Sharkstooth Trailhead. Ride straight ahead and start climbing. The trail starts out rocky and tough, then becomes smoother.

19.0 Stay right at a fork in the trail and climb the switchbacks. Left is the interpretive Windy Williams Trail.

19.2 Windy Williams Trail comes in on left, stay right. Enjoy awesome views of Hesperus Mountain along this section of trail.

19.7 Hike a bike to the summit of Sharkstooth Pass.

19.9 Reach Sharkstooth Pass, 11,945' and enjoy great views of the La Plata Mountains. Start a challenging descent on steep, loose switchbacks and scree slopes with some hike a bike.

20.4 Ride a short uphill and contour across the scree mountain side. Enter the woods.

21.1 Cross a small creek and head up the creek and across the basin.

21.5 Turn left and down Bear Creek Trail 607 at a signed intersection. Sharkstooth continues straight ahead and climbs to Taylor Lake and Kennebec Pass. There are a couple signs high in the trees. The Bear Creek Trail starts out with steep switchbacks, exposure, rocks and roots. It is a real wilderness experience here; raw with evidence of avalanches along the sides.

23.8 Cross a bridge.

25.1 (approx mileage.) Start riding in meadows.

27.0 Pass the signed Grindstone Trail on the right. See page 140 for details of this ride.

28.7 Stay right and pass the Gold Run Trail, which starts just over the bridge on the left.

30.8 Cross Little Bear Creek, ride straight ahead and climb, passing the Little Bear Creek Trail to the right.

33.2 Ride straight past the Little Bear Creek Pack Trail on the right, and climb.

34.5 Stay right and climb a short steep hill on the main trail. In 1/10th mile at a signed junction, pass a trail to the right. Soon start descending switchbacks.

34.9 Stay right and pass the signed Morrison Trail.

35.2 Cross the bridge to the parking area.

★★★☆☆

SHARKSTOOTH, BEAR CREEK AND GOLD RUN

See map pages 128-129

Description: This is a big adventurous ride, with amazing views and trails, and strenuous high alpine riding and hike a bike. The Sharkstooth Trail climbs to almost 12,000', and descends by challenging switchbacks into a high basin in the La Plata Mountains to the headwaters of Bear Creek. Bear Creek starts with exposure and challenging terrain, rolls through dark forest where you might hear elk bugling in the fall, then mellows gradually to miles of rambling trail through meadows down lower. The aspens in this area are phenomenal in the fall. The Gold Run Trail is an extremely difficult uphill; steep, rutted and with lots of loose rock, and will require quite a lot of hike a bike. Using a shuttle to ride Sharkstooth and Bear Creek might be preferable to riding/hike a biking up Gold Run Trail as described here, but involves a very long shuttle, see below. For a much longer ride that includes the Sharkstooth Trail, see page 134.

Distance: 18.4 mile loop, 12.4 miles of singletrack, 6 miles of dirt road and ATV trail.
Time: 4 ½ - 6 ½ hours
Difficulty: Expert/Epic ride due to the isolated area and difficulty of some of the trail sections, with a few extreme/very difficult sections.
Aerobic Effort: Very Strenuous
Elevation: Top: 11,945' **Gain:** 3,937'
Season: July through September or early October
Finding Route: Moderate. Most turns are marked. Several spur roads might confuse route finding on the road climb. The Sharkstooth Trail is faint near the top of Bear Creek Trail.
Map: Latitude 40 Southwest Trails or Mountain Bike Map for Cortez, Dolores, Mancos and Rico
Location: This ride is located in the La Plata Mountains and can be accessed from Mancos or Dolores. To get to the trailhead from Durango, drive 26.3 miles to Mancos and turn right at the light on State Hwy 184. Drive 3/10ths mile and turn right on CR 42 toward Mancos State Park, and start your mileage here. Pass the turn to Mancos State Park and continue straight toward Transfer Campground and onto West Mancos Road/FS 561 at mile 5.4. Stay on the well signed FS 561 to the trailhead: At 9.4 miles, stay left passing the Transfer Campground. At 10.2 go straight ahead, staying on FS 561. Pass the Aspen Guard Station. At 11.5 stay left on FS 561 toward the Gold Run Trailhead. At 15.8 miles, turn right toward the Gold Run Trailhead (left is FS 556 to Dolores.) At 18 miles, the signed Gold Run trailhead is on left. See page 138 for directions to the trailhead from Dolores, and for shuttle directions to the Sharkstooth trailhead.

Mileage Log:

0.0 Turn left and start riding up the road from Gold Run Trailhead. The road gradually becomes more narrow and primitive.

SHARKSTOOTH, BEAR CREEK AND GOLD RUN

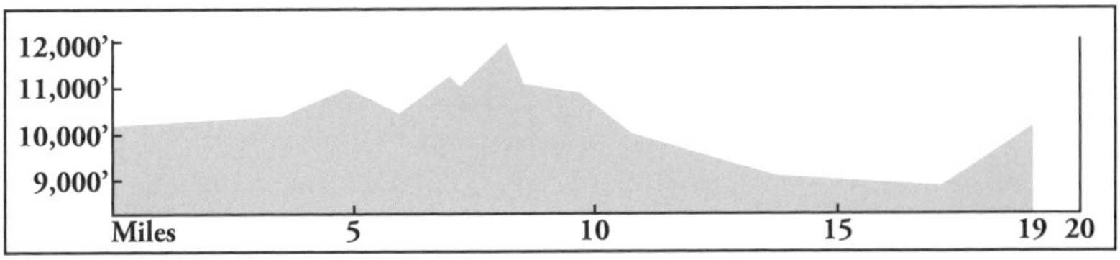

4.5 Arrive at a many way intersection. Go straight ahead on an unsigned ATV Trail. (Right is the main road, FS 350, which will arrive in the same place but in a more roundabout fashion; left is a closed logging road.) In 2/10ths mile, stay right on the main ATV trail marked with brown carsonite signs.

5.5 Turn left on FS Road 346.

6.0 Arrive at the Sharkstooth Trailhead. Ride straight ahead and start climbing. The trail starts out rocky and tough, then becomes smooth and pine needle covered.

6.9 Stay right at a fork in the trail and climb the switchbacks. Left is the interpretive historic Windy Williams trail that comes back in up higher.

7.1 Windy Williams Trail comes in on left, stay right. Enjoy great views of Hesperus Mountain along this section of trail.

7.6 Hike a bike to the summit of Sharkstooth Pass.

7.8 Reach Sharkstooth Pass, 11,945' and enjoy great views of the La Plata Mountains. Start a challenging descent on steep, loose switchbacks and scree slopes with some hike a bike.

8.3 Ride a short uphill and contour across the scree mountain. Enter the woods.

9.0 Cross a small creek and head up the creek and across the basin.

9.4 Turn left and down Bear Creek Trail 607 at a signed intersection. Sharkstooth continues straight and climbs to Taylor Lake and Kennebec Pass. The Bear Creek Trail starts with steep switchbacks, exposure, rocks and roots.

14.6 Cross signed Grindstone Creek.

14.9 The signed Grindstone Trail turns off to the right, see page 140 for details of this ride.

16.5 Turn left and cross Bear Creek on a big bridge to the Gold Run Trail. The bottom section of the trail is somewhat rideable, the middle section through scree and cliffs is too steep and rocky to ride, and the top half of the trail is rideable back to the trailhead. This is a fun and challenging descent, see Morrison and Gold Run to Bear Creek page 132.

18.4 Back to the trailhead.

SHARKSTOOTH, BEAR CREEK AND GOLD RUN TRAILS

Shuttle to the Sharkstooth Trailhead: On 2WD gravel and some high clearance road, continue with the driving directions, page 136, Location, to mile 11.5 and turn right on FS 350/ Spruce Mill Road. Continue to FS 346 and turn right to the trailhead. To leave a car at the bottom at the Bear Creek Trailhead on Hwy 145, drive 23 miles north of Dolores to the signed trailhead on the right, one mile before the Priest Gulch Campground. Return through Dolores and south 6/10ths mile, and turn left on Hwy 184. Go 3.2 miles and turn left on CR S/Rock Springs Rd/FS 556 and drive 24 miles and turn right onto FS 561. Continue 4.3 miles to Spruce Mill Road/ FS 350 and turn left. Turn right on FS 346 to the Sharkstooth Trailhead.

Directions to the trailhead from Dolores: Drive south from Dolores 6/10ths mile on Hwy 145 and turn left on Hwy 184. Go 3.2 miles and turn left on CR S/FS 556 and drive 24 miles. Go left onto FS 561 and continue 2.3 miles to the trailhead for the loop. These are good gravel 2WD roads.

La Plata Canyon shuttle directions: To access the Sharkstooth Trail from Kennebec Pass, drive 11 miles on Hwy 160 west (toward Cortez) to Hesperus and turn right on CR 124. Drive 5.5 miles on graded dirt, then continue up very steep high clearance road with a few serious 4WD sections. Take the Colorado Trail west (left) out of the parking area 1.2 miles to Taylor lake and on to the Sharkstooth Trail. Ride 3.9 miles and join the above description at mile 9.4. Hermosa Tours does shuttles, 877-765-5682

Sharkstooth Trail | *Rob Mahedy*

★★★☆☆

BEAR CREEK TRAIL

See map pages 128-129

Description: The Bear Creek Trail rolls through an amazing high alpine valley. This is one of the few Rico trails that doesn't start out with a really big climb, but there are still some sections of hike a bike. It starts out steeply in aspen forest with a few difficult sections, then climbs into Ponderosa Pines on wide, smooth trail. Next the trail climbs and descends on almost all rideable but many places narrow and challenging singletrack, through aspen forest and alpine meadows, next to scenic Bear Creek. It is a fun out and back. A good place to turn around is at mile 6.6 at the Gold Run Trail. Enjoy a really fun and playful downhill with some technical, interspersed with some steep uphills. It is a great downhill part of a loop with Sharkstooth, Gold Run, Morrison or Grindstone Trails, see pages 132, 134, 136 and 140.

Distance: Up to 27.4 miles, all singletrack
Time: 3-4 hours
Difficulty: Advanced intermediate to expert
Aerobic Effort: Moderately high to very high, depending on how far you ride.
Elevation: Top: 8,818' (or higher) **Gain:** 1,909' (or more)
Season: June through October
Finding Route: Easy
Map: Mountain Bike Map Cortez, Dolores, Mancos and Rico or Latitude 40 Durango or Southwest Colorado Trails
Location: Park at the signed bottom of the Bear Creek Trail, 23 miles north of Dolores on Highway 145, on the right, or 12.5 miles south of Rico. The trailhead is 1.2 miles south of the Priest Gulch Campground.

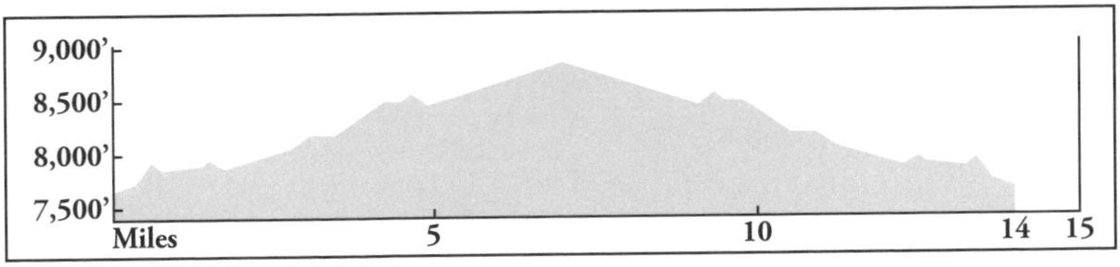

Mileage Log:

0.0 From the parking area, cross the bridge and turn right on the Bear Creek Trail.

0.3 Stay left and pass the signed Morrison Trail.

0.7 Pass a trail on the left, descend a short steep hill, and pass a trail on the right.

2.0 Pass the Little Bear Creek Pack Trail on the left.

4.5 Pass the Little Bear Creek Trail on the left and cross Little Bear Creek. The trail starts to get more technical.

6.6 Pass the Gold Run Trail, over a bridge on the right. Soon the trail becomes more technical. Or, turn around here.

8.3 Pass the Grindstone Trail on the left, and cross Grindstone Creek.

13.7 Top of the trail and junction with the Sharkstooth Trail.

★★★★★

HILLSIDE DRIVE, GRINDSTONE AND BEAR CREEK

HILLSIDE DRIVE TO SALT CREEK OR SHARKSTOOTH

See map page 128-129

Description: This is an amazing long loop through very scenic country near Rico and the Colorado Trail (CT). The lower parts of the ride have miles of great aspen forest for a beautiful ride in the fall. The upper part of the singletrack has terrific views of the La Plata Mountains from high altitude meadows. The climb is very long, mostly on gradual graded dirt road, with a little rough dirt road and singletrack. The descent is quality singletrack with a few sections of eroded rocky trail. The Grindstone Trail would not be a good uphill. Riding up Hillside Drive is good access to the CT and more high country singletrack; descend Salt Creek Trail back to Rico, or traverse Indian Ridge to descend from Taylor Lake on the Sharkstooth and Bear Creek Trails, or continue on to Durango. See options below.

Distance: 32.7 miles, 12.5 miles of singletrack, 17.2 miles of dirt road, 3 miles of pavement.
Difficulty: Expert
Time: 5-8 hours
Aerobic Effort: Strenuous
Elevation: Top: 11,506' **Gain:** 5,209'
Season: July through September or early October
Finding Route: Easy
Map: Latitude 40 Durango or Southwest Colorado Trails or National Geographic Durango/ Cortez
Location: Park at the signed bottom of the Bear Creek Trail, 23 miles north of Dolores on Highway 145, on the right, or 12.5 miles south of Rico. The trailhead is 1.2 miles south of the Priest Gulch Campground.

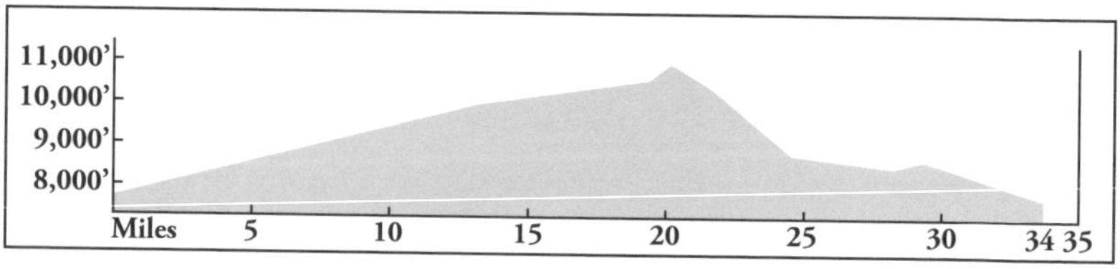

Mileage Log:

0.0 Turn right out of the parking area and ride the highway shoulder.

3.0 Turn right on Hillside Drive Road/FS 436 (marked with a big sign,) cross the bridge and begin climbing. Stay right in 1/10th mile.

14.0 Ride straight ahead passing FS 358.

14.3 Pass a dirt road spur on the left.

14.6 Ride past Little Bear Creek Trail 609 (difficult to follow/ not great bike trail) on the right, and signed Rough Canyon Trail 435 on the left (a fun early summer trail to ride down to Roaring Fork Road.) Ride into the coniferous forest.

HILLSIDE DRIVE, GRINDSTONE AND BEAR CREEK
HILLSIDE DRIVE TO SALT CREEK OR SHARKSTOOTH

15.2 Pass a road spur to left. Swing to the right and FS 436 gets rougher.

20.2 Turn left to the end of the road and right on the signed Hillside Connection Trail and climb.

20.7 Ride over the top of the hill to a T-intersection and turn right on the Grindstone Trail. Amazing views of Hesperus Mountain and the La Plata Mountains are straight ahead. Left goes to the CT, see options below.

20.8 Ride straight ahead and down through the forest, the next section being a great downhill. The Grindstone Loop Trail goes right and up, and then descends to join the Grindstone Trail down lower, but is not a great trail.

21.2 Cross an old road and stay on the singletrack. The trail descends through trees and then contours on buff singletrack through big high altitude meadows.

22.5 Ride into the forest on a sudden tight switchback, descend a rough section, and then roll long switchbacks through aspen forest.

24.2 Ride into the open for a moment, cross a creek, and pass the Grindstone Loop Trail coming in on the right. Stay left.

24.4 Intersect the Bear Creek Trail, ride straight ahead (right) and uphill a little. This is fun and playful through here, up and down with a few technical sections.

26.1 Stay right and pass the Gold Run Trail, left and over the bridge.

28.2 Cross Little Bear Creek and ride straight ahead and climb, passing the Little Bear Creek Trail on the right.

30.7 Ride straight past the Little Bear Creek Pack Trail, to the right, and climb.

32.0 Stay right and climb a short steep hill on the main trail. In 1/10th mile at a signed junction, stay left and pass a trail to the right. Soon start descending switchbacks.

32.4 Stay right and pass the signed Morrison Trail.

32.7 Cross the bridge to the parking area.

Option 1: Park on Hillside Drive. Climb Hillside Drive and the Hillside Connection Trail to mile 20.7 above. Turn left and climb to the CT, turn left and ride (approx.) 7.3 miles to Salt Creek Trail. Descend 5.2 miles on Salt to Highway 145 and turn left and ride 5.5 miles to your car. This is 36 mile loop, and takes 5-7 hours. See page 142 for details on the Salt Creek Trail.

Option 2: Climb Hillside Drive and the Hillside Connection Trail to mile 20.7. Go left and climb to the CT, turn right and ride 4.2 miles along Indian Trail Ridge and descend to Taylor Lake. Go right on the signed Sharkstooth Trail and descend with some hike a bike 3.9 miles to the Bear Creek Trail, and turn right and ride 9 miles to the Bear Creek Trailhead. See page 134 for details. This loop is 39 miles and take 6 ½ -9 hours. Or continue on to Durango on the CT if you are bikepacking.

★★★★☆

SCOTCH CREEK TO THE SALT CREEK TRAIL

RYMAN TRAIL

See map page 128-129

Description: This is a great loop that incorporates a smooth section of the Colorado Trail (CT) and a lively descent on the non-motorized Salt Creek Trail just 2 ½ miles from Rico. Scotch Creek Road is a great way to ride up to the CT, a moderate grade most of the way up. The CT contours and climbs along a high and mostly forested ridge interspersed with alpine meadows and views of Molas Pass, the Weminuche Wilderness, Engineer Mountain and the La Plata Mountains. The majority of Salt Creek is a narrow little singletrack that rolls through a huge aspen grove and Douglas Fir forest down lower, with some exposure over steep hillsides to keep it exciting. It is a lovely fall ride when the colors are changing. Close the loop with a short stint on Highway 145. Unlike many Rico rides that are quite long and with a fair amount of hike a bike, this loop is all rideable and moderate length, but still an alpine ride.

Distance: 18.6 mile loop, 8 miles singletrack, 6.7 miles dirt road, 1.3 mile doubletrack narrowing to singletrack, 1.5 miles paved road.
Time: 3 ½ - 5 ½ hours
Difficulty: Expert
Aerobic Effort: High
Elevation: Top: 10,919' **Gain:** 3,398'
Season: July through mid-October
Finding Route: Moderate to moderately difficult in places. Some of the trail links old logging roads and sections of singletrack (many turns.) Signed, but could be confusing if you don't see the signs.
Map: Mountain Bike Map for Cortez, Dolores, Mancos and Rico or Latitude 40 Durango or Southwest Colorado Trails. Older maps don't show changes to the upper Salt Creek trailhead.
Location: Start at the signed bottom of Scotch Creek Road and Hwy 145, 2 ½ miles south of Rico, 31 miles north of Dolores.

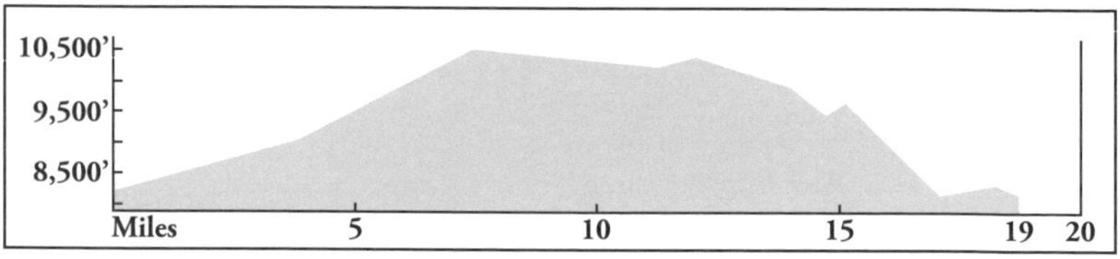

Mileage Log:

0.0 Ride up Scotch Creek Road. The first ¾ mile is rocky but rideable, and the first 3 miles are a very moderate grade.

2.2 After a short, steep, rocky hill, ride straight ahead. Pass a spur to the left and cross a side creek.

3.2 Cross the main creek to the right, and climb. In 3/10ths mile, switchback left, passing a spur road to the right. After a short level section, climb steadily.

SCOTCH CREEK TO THE SALT CREEK TRAIL
RYMAN TRAIL

6.2 Top out. FS 550 continues straight down Hotel Draw. Turn right on FS 564 and left on the signed CT in 1/10th mile.

7.7 Pass the signed Corral Draw Trail to the left.

8.7 Turn left on FS 564 at the end of the singletrack. In 1/10th mile, turn left again on signed CT singletrack. Stay on the CT for the next three miles following triangle CT markers as the trail goes on the road for short distances and quickly back to singletrack.

8.9 Cross FS 564, climb, and cross the road again, passing a "road closed" sign.

9.7 Turn left on FS 564, go around a small hill, then left again on the singletrack.

10.4 Turn left on the road for a very short distance, then left on the trail.

11.2 Pass the Big Bend Trail.

11.7 Ride out of the trees next to the road. Veer left and up more steeply on bumpy singletrack, and onto a section of old road up higher. In 2/10ths mile, turn right on the signed Salt Creek Trail in a level area. The trail is faint at first.

12.2 Cross a road to the right and near the junction of FS 564A (on the left,) staying with the signed trail. Meander downhill, left and then uphill, then ride down a small open ridge above a road below and left.

13.0 Turn sharp right off the ridge onto signed singletrack and into aspen forest.

13.1 Merge straight ahead onto old road (right.)

13.8 Turn left at signed intersection, on old road.

14.0 Turn left on a signed singletrack. Careen steeply down through the aspens, then climb for 2/10ths mile. Descend the ridge into Douglas Fir forest. Ride down many steep sections on narrow trail, with a few rutted and rocky sections.

16.8 Merge left onto the Ryman Creek Trail.

16.9 Turn right on gravel road at the end of the trail.

17.1 Turn right on Highway 145 and ride the shoulder carefully uphill.

18.6 End at Scotch Creek Road.

Option: The Upper Ryman Creek Trail is a fun descent, but has some very rutted sections. Repairing the trail is proposed, but until then Salt is the better trail. Ride as above to mile 8.9. After crossing the road once, turn right on the road instead of crossing a second time. Contour and start downhill. At mile 10, turn right on the signed Ryman Trail, an old closed road at first. Great views open before a very steep rutted section at 11.5 (hike a bike for most.) At 11.6 stay right passing Lower Ryman and contour, then descend. Stay right again when Lower Ryman and Salt merge in. End at the same trailhead as Salt Creek Trail. Lower Ryman is overgrown and mostly hike a bike.

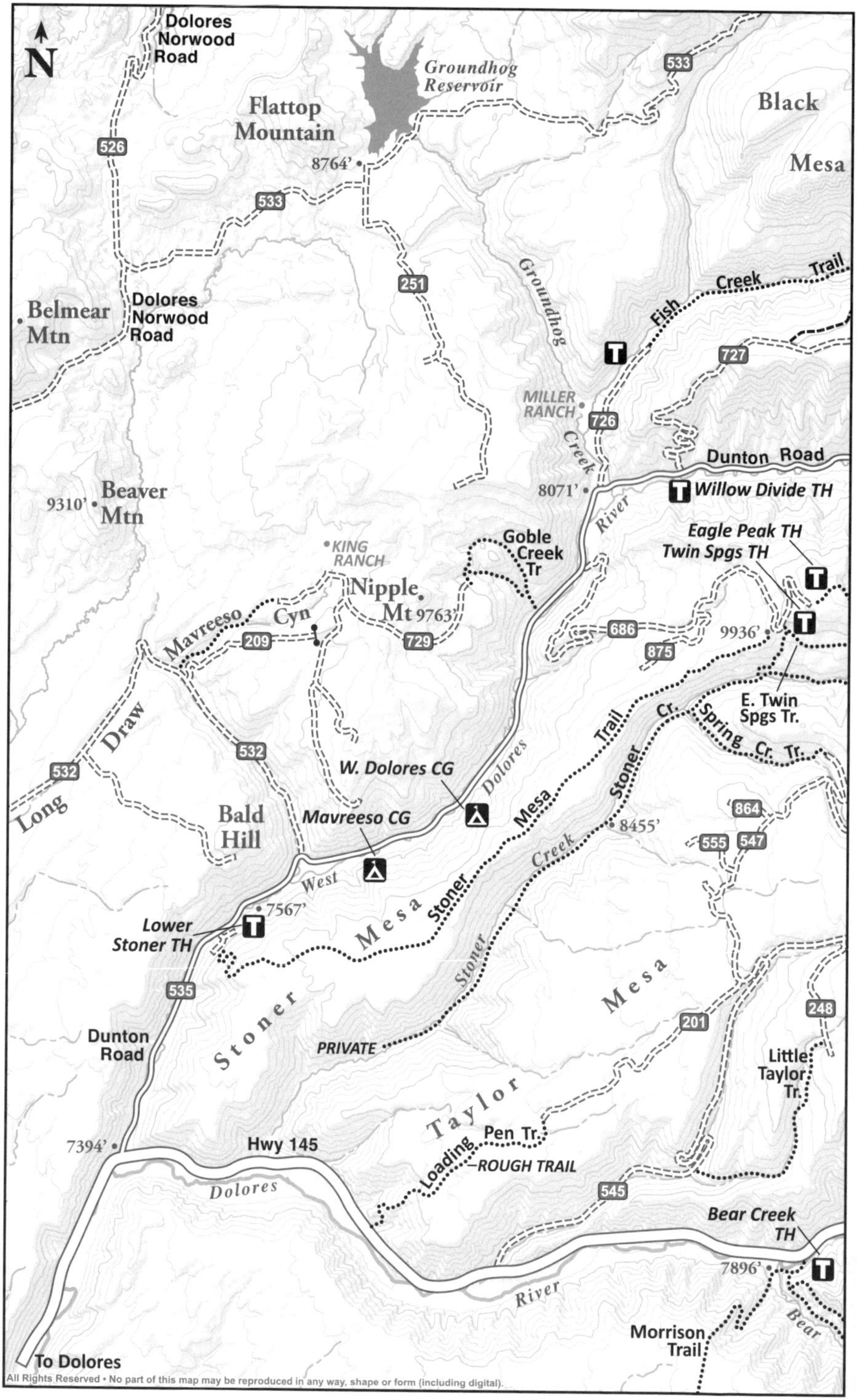
N
Dolores Norwood Road
Groundhog Reservoir
Flattop Mountain
8764'
Black Mesa
526
533
251
Belmear Mtn
Dolores Norwood Road
Groundhog
Fish Creek Trail
727
MILLER RANCH
726
Creek
Dunton Road
Beaver Mtn
9310'
8071'
Willow Divide TH
River
Eagle Peak TH
Twin Spgs TH
KING RANCH
Goble Creek Tr
Nipple Mt 9763'
Mavreeso Cyn
209
729
686
875
9936'
Long Draw
E. Twin Spgs Tr.
Spring Cr. Tr.
Cr.
Trail
532
532
W. Dolores CG
Dolores
Stoner
Mesa
Bald Hill
Mavreeso CG
8455'
864
555
547
West
Creek
7567'
Stoner
Mesa
Lower Stoner TH
Stoner
535
Mesa
Stoner
248
Dunton Road
201
PRIVATE
Little Taylor Tr.
Taylor
Pen Tr.
Loading
7394'
Hwy 145
ROUGH TRAIL
Dolores
545
Bear Creek TH
7896'
River
Bear
Morrison Trail
To Dolores

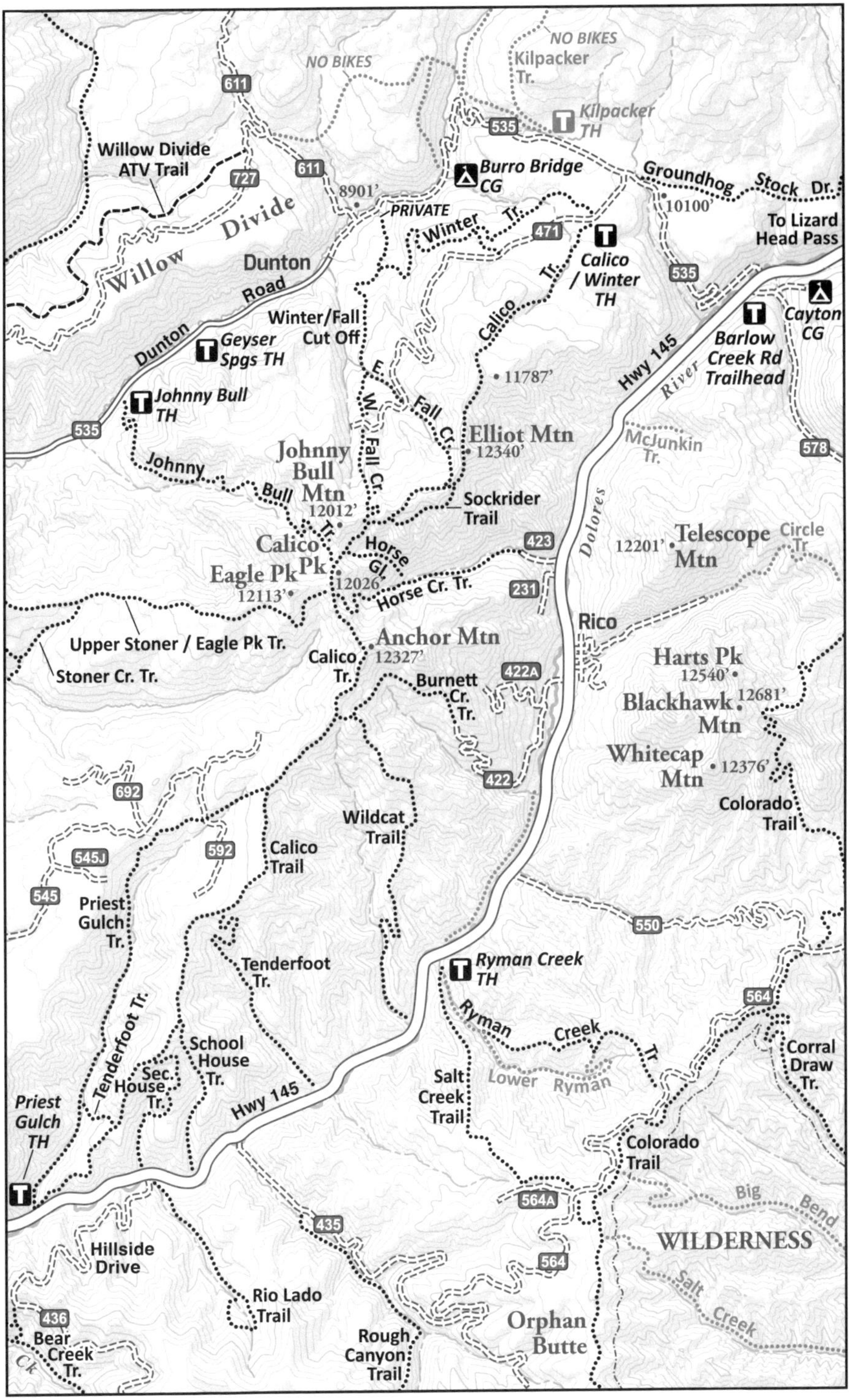
NO BIKES
Kilpacker Tr.
NO BIKES
611
Kilpacker TH
535
Willow Divide ATV Trail
727
611
Burro Bridge CG
Groundhog Stock Dr.
8901'
PRIVATE
Winter Tr.
10100'
471
To Lizard Head Pass
Willow Divide
Dunton Road
Calico / Winter TH
535
Calico Tr.
Cayton CG
Winter/Fall Cut Off
Barlow Creek Rd Trailhead
Dunton Road
Geyser Spgs TH
Hwy 145
River
Johnny Bull TH
E. Fall Cr.
11787'
W. Fall Cr.
Elliot Mtn
535
12340'
McJunkin Tr.
578
Johnny Bull Tr.
Johnny Bull Mtn
12012'
Sockrider Trail
Dolores
Calico Pk
Horse Gl.
423
12201'
Telescope Mtn
Circle Tr.
Eagle Pk
12026'
12113'
Horse Cr. Tr.
231
Rico
Upper Stoner / Eagle Pk Tr.
Anchor Mtn
12327'
Stoner Cr. Tr.
Calico Tr.
Harts Pk
12540'
422A
Burnett Cr. Tr.
Blackhawk Mtn
12681'
Whitecap Mtn
12376'
692
422
Colorado Trail
Wildcat Trail
545J
592
Calico Trail
545
Priest Gulch Tr.
550
Tenderfoot Tr.
Ryman Creek TH
564
Tenderfoot Tr.
School House Tr.
Ryman Creek Tr.
Corral Draw Tr.
Sec. House Tr.
Lower Ryman
Priest Gulch TH
Hwy 145
Salt Creek Trail
Colorado Trail
Big Bend
564A
435
WILDERNESS
Hillside Drive
564
Salt Creek
Rio Lado Trail
436
Orphan Butte
Bear Creek Tr.
Rough Canyon Trail
Ck

★★★☆☆

TAYLOR CREEK ROAD TO PRIEST GULCH

See map pages 144-145

Description: Priest Gulch is a long, quite fun, very fast and narrow descent through spruce and fir forest, aspens and meadows. It has quite a few short technical sections. There are smooth contouring sections, fast downhills, some very rocky, rough and rutted sections, some overgrown trail sections and some climbs. Riding it as a loop with Taylor Creek Road and down Priest Gulch is long, scenic loop with an almost all rideable downhill that opens just a little earlier than other high alpine rides. Taylor Creek Road is a very long dirt road approach (14 miles,) but is mostly moderate climbing on good gravel and dirt road. It is the most rideable approach to trails in this area, although somewhat monotonous. Priest Gulch is better before plants overwhelm it, by mid July. Riding up Priest Gulch would involve quite a bit of hike a bike on the narrow rutted trail and steep sections.
Distance: 26.8 mile loop, 6.5 miles of singletrack, 14.3 miles of dirt road, 6 miles of pavement.
Time: 5 -7 hours
Difficulty: Expert
Aerobic Effort: Very High
Elevation: Top: 11,183' **Gain:** 4,264'
Season: Late June through mid-October
Finding Route: Easy to moderate
Map: Mountain Bike Map Cortez, Dolores, Mancos and Rico or Latitude 40 Durango or Southwest Colorado Trails
Location: Start at the Priest Gulch Trailhead, 24 miles north of Dolores and 11.3 miles south of Rico on Highway 145, across from the Priest Gulch Campground. Drive to the trailhead on the dirt road next to a small cabin.

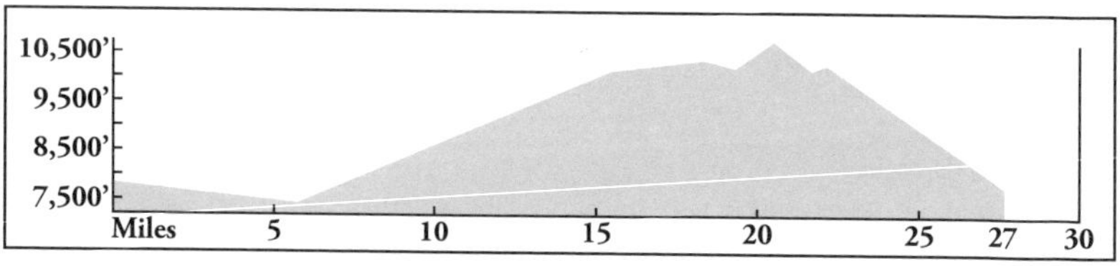

Mileage Log:

0.0 Ride down the dirt road from the trailhead and turn right on Highway 145. Ride carefully on the shoulder as many people drive quite fast on this narrow road.

5.9 Turn right on Taylor Creek Road. It has a big green highway sign. Start a moderate climb for several miles.

9.5 Pass the Little Taylor Trailhead and climb a couple of long switchbacks, all through aspen forest.

13.7 Ride straight ahead on FS 545 when the road forks and continue climbing. Left is Taylor Mesa Road to Spring Creek.

TAYLOR CREEK ROAD TO PRIEST GULCH

14.9 Pass signed 248 on the right.

16.4 Pass a big meadow on the left and signed FS 545J on the right. The road levels.

18.1 Pass signed FS 692 on the left.

19.5 Turn right at the Y-intersection on FS 592, after a downhill. Go downhill and around a corner.

20.3 Turn right on the signed Priest Gulch Trail. Left and up leads to the Calico, with some hike a bike, for other options.

25.3 Pass signs for the Tenderfoot Trail in a meadow on the left.

26.5 Ride through a gate.

26.8 End the trail at the parking area.

Options: An alternative descent to Priest Gulch Trail is on the Calico Trail. At mile 20.3 go left and climb steeply one mile to the Calico Trail (with some hike a bike), turn right and descend this fun trail section to the same parking area. Local Dolores and Rico riders climb Taylor Creek Road and the Calico Trail, then descend Eagle Peaks and Stoner Mesa Trail and connect the loop with pavement on Dunton Road and left on Hwy 145 for an epic ride.

Calico Trail | *Holly Annala*

★★★☆☆

STONER MESA TRAIL

See map pages 144-145

Description: The Stoner Mesa Trail is a moderate singletrack that rolls along an incredibly flat mesa through aspen forest, and it can be magical when the aspens are changing. If you ride the loop with Dunton Road and up FS 686, it is a big ride with a long dirt road climb and fast singletrack down. With a shuttle it is a quick ride and much less difficult aerobically. It is a good intermediate ride, but expect some hike a bike at the end. In the summer it is slightly monotonous as a solo ride. There are quite a few cows on the trail in the summer. Drive up FS 686 for many dispersed camping sites after 2 miles. For a great, more difficult ride, shuttle to West Fall and Eagle Peaks/Upper Stoner Mesa Trail, see page 150, and continue to ride Stoner Mesa at the end.

Distance: 26.7 mile loop, 11.2 miles of singletrack, 7.5 miles of paved road, 8 miles of graded dirt road.
Time: Loop: 4-6 hours. **With a shuttle, trail only:** 2 -3 hours
Difficulty: Advanced intermediate with a couple rocky expert sections and 2 miles of advanced/expert switchbacks at the end.
Aerobic Effort: Loop: Very high. **With a shuttle, trail only:** Low to moderate
Elevation: Top: 9,928' **Gain:** 2,823' **With a shuttle: Gain:** 515' **Loss:** 2720'
Season: June through mid-October
Finding Route: Fairly easy. The trail is straightforward (spurs are faint) and the road junctions are signed.
Map: Mountain Bike Map for Cortez, Dolores, Mancos and Rico or Latitude 40 Southwest Colorado Trails
Location: To get to the bottom of the Stoner Mesa Trail, drive 12 miles north of Dolores on Highway 145, and turn left on West Dolores/Dunton Road/ FS 535. Go 3.3 miles to the signed Lower Stoner Mesa Trailhead on the right. Start riding here for the loop, or leave a shuttle vehicle. To shuttle to the top drive 8.1 miles on FS 535 and turn right on Stoner Mesa Road. Drive 7.2 miles to the trailhead on the right, in a big pullout. If you come to the corrals, you have gone past the trailhead.

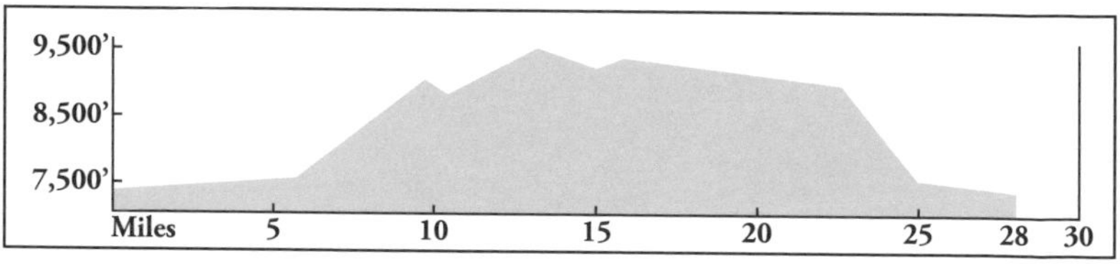

Mileage Log:

0.0 Ride uphill on pavement out of the parking area to Dunton Road and turn right. Ride on pavement, then dirt road to Stoner Mesa Road 686.

8.2 Turn right, cross the bridge, and climb on Stoner Mesa Road. The road starts somewhat steeply, then after two miles is quite moderate, even fast and flat for a while through beautiful aspen forest.

14.0 Cross a cattleguard, the climb gets steeper.

15.4 After the steeper climb, on the right on a big switchback is a pullout with trail and no camping signs. Last time I was here there was no trail name on the sign. Start riding on the moderate trail through the aspens. (If you arrive at a corral and the Twin Springs Trailhead, you have gone too far.) There are some rocks and roots, then the trail rolls along the edge of a forested canyon.

17.4 Hike a bike up a short, steep hill (either trail) and straight up through a gate, passing a dead end trail on the left.

18.7 Pass a cattle pond.

19.2 Pass a couple spur trails to the left to a hunting camp area.

21.5 Go through a gate and close it behind you. Ride through meadows and pass another spur to the left and a pond in about ½ mile. The trail is amazingly flat through here. If the trail is not obvious through the meadows, follow the posts.

23.5 Go through a gate and swerve left and then right through a big meadow.

24.2 Cross the dam of another pond and climb through a meadow with great mesa views ahead. In 2/10ths mile, start down a more difficult section of fun switchbacks.

26.4 End of the trail on a gravel road. Turn right, cross a bridge, and turn right on singletrack just after the bridge and follow the creek up.

26.7 End at parking area.

Stoner Mesa | *Holly Annala*

★★★★★

EAGLE PEAK AND STONER MESA TRAILS

See map pages 144-145

Description: This is an awesome high country shuttle ride with great views, landscape and singletrack, accessible from the Calico/Winter Trailhead. It has an incredibly long and varied downhill, with lots of smooth track and lots of rocky technical riding. Start the ride with Eagle Peaks Road and West Fall Trail as described here, or alternately ride the Calico Trail first. Eagle Peak Road, a moderate spin, and West Fall Trail, which is mostly rideable with a few short steep and difficult sections, is about ½ hour quicker and has less hike a bike than the alternate start on the Calico Trail, but the Calico has amazing views and high alpine trail. The Upper Stoner Mesa/ Eagle Peak Trail contours around a high alpine basin, climbs to a saddle, and descends smooth and fast singletrack down the edge of a ridge, then continues on rocky, rutted and technical trail. Be sure to stop and look at the view off the cliff to the right. At the end of the trail, a few minutes downhill on Stoner Mesa dirt road leads to the mostly fast and smooth singletrack on the Stoner Mesa Trail. See pages 152 for details on the Calico Trail, and page 148 for details on Stoner Mesa Trail.

Distance: 27.8 mile shuttle ride, 20.2 miles of singletrack and 7.6 miles of moderate dirt road. Or ride the Calico Trail first: 26 mile shuttle ride, 24.6 miles singletrack, 1.4 dirt road.
Time: 4 ½ - 6 hours
Difficulty: Expert
Aerobic Effort: Strenuous
Elevation: Top: 11,778' **Gain:** 2,974' **Loss:** 5,691'
Season: July through September or mid-October.
Finding Route: Fairly easy. Most junctions are signed.
Map: Mountain Bike Map for Cortez, Dolores, Mancos and Rico and/or Latitude 40 Southwest Colorado Trails (older versions are incorrect at the West Fall and Calico Trails junction.)
Location: Leave a shuttle vehicle at the Lower Stoner Mesa Trailhead. Drive 12 miles north of Dolores on Highway 145 and turn left on the West Dolores/Dunton Road/ FS 535. Drive 3.3 miles and turn right and down to the signed Lower Stoner Mesa Trailhead. Return to FS 535, turn right and drive 24.1 miles on paved and then dirt road to Eagle Peak Road. Turn right and continue 8/10ths mile to the Calico and Winter Trailhead on the left.

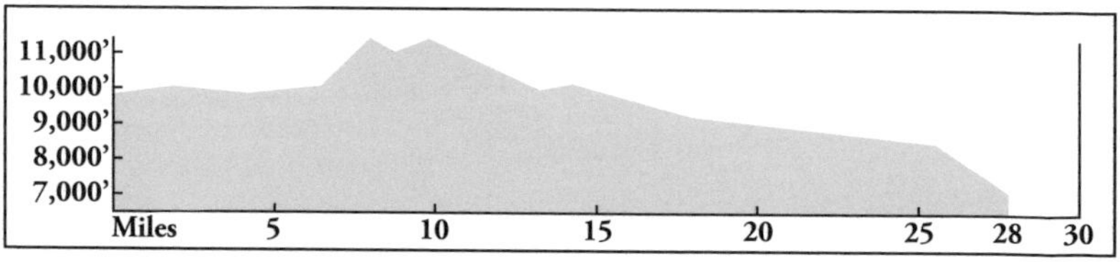

EAGLE PEAK AND STONER MESA TRAILS

Mileage Log:

0.0 Turn left out of the parking area and ride up Eagle Peaks Road. Pass the Calico Trail on the left. The road has moderate climbing and some descending.

5.1 Pass signed East Fall Trail (aka East Fork) on the right to the Winter Trail, then in 2/10ths mile, the continuation of East Fall to the Calico Trail on the left.

6.2 Reach signed West Fall Trail crossing the road at a pullout. If you reach the end of the road you have gone too far. Turn left and climb long switchbacks, sometimes moderate, sometimes steep.

7.9 Top out on the Calico Trail. Turn right and downhill, pass some old mines, then climb.

8.5 Pass the Horse Gulch Trail on the left, and descend straight ahead.

8.7 Pass the signed Johnny Bull Trail and continue left and uphill. Hike a bike up through a scree field.

9.0 Turn right on the signed Upper Stoner Mesa/Eagle Peak singletrack. To the left is Horse Creek Trail, which joins Horse Gulch Trail, and straight ahead the Calico continues. Climb and contour around a big basin on Upper Stoner Mesa/Eagle Peaks, then start an awesome and very fast, rugged downhill of smooth track intermixed with rooty, rocky, technical singletrack.

13.0 After a meadow and a short, steep, rooty section, turn hard right on signed Eagle Peak Trail for some welcome smooth riding. Straight ahead is Stoner Creek Trail, which leads to the rough Twin Springs Trail and eventually to private. Twin Springs is not a good biking trail.

14.0 Go through a gate and climb.

15.0 End of the trail at the top of the road, FS 686. Ride down the road and swing sharp left past a spur, then pass the Twin Springs Trailhead with pullout and corrals. Just past this is the Stoner Mesa Trailhead on the left.

16.3 On the left is a pullout and the Stoner Mesa Trail, with trail and no camping signs, but no name on the sign. If you go around a big switchback and start downhill more steeply on the road, you have gone too far. Take the moderate trail straight through the aspens. See page 148 for details on Stoner Mesa Trail.

27.5 End of the Stoner Mesa Trail. Turn right on the gravel road, cross the bridge and turn right on the singletrack to your vehicle.

27.8 Back to the trailhead and shuttle vehicle.

★★★★★

CALICO TRAIL

See map pages 144-145

Description: The Calico Trail is one of the most interesting rides in the Rico area, an amazing ridge-top singletrack at high altitude that rolls up and down for miles before descending what feels like forever to Highway 145. The Calico Trail has awesome views nearly from start to finish, and is all singletrack, 18.8 miles of it! The descent at the end of the ride is really fun, and technical in several places. The climbs are very difficult with a fair amount of hike a bike. A fun way to do Calico is with a long shuttle, as described here, but several other trails in the area exist for explorations and other loops, see options, below. All of the trails require some hike a bike in an uphill direction, as they are fairly steep and rough in places, as does the Calico, no matter which section or direction you ride it. A great alternative start to the ride is to add on the Groundhog Stock Trail at the beginning, see page 159 for details on this ride. This adds 6.7 miles and 1-2 hours to the ride. There is good dispersed camping near the Calico/Winter Trailhead, and in campgrounds along the lower (southern) end of Dunton Road.

Distance: 18.8 mile shuttle ride, all singletrack.
Time: 4 ½ - 6 hours
Difficulty: Expert/Epic
Aerobic Effort: Strenuous
Elevation: Top: 12,102' **Gain:** 3,515' **Loss:** 5,756'
Season: July through September or early October
Finding Route: Fairly easy, well signed. The area above Burnett Creek and Wildcat Trails is a little confusing (junctions mile 8.8 and 9.4).
Map: Mountain Bike Map Cortez, Dolores, Mancos and Rico or Latitude 40 Telluride, Silverton and Ouray or Southwest Colorado Trails (The turn onto West Fall Trail and the hiking trail over Sockrider Peak are not shown accurately on the older versions of the Lat 40 maps-bring these directions if you have one of them.) Bring one of the Latitude 40 maps above if you ride Groundhog first.
Location: Leave one car at the bottom at the Priest Gulch Trailhead, 24 miles north of 11th Street in Dolores (the turn to Boggy Draw/McPhee Reservoir) and 11.3 miles south of Rico on Hwy 145. Look for the big Priest Gulch Campground across from the turn to the trailhead. Drive 1/10th mile into the parking area, then continue with bikes and riders north 17.8 miles to the Dunton Road/ FS 535 (6.5 north of Rico) and turn left. Climb 3.9 miles to Eagle Peak Road and turn left, drive 8/10ths mile to the Calico/Winter Trailhead, on the left. This end of Dunton Road has some very narrow sections and exposure. If you are nervous in this situation, drive up the Dunton Road from the southern end. To get here from the Priest Gulch Trailhead, go 10.5 miles south on Hwy 145 and turn right on Dunton/West Dolores Road/FS 535, and continue 27.4 miles to Eagle Peak Road and right to the trailhead. To get to the Groundhog Stock Trail, continue 3.4 miles farther up Hwy 145 past the north end of Dunton Road to the Cross Mountain Trailhead on the left and start here. This is an easier shuttle with no dirt roads.

CALICO TRAIL

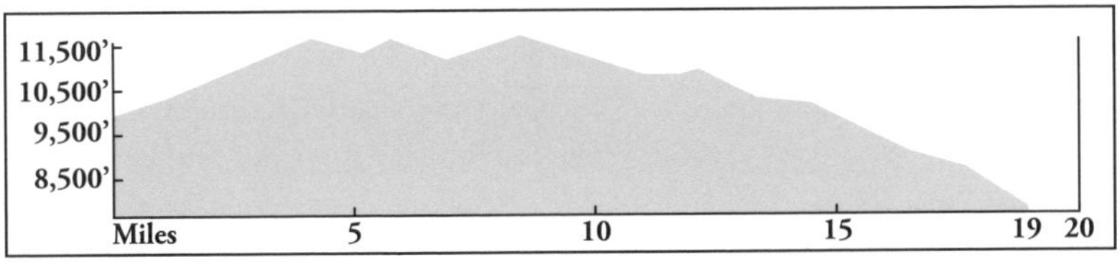

Mileage Log:

0.0 Ride out of the parking area and turn left in 200 feet on the signed Calico singletrack. The trail is moderate for about one mile with bridging over some boggy areas, then starts a big climb with a couple short sections of hike a bike.

3.0 The trail levels after some switchbacks. Enjoy amazing views of Lizard Head and the San Miguel and San Juan Mountains, and some flat trail. Next comes a couple more hike a bike sections and an amazing, mostly rideable side-hill trail that contours around Elliot Mountain.

4.5 Reach a fork on the ridge. Turn right and descend a rutted section toward East Fall Trail (aka East Fork) on the motorcycle and horse trail. (Straight ahead and steeply up to Sockrider Peak is hiking only.)

4.7 Pass the signed East Fall Trail (aka East Fork), and contour and climb through the basin.

5.7 After a strenuous section of hike a bike, reach the ridge and rejoin the hiking trail. Turn right and roll along the ridge with amazing views of Calico Peak straight ahead, and descend a couple rutted switchbacks.

6.1 Continue straight (left) and contour downhill, passing West Fall Creek on the right in a saddle. Pass some old mines and climb a short loose hill.

6.8 Horse Gulch Trail is on the left, continue straight ahead and downhill.

7.0 Pass signed Johnny Bull Trail to the right. Swing left and climb, then hike a bike up a big scree field.

7.3 Right is the Upper Stoner Mesa/ Eagle Peak Trail, left is Horse Creek 626. Ride straight ahead along the ridge, climbing and descending a few short, stinger hills.

8.8 After an enjoyable flat section and a descent, arrive at an unsigned junction above a cliff area to the left. Turn right and contour around the peak on the more well used trail.

9.4 After another stinger uphill ride up to a small red cliff face that divides the trail, next to a trail sign. Turn left and ride downhill (right of the small cliff is a cow trail) and then swing right to contour again toward the southwest. The signed Burnett Trail goes left. After a flat section and a short uphill, start the downhill.

10.9 Pass the Priest Gulch Trail, to the right.

13.0 After a big meadow stay right at a fork, then pass the signed intersection to the Tenderfoot Trail on the left. Descend through meadows and aspen forest.

CALICO TRAIL

15.3 Pass the Schoolhouse Trail on the left.

15.6 Pass the signed Section House Trail on the left, by a corral. Continue down, down, down fast singletrack with some technical and some rutted trail.

16.9 Stay left at the Y intersection, passing the continuation of the Tenderfoot Trail. The descent gets technical with a little exposure, then rolls down great switchbacks through the Ponderosa Pines.

18.8 Roll across a bridge to the end of the trail and the parking area.

Other trails in the area:
East Fall Trail (aka East Fork): A fun descent to Eagle Peak Road for a spin back to the Calico and Winter Trailhead, or continue across the road and descend to join West Fall Creek Trail and the Winter Trail, see page 155.
West Fall Creek Trail is good up or down, some hike a bike uphill, see page 150.
Horse Gulch/Horse Creek: Rough, but ok for downhill; neither is a great uphill. Horse Gulch is a better trail. Trails merge down lower and end in Rico.
Johnny Bull: Rocky and steep, but a fun trail down. Challenging with a lot of hike a bike uphill unless you are very strong.
Eagle Peak/Upper Stoner Mesa: Technical and awesome downhill. Challenging with quite a bit of hike a bike uphill. See page 150.
Schoolhouse, Section House and Tenderfoot: Rough horse and hike trails with lots of hike a bike, hard to follow.
Burnett: Some good downhill on trail, mostly road, however. Fast exit in bad weather.
Wildcat: Fun and rough downhill but very hard to follow, not a good emergency exit.
Priest Gulch: Really fun technical descent, lots of hike a bike uphill, see page 146.
Loading Pen: Not great up or down. Very steep and rocky.

Burnette to Wildcat Loop: This loop starts right in the town of Rico. It combines a grind on rocky FS 422 and the Burnett Creek Trail with a rough but fun downhill on the Wildcat Trail. After much deliberation I decided to leave this ride out due to the difficulty of following the loop, the rough nature of the trails, and the amount of hike a bike involved. It is a fun loop through beautiful countryside, but involves a fair amount of route finding. If you are curious, ride it with someone who knows the loop.

★★★★☆

CALICO, WEST FALL AND WINTER TRAILS LOOP

See map pages 144-145

Description: This loop is nearly all singletrack with great views and high altitude adventure riding. The Calico Trail is difficult climbing with quite a bit of hike a bike, but is worth it for the unique nature of the trail. West Fall Creek is a great descent on singletrack up top with smooth sections and switchbacks through conifer forest. Once it crosses Eagle Peak Road it is old eroded road and not very exciting for 2 miles. The Winter Trail climbs moderately through the forest to the Calico/Winter Trailhead to complete the loop. The East Fall Trail (aka East Fork) is a fun alternative descent. It starts on the Calico Trail, crosses Eagle Peak Road, and continues to join West Fall Creek and the Winter Trail. The upper section of West Fall Creek is mostly rideable uphill, accessed from Eagle Peak Road/FS 471, for a different way to reach the Calico Trail for other loops in the area.

Distance: 15 mile loop, all singletrack
Time: 4-6 hours
Difficulty: Expert
Aerobic Effort: Strenuous
Elevation: Top: 12,016' **Gain:** 3,683'
Season: July through September or early October
Finding Route: Moderate, some signs here have disappeared and West Fall Creek has some unmarked turns.
Map: Mountain Bike Map Cortez, Dolores, Mancos and Rico (East Fork Trail is not shown accurately on this map) or Latitude 40 Telluride, Silverton and Ouray or Southwest Colorado Trails (The turn onto West Fall Trail and the hiking trail over Sockrider Peak are not shown accurately on the older versions of these maps-bring these directions if you have one of them.)
Location: Start at the Calico and Winter Trailhead. Drive 12 miles north of Dolores on Hwy 145 and turn left and drive 27.4 miles up West Dolores/Dunton Road/ FS 535. Turn right on signed Eagle Peak Road and continue 8/10ths mile to the trailhead on the left. From the north end of Dunton Road/FS 535 (6.5 miles north of Rico) drive 3.9 miles to Eagle Peak Road. This end of the road has some very narrow sections and exposure. If you are nervous in this situation, drive from the southern end.

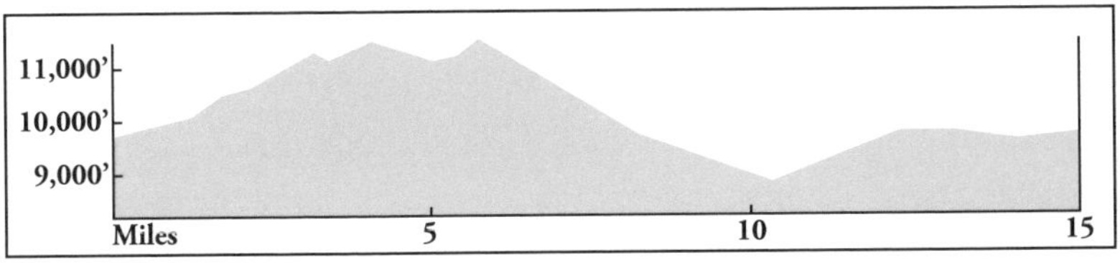

CALICO, WEST FALL AND WINTER TRAILS LOOP

Mileage Log:

0.0 Ride left out of the parking area and go 200 feet to the signed Calico Trail singletrack and turn left. Ride moderate trail for about one mile, then start a big climb with a couple short sections of hike a bike.

3.0 The trail levels after some switchbacks. Enjoy amazing views of Lizard Head and the San Juan Mountains and some flat trail. Next comes a couple more hike a bike sections and an amazing side-hill trail that contours around Elliot Mountain.

4.5 Reach a junction on the ridge. Turn right and descend rutted trail toward East Fall Trail (aka East Fork) on the motorcycle and horse trail. (Hikers go straight.)

4.7 Pass the East Fall Trail (aka East Fork) on the right (a good exit in case of bad weather.) Contour and climb through the basin, then hike a bike up to the next junction.

5.7 Reach the ridge and rejoin the hiking trail. Turn right along the ridge with views of Calico Peak ahead, and descend a couple rutted switchbacks.

6.1 Turn right on West Fall Creek, in a small saddle. Recently the trail sign was missing and only the post remained. Descend smooth trail on long switchbacks.

7.9 Cross FS 471, Eagle Peak Road. Continue on the signed West Fall Creek Trail 640. The trail starts as singletrack but soon follows old roads to the bottom.

8.8 Turn left at a post on an old road and descend past an old cabin. This is where East Fall comes in.

10.1 At a signed junction turn right on the Winter Trail. Left goes to Dunton and is private, no access.

10.6 Swing right in a big meadow and climb. (Straight ahead is overgrown and has a no motor vehicle sign.) Ahead is some contouring trail, a few stiff climbs, but mostly rideable track.

12.5 The trail levels and is super fun, rolling, middle chain ring riding.

13.2 Cross a creek and stay left, passing a signed spur to Eagle Peak Road. Soon ride into a meadow with great views of the San Miguel Mountains straight ahead.

15.1 Cross Eagle Peak Road to the trailhead.

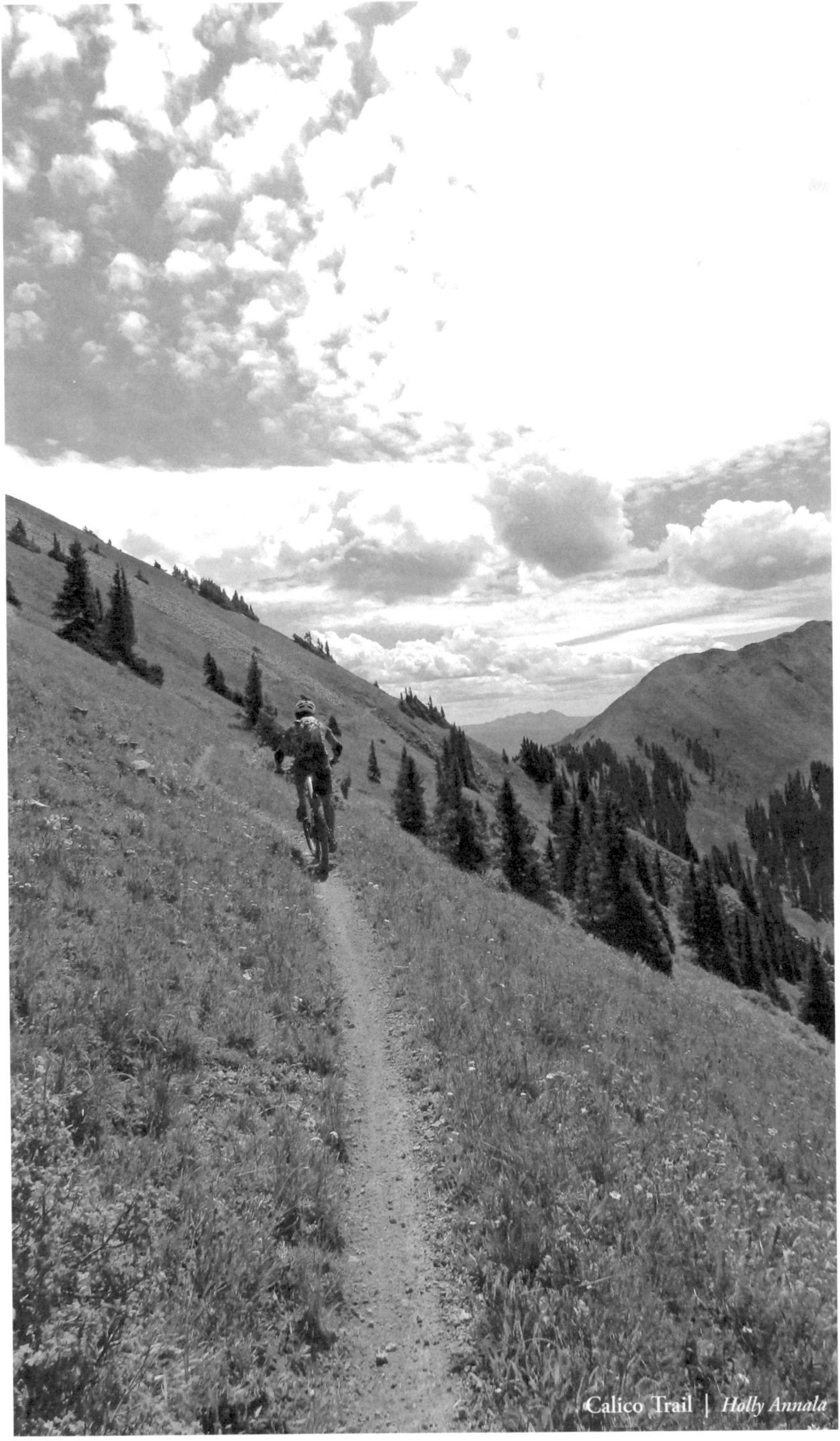

Calico Trail | *Holly Annala*

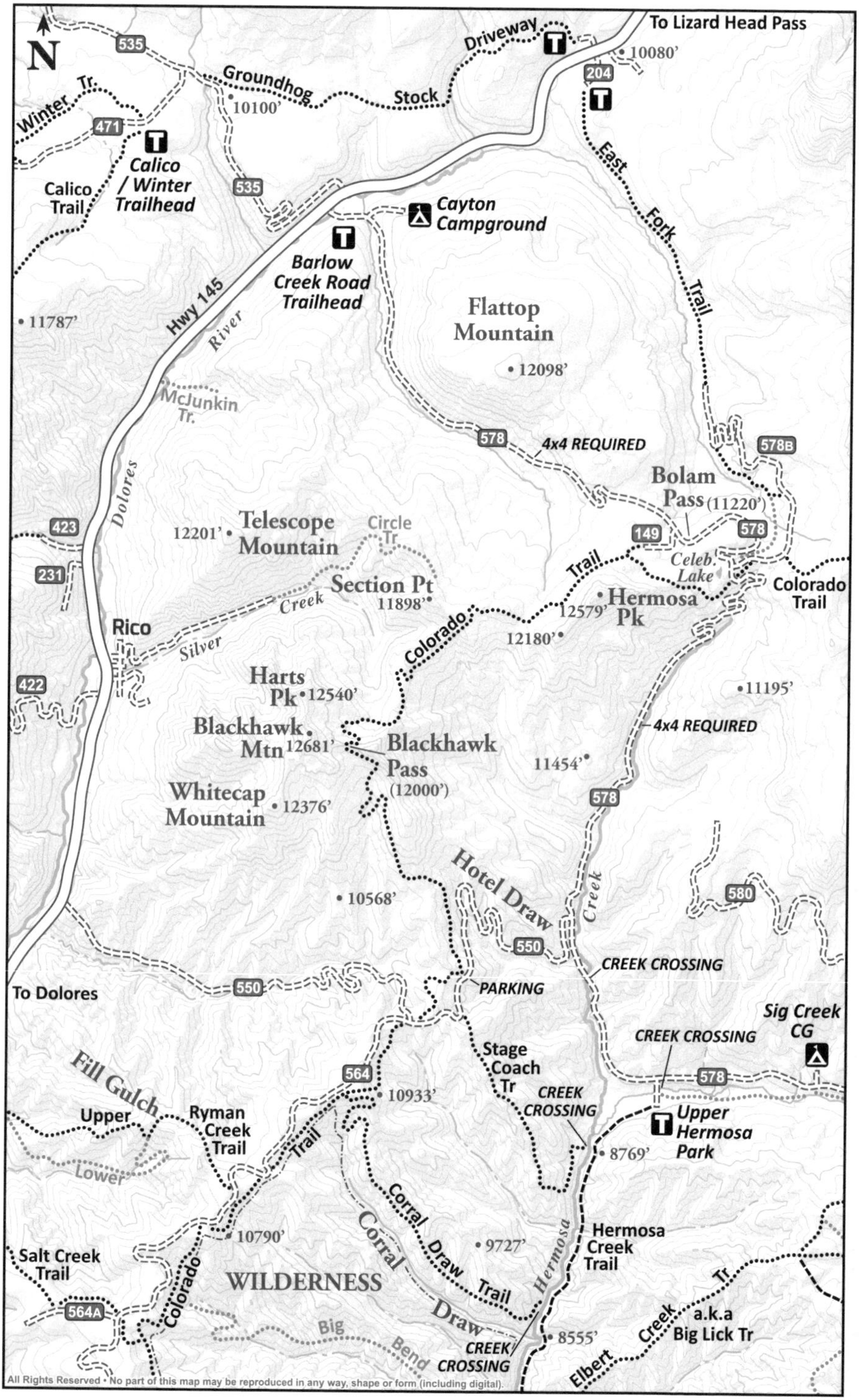
N
535
Winter Tr.
Groundhog
Stock
Driveway
To Lizard Head Pass
10080'
204
10100'
471
Calico / Winter Trailhead
Calico Trail
535
East Fork Trail
Cayton Campground
Barlow Creek Road Trailhead
Hwy 145
River
11787'
Flattop Mountain
12098'
McJunkin Tr.
578
4x4 REQUIRED
578B
Bolam Pass (11220')
Dolores
423
12201'
Telescope Mountain
Circle Tr.
149
578
Celeb. Lake
231
Section Pt
11898'
Creek
Trail
Hermosa Pk
12579'
Colorado Trail
Rico
Silver
Colorado
12180'
422
Harts Pk
12540'
11195'
Blackhawk Mtn
12681'
Blackhawk Pass (12000')
4x4 REQUIRED
11454'
Whitecap Mountain
12376'
578
Hotel Draw
Creek
10568'
580
550
CREEK CROSSING
To Dolores
550
PARKING
Sig Creek CG
Stage Coach Tr
CREEK CROSSING
Fill Gulch
564
10933'
578
Upper
Ryman Creek Trail
CREEK CROSSING
Trail
Upper Hermosa Park
8769'
Lower
10790'
Corral Draw Trail
9727'
Hermosa Creek Trail
Salt Creek Trail
Colorado
WILDERNESS
Corral Draw
Hermosa
Tr.
564A
Big
Bend
CREEK CROSSING
8555'
Creek
a.k.a Big Lick Tr
Elbert

★★★★☆

GROUNDHOG STOCK DRIVEWAY

Description: This is a beautiful high altitude out and back ride, or loop with dirt road and Hwy 145. There are great views of Lizard Head, Cross Mountain, Mount Wilson and El Diente as the trail skirts along the Lizard Head Wilderness boundary. It is short ride, but has all the characteristics of a high alpine ride with awesome mountain terrain, big stream crossings, and possibly very stormy weather. Descend Dunton Road through aspen forest, and climb Hwy 145 to close the loop. It is also a great way to access the Calico Trail, see page 152. Camping at the Calico/Winter Trailhead area offers quick access to Groundhog Stock Driveway and the Calico and Winter Trails, see page 155. Groundhog Stock tends to be quite swampy after rains and snow melt. In thunderstorm season, get an early start to avoid lightning and rains.

Distance: 13.1 mile loop with Dunton Road and Highway 145, 5.6 miles of singletrack, 4 miles dirt road, 3.5 miles of paved road.
Time: 2 ¼- 3 hours
Difficulty: Advanced intermediate with expert sections.
Aerobic Effort: Moderately high
Elevation: Top: 10,649' **Gain:** 1,835'
Season: July through September or early October
Finding Route: Moderately difficult. Some signs. A couple of the intersections can be confusing but with a little looking around are fairly straightforward.
Map: Latitude 40 Telluride, Silverton, Ouray Trails
Location: Start at the Cross Mountain Trailhead, located two miles south of Lizard Head Pass on Hwy 145 on the north side of the highway. This is 10 miles north of Rico (turn left to the trailhead) and 13.8 miles south of the turn to Telluride.

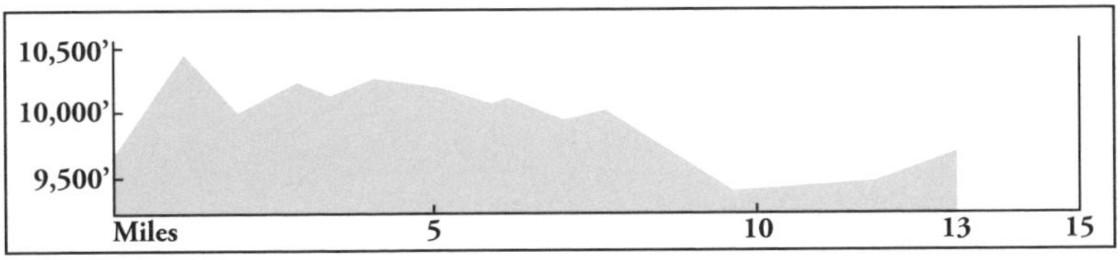

Mileage Log:

0.0 Cross the bridge on the signed trail and ride up an old road/braided trail.

0.5 Ride straight ahead (left) at the signed intersection onto the Groundhog Stock Trail. Right is Cross Mountain Trail, no bikes allowed.

0.7 The wide and braided trail climbs and contours left through the forest.

1.1 Descend and stay right across a small bridge, contour, and then switchback down through meadows.

1.8 Descend a switchback to Slate Creek and cross a big bridge. Head left and downstream while contouring and climbing gradually out of the drainage.

GROUNDHOG STOCK DRIVEWAY

2.5 Turn right on the main trail, ride over a saddle and into the forest briefly, then out into meadows.

3.4 Cross big Coke Oven Creek.

3.6 Ride straight ahead and downhill for a short distance, passing a less used trail going right and up (the trails rejoin shortly.) Next pass a spur on the left, swing right and climb a braided section, and swing left at a pole trail marker. Ride through a big meadow following the pole markers and past old corral posts on the left. Lizard Head and Cross Mountain to the right.

3.8 Cross a creek and merge left at the end of the meadow.

5.6 End Groundhog Stock Trail on Dunton Road/ FS 535. Turn left. Right leads to the Calico and Winter Trails if you are continuing on.

9.5 Turn left on Hwy 145. Climb gradually and then more steeply.

13.0 Turn left into the parking area and back to your vehicle.

Groundhog Stock Driveway | *Holly Annala*

★★★★★

BARLOW CREEK ROAD TO BOLAM PASS AND EAST FORK TRAIL

See map page 158

Description: This in an excellent mountain bike ride with spectacular scenery and great singletrack. The East Fork Trail is an awesome descent on a long, narrow singletrack in the San Juan Mountains near Telluride and Rico. There are smooth sections, technical sections, big creek crossings, and great views of Lizard Head and the San Miguel Mountains. Riding up Barlow Creek to the East Fork Trail is fairly direct and quite steep and grinding for a couple miles, at high altitude. In high summer, there can be quite a bit of 4-wheel drive traffic on the road, so get an early start to avoid the dust. The East Fork Trail is a good, mostly moderate uphill if you prefer an out and back, or to continue up to the Colorado Trail (CT) for a long loop with some of the other trails in the area. If you are bike packing from Durango toward Rico or Telluride, a nice option is to ride Hermosa Creek Trail and Bolam Pass Road up and down East Fork. From here you can cross the highway and ride Groundhog Stock Driveway and the Calico Trail and continue back to Durango on Hillside Drive and the CT, see pages 140 and 102. The crossing of Twin Creeks can be dangerous early summer, plan on turning back if they are too swift and deep to cross safely. The top of Barlow Creek Road has great views and camping if you are willing to 4-wheel up, or if you are bike packing.

Distance: 19.8 miles, 10.6 miles of dirt forest road and doubletrack, 5.3 miles of singletrack, and 3.9 miles of paved road.
Time: 3 ½ to 5 hours
Difficulty: Expert; out and back on East Fork is advanced intermediate/expert
Aerobic Effort: Strenuous
Elevation: Top: 11,413' **Gain:** 2,890'
Season: July through September or early October
Finding Route: Moderate overall. Easy on Barlow Creek Road and on the East Fork Trail, somewhat difficult from Bolam Pass to the singletrack.
Map: Singletrack Maps Durango Trails, the Mountain Bike Map for Cortez, Dolores, Mancos & Rico, and Latitude 40 Southwest Colorado show the ride, but the top of the East Fork Trail is incomplete. Take one of these maps and the directions and map here.
Location: The Barlow Creek Trailhead is located on Hwy 145 between Telluride and Dolores, 17.7 miles south of the turn to Telluride from Hwy 145 and 6 miles north of Rico. When driving north it is on the right side of the highway, look for the Cayton Campground sign. There is a parking area just off the highway on the right. The East Fork trailhead is located just south of Lizard Head Pass, 10 miles north of Rico and 13.8 miles south of Telluride, for an out and back.

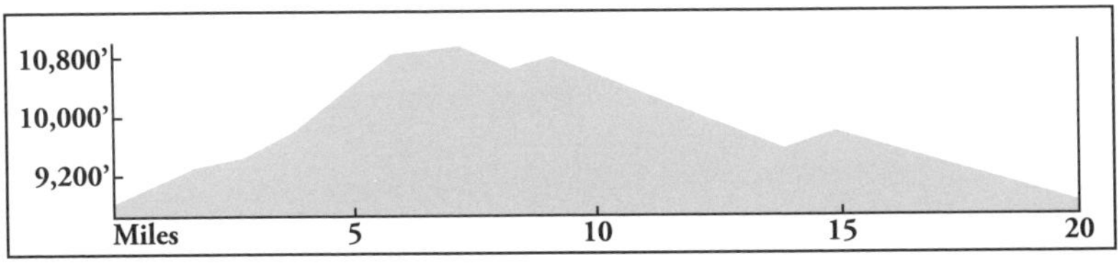

BARLOW CREEK ROAD TO BOLAM PASS AND EAST FORK TRAIL

Mileage Log:

0.0 Turn right out of the parking area, cross the Dolores River, and ride up Barlow Creek Road toward Bolam Pass. Stay right in 3/10ths mile, passing the Cayton Campground on the left. The road starts moderately.

2.5 Pass a spur to the right, cross a creek and climb. The road gets rockier.

3.5 Pass the historic Dunning claim and cabin. Grind up sustained steep and rocky road. Pass a spur on the right in 2/10ths mile.

5.0 Ride around some switchbacks, then the grade eases.

5.6 Nice views to the northeast of Grizzly Peak and Sliderock Ridge.

6.3 Turn left at the road junction at the top of the cliff area, and cross the headwaters of the East Fork of the Dolores River. The unsigned right fork of the road, FS 149, leads to the Colorado Trail (CT) near Hermosa Peak.

7.4 Ride over Bolam Pass. Descend on the road to Celebration Lake.

8.1 Ride straight past the lake 1/10th mile on FS 578 (pass FS 578B to the left) and turn left on the signed CT singletrack.

8.4 Merge right onto FS 578B.

9.0 Ride straight past the continuation of the CT on the right, and descend on the road. Watch for the next turn on the left in less than one mile, an obscure singletrack marked with a small brown carsonite user sign.

9.8 Turn left on the East Fork singletrack. Watch for down trees.

10.1 Turn right at the junction on the East Fork Trail, marked with a post, and descend. (The left fork comes in from mile 8.4 above, directly across from the CT singletrack, but is a very swampy, rutted trail.)

10.9 Ride downhill (left) on the dirt road, at the end of the singletrack.

11.6 At the end of the road ride onto the signed singletrack.

12.7 Cross two big creeks, South and North Twin Creeks.

13.6 Start a long climb, with a couple of breaks.

14.9 Ride straight ahead, passing another singletrack that turns sharply to the right. Descend and cross a big flat (sometimes swampy) area to the trailhead.

15.5 Reach the East Fork Trailhead. Ride down to the highway.

15.9 Turn left on Hwy 145 and roll down to Barlow Creek Road.

19.8 Turn left on Barlow Creek Road and return to your vehicle.

East Fork Trail | *Rob Mahedy*

Barlow Creek Road | *Rob Mahedy*

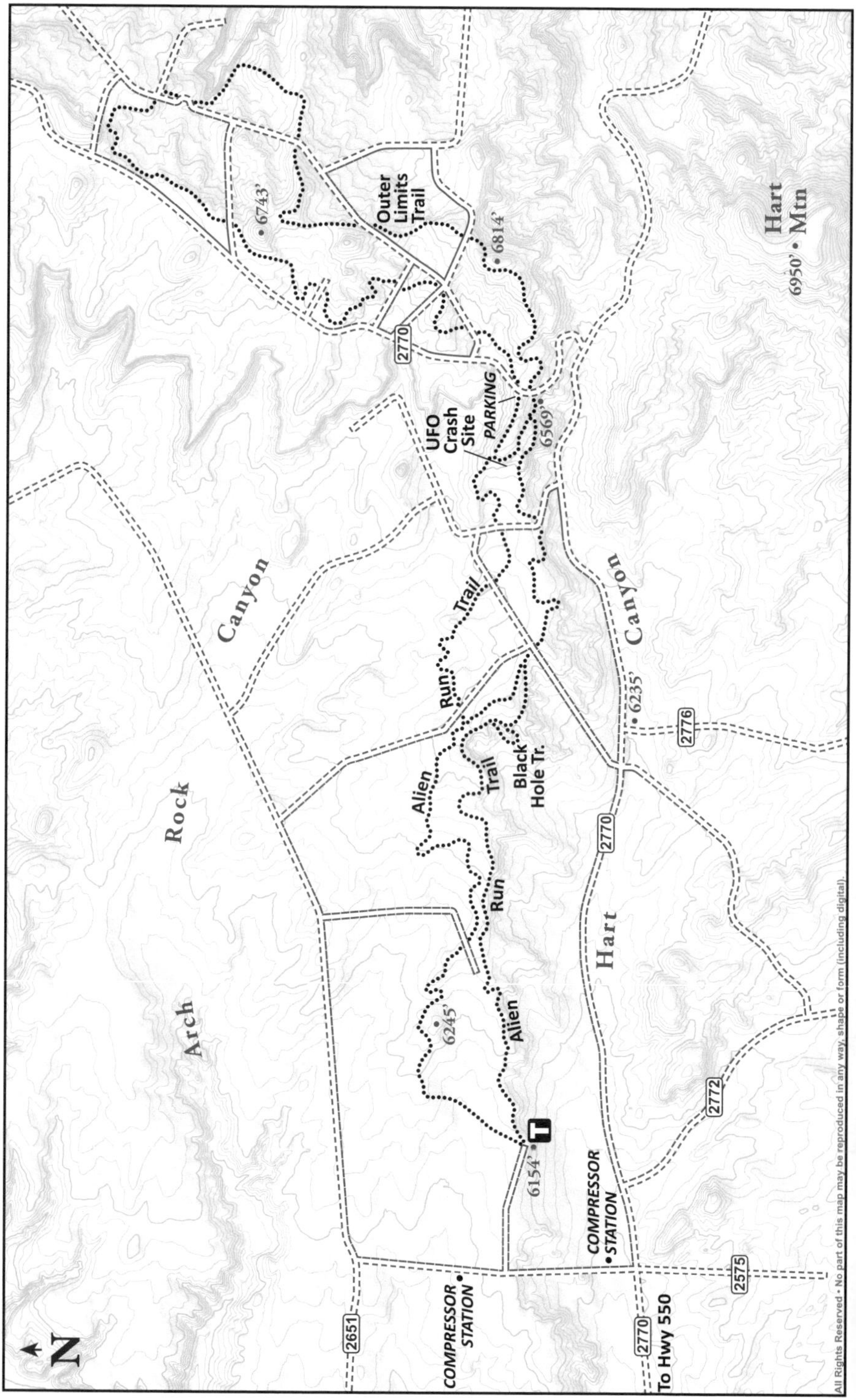

Outer Limits Trail
6743'
6814'
Hart Mtn
6950'
2770
UFO Crash Site
PARKING
6569'
Canyon
Trail
Canyon
Rock
Alien Run
Trail
Black Hole Tr.
6235'
2776
2770
Alien
Run
Hart
Arch
6245'
Alien
2772
6154'
COMPRESSOR STATION
COMPRESSOR STATION
2575
2651
2770
To Hwy 550
N
All Rights Reserved • No part of this map may be reproduced in any way, shape or form (including digital).

★★★☆☆

THE ALIEN RUN TRAIL

Aztec, NM (45 minutes south of Durango)

Description: This is a really fun and moderate singletrack loop system created especially for mountain bikes, and you can visit the alien crash site just a few miles out, complete with interpretive signs. The trails roll moderately through Pinyon-juniper forest and along the edge of small sandstone cliffs. There are three stacked loops for different abilities of riders. The short beginner loop is mostly smooth with a few short more advanced sections of slickrock. The original Alien Trail Loop is 10 miles long, and quite fun and winding. It has moderate climbs, a few short technical sections, some easy slickrock and lots of rolling singletrack. The longer Outer Limits loop is more remote and quiet (past a lot of the gas drilling activity.) The beginning is rocky with some rutted descents, the second half is smooth and flowing. All the loops share the last few miles of fast, smooth singletrack with lots of great turns that will make you smile! The downfall of this ride is all the compressor stations, gas wells, and gas well road crossings. Cross these roads with care as they are busy. The trails are rideable nearly all year, just a couple months in winter get snow and mud that make it impassable. The trails are one way only, counterclockwise, and easy to follow.

Distance: Beginner Short Loop: 6 miles **Alien Run Intermediate Loop:** 8.3 miles **Outer Limits:** 14.7 miles. All singletrack.
Time: Short Loop: 1 hour **Alien Loop:** 1 ½ to 2 hours **Outer Limits:** 2 ½ to 3 ½ hours
Difficulty: Short Loop: Beginner/easy intermediate. **Alien loop:** Intermediate with a couple of expert sections. **Outer Limits:** Advanced intermediate.
Aerobic Effort: Moderate except one longer climb on the Outer Limits
Elevation: Top: Short Loop: 6,035' **Alien Loop:** 6,140' **Outer Limits:** 6,381'
Gain: Short Loop: 435' **Alien Loop:** 656' **Outer Limits:** 1,450'
Season: March through December
Finding Route: Easy. The Outer Limits is more difficult; the trail is slightly hard to follow in a few places. Bring these directions.
Map: The map in this book, preceding page.
Location: To get to the Alien Trail, drive south 4.2 miles on Highway 550/160 from Durango. Turn right where Highway 550 splits off and drive up Farmington Hill. Continue 26 miles toward Farmington and turn left on CR 2770 and stay left. There is a big yellowish warehouse with a NM flag on it by the turn. Continue out 2.7 miles and turn left, cross a wash, pass a compressor station and climb the hill. Signed CR 2575 goes to the right, across the main road from this turn. Cross a cattleguard at the top of the hill and turn right just past the fence. There is a brown BLM Alien Trail sign here. Follow this to the trailhead at the end, a total of 3.7 miles from the highway.

THE ALIEN RUN TRAIL

Aztec, NM (45 minutes south of Durango)

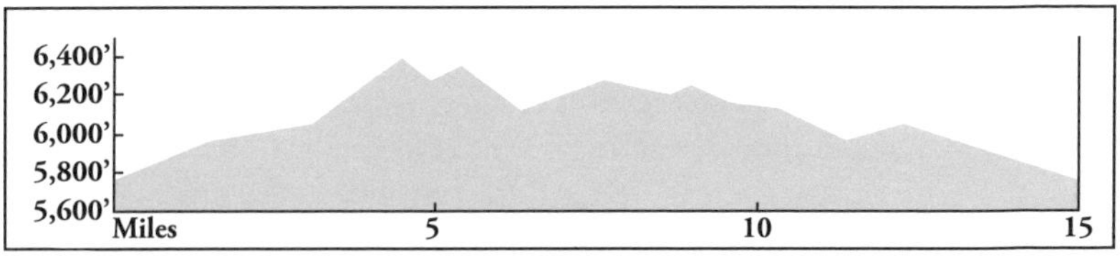

Mileage Log:

0.0 From the parking area, cross the rollover and stay right. Roll on smooth singletrack and intermittent slickrock. Paint spots guide you over the slickrock.

2.2 Turn left at a signed fork in the trail. To the right is the short, very technical Black Hole. It rejoins the main trail in a short distance.

2.5 Signed intersection. The short, easier loop turns left and merges with the return route of the Alien Trail in ½ mile. For the Alien and Outer Limits Loops, turn right.

2.6 Cross two gas well roads. In 7/10ths mile, cross another gas well road and climb.

3.7 Ride through a short technical area and climb a steep hill. In 1/10th mile, look left for a big flat area and the site for the Alien Spacecraft crash in 1948.

3.9 Signed junction. To ride the Alien Trail, turn left and climb a short, rocky section. To add the Outer Limits Loop, turn right. See option below for details.

4.2 Pass the unsigned Outer Limits return trail on the right, and descend a steep, technical, advanced section. Caution!

4.6 Ride straight across an intersection of gas well roads, the trail is caddy-corner and signed. Cross two more gas well roads in the next mile.

5.8 The easy loop merges back in. Ride straight ahead on the smooth, rolling trail.

7.0 Cross a gas well road.

7.8 Caution! Trail comes close to the fence on a fast descent!

8.3 Back to the Trailhead.

Option: For the Outer Limits turn right at mile 3.9:

4.0 Cross a rollover, climb a loose, rocky hill and swing right. Cross a gas well road. Start a rocky climb. Look for the worn area and the cairns to follow the faint parts. Pass a cool old corral.

5.0 Cross a gas well road. Soon the trail gets less rocky. In 4/10ths mile, cross a gas well road.

THE ALIEN RUN TRAIL
Aztec, NM (45 minutes south of Durango)

6.9 Wind around the head of a scenic canyon.

7.0 Pass an Outer Limits Trail sign, turn right on the road and ride uphill.

7.1 At the top of the hill, take a singletrack on the right along the road. In 1/10th mile turn left and cross the road at an intersection and continue on the signed singletrack.

8.2 Cross two roads and descend smoothly. Continue following the singletrack, crossing 4 more roads in the next 2 miles.

10.3 Caution sign and dangerous road crossing. Ride straight ahead through the parking area and onto the signed singletrack.

10.7 Intersect the Alien Loop after a cobbled descent. Turn right and descend a short technical section.

11.1 Ride straight across an intersection of gas well roads, the trail is caddy-corner and signed. Cross two more roads in the next mile.

12.3 The easy loop merges back in.

13.5 The trail crosses one more road. In 8/10ths mile, caution! Fence is close to the trail.

14.7 Back to the trailhead.

Alien Trail | *Holly Annala*

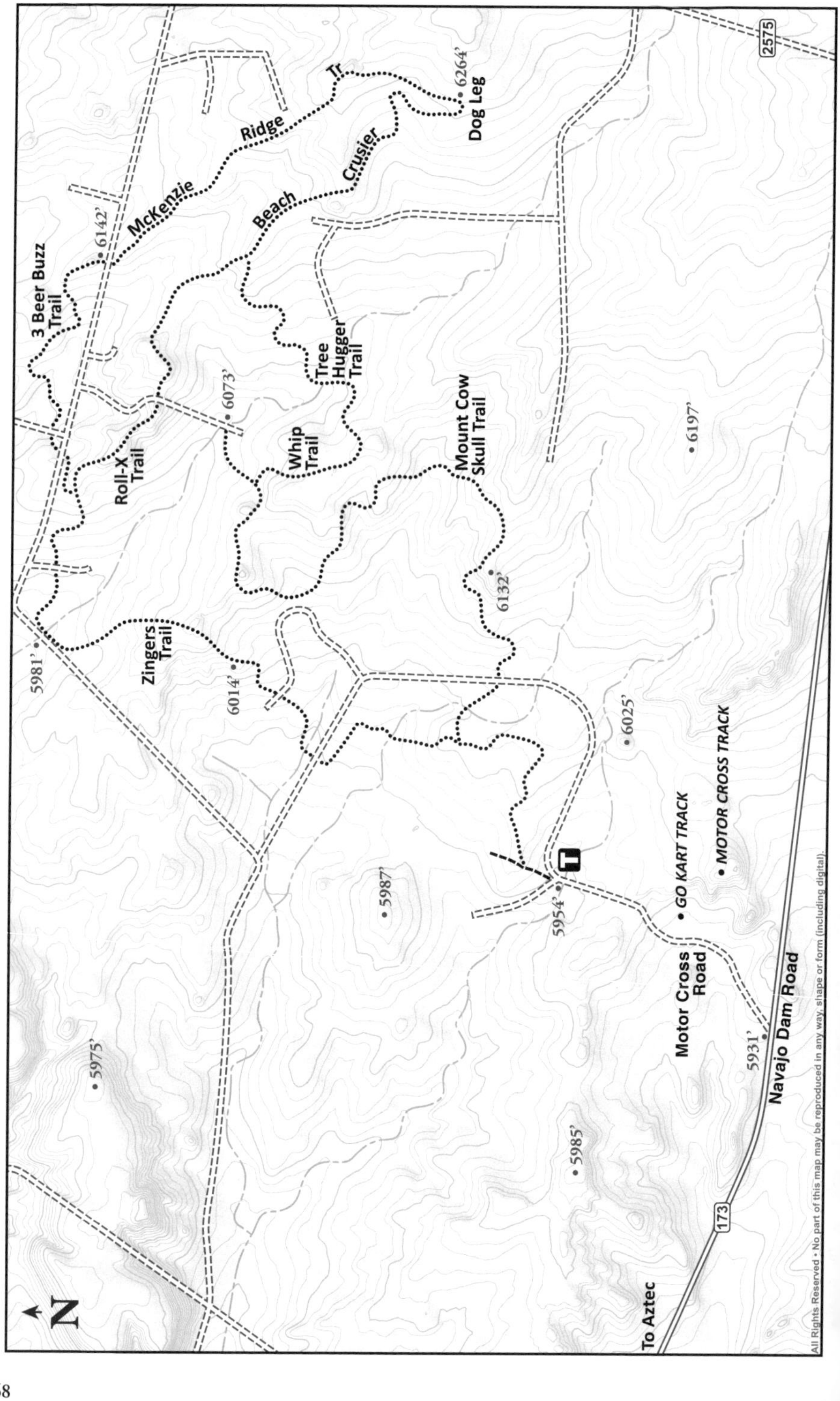

N
2575
Tr
6264'
Dog Leg
McKenzie
Ridge
Beach
Crusier
6142'
3 Beer Buzz Trail
Tree Hugger Trail
6073'
Mount Cow Skull Trail
Whip Trail
Roll-X Trail
6197'
6132'
5981'
Zingers Trail
6014'
6025'
GO KART TRACK
MOTOR CROSS TRACK
5987'
5954'
Motor Cross Road
5931'
Navajo Dam Road
5975'
5985'
173
To Aztec
All Rights Reserved • No part of this map may be reproduced in any way, shape or form (including digital).

★★★☆☆

MOUNTAIN VIEW TRAILS

Aztec, NM (45 minutes south of Durango)

Description: The Mountain View trails are a little known gem in the rolling Pinyon-juniper hills just outside Aztec. There is 10 miles of singletrack here, built with love. The trails wind through the desert and across washes, climb to interesting narrow ridges, and cross slickrock. There are great views of the La Plata Mountains and the interesting hills around Aztec. These trails are open nearly all year with the exception of a couple months in the winter when they may have snow and mud. It can be quite hot in the summer. The trails are non-motorized but there is evidence of some minor poaching. Below is a tour of all the trails, a loop within a loop. It is easy to shorten the ride by skipping the Beach Cruiser Trail at mile 3.2 (go left,) or turning right on Zingers at mile 5.5. The trails are one way.

Distance: 9.7 miles loop, 9.4 miles of singletrack, 0.3 miles dirt road.
Time: 1 ½ to 2 hours
Difficulty: Easy intermediate and intermediate.
Aerobic Effort: Low to moderate.
Elevation: Top: 6,279' **Gain:** 863'
Season: March through December
Finding Route: Moderate. Follow the singletrack and signs to connect sections. Some of the signs were torn off and hidden when I was here last. Most of the signs are brown carsonite, some trails are marked with handmade signs.
Map: The map in this book or get a print out from Cottonwood Cycles in Farmington, 505-326-0429
Location: To get to the trailhead, drive south on Hwy 550/160 from Durango 4.2 miles and turn right on Highway 550, and climb Farmington Hill. Continue 28.7 miles and turn left on NM Hwy 173 East toward Navajo Dam, just before downtown Aztec, marked with a big brown sign. Drive one mile and turn left at the major intersection on NM Hwy 173. Drive one more mile and turn left at a big white sign for Kart Canyon Speedway. Drive ½ mile past the race track and up the hill to the carsonite signed singletrack and the start of the Mountain View Trails. Park somewhere off the road.

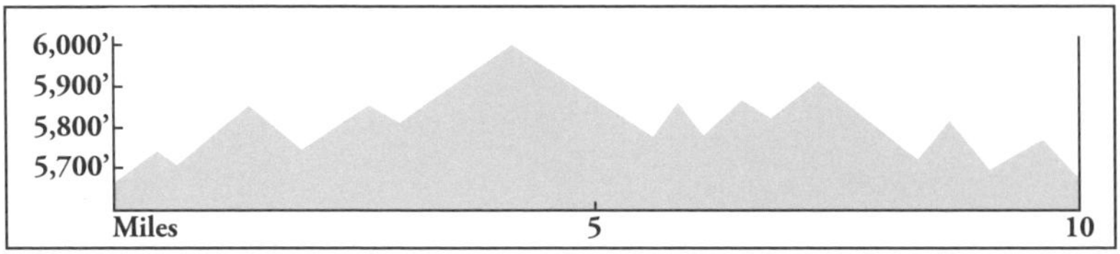

Mileage Log:

0.0 Start up the ATV trail. In 300 feet turn right at a big cairn and sign.

0.5 Turn right on the trail signed with 2 big orange arrows. In 2/10ths mile cross two dirt roads. Stay on the singletrack as it travels next to an ATV trail at the top of the hill.

MOUNTAIN VIEW TRAILS

Aztec, NM (45 minutes south of Durango)

1.5 Stay left with the orange arrows. A faint spur is right. Pass a gas well to the left.

2.0 Turn right on a road and then immediately left.

2.3 Turn right on the trail with blue arrows, Whiptail, marked with a river rock cairn and a dead tree. The "Whiptail/ non-motorized" sign was torn off and hidden.

2.6 Pass the connector from 1.5 on the right. In 3/10ths mile, cross a big wash.

3.2 Junction at the top of the hill. Turn right on Beach Cruiser with blue arrows and pass a decorated Christmas tree. Left (green arrows) leads to Roll-X.

3.5 Descend and then go left on slickrock around the corner. Continue straight to the trail.

4.0 Turn sharp left as the trail doglegs to the north.

4.2 As you approach a sandstone bluff, turn right and up toward a power pole, above the small bluff. On top head left to the sign and singletrack.

4.4 Ride straight across the well pad to the singletrack.

4.9 Roll along a small ridge with great views of the La Plata and Needle Mountains near Durango. Be careful of a few very sharp turns in here, and a road crossing.

5.4 Cross a road, turn right on another road and left onto the singletrack.

5.5 Intersection. Turn left (orange arrows) on Roll-X and climb another fun ridgetop trail. Right on Zingers (yellow arrows) goes to the parking area.

5.7 Turn right on a road. Straight across is the green arrow connector to Beach Cruiser.

5.9 After Crossing the big wash, turn right immediately on a signed singletrack.

6.1 Back to the Whiptail junction, turn left and ride this section again up to Christmas tree junction.

7.0 Turn left on the green arrow trail and descend then climb to an interesting salmon colored ridge.

7.4 Cross the road and ride the opposite direction on Roll-X.

7.6 Turn left with the yellow arrows on Zingers. In 3/10ths mile cross a road.

8.0 Turn left on a wide, sandy road, go 1/10th mile and cross the wash. Turn left on singletrack. Climb and descend, and cross two more roads in the next mile.

9.2 Turn right at the intersection marked by an old bucket.

9.7 Turn left on the ATV trail and head down to the parking area.

Alien Trail | *Holly Annala*

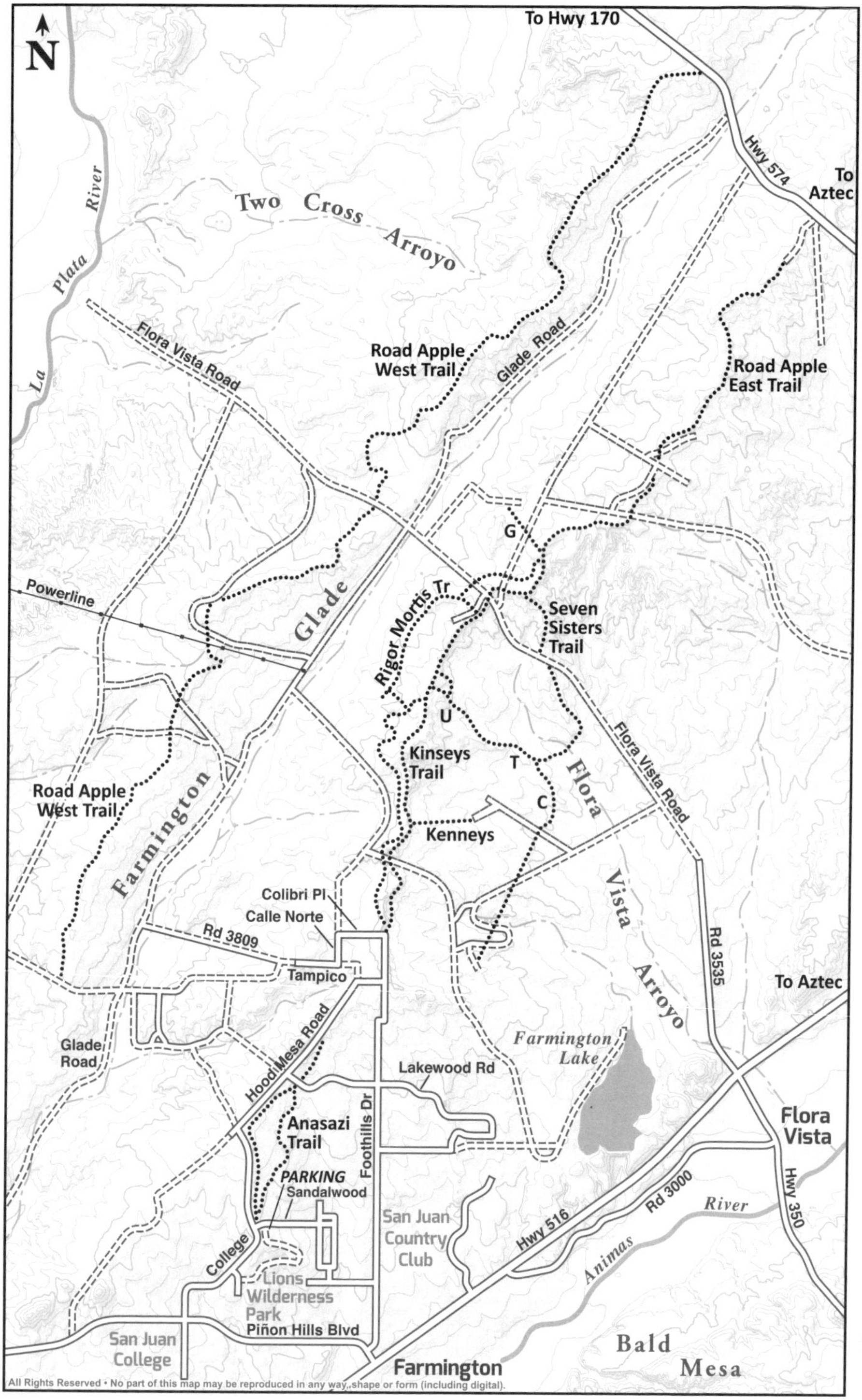
N
To Hwy 170
Hwy 574
To Aztec
La Plata River
Two Cross Arroyo
Flora Vista Road
Road Apple West Trail
Glade Road
Road Apple East Trail
G
Powerline
Glade
Rigor Mortis Tr
Seven Sisters Trail
U
Kinseys Trail
T
Flora Vista Road
Road Apple West Trail
Farmington
C
Flora
Kenneys
Vista
Colibri Pl
Calle Norte
Rd 3809
Tampico
Arroyo
Rd 3535
To Aztec
Glade Road
Hood Mesa Road
Lakewood Rd
Farmington Lake
Anasazi Trail
Foothills Dr
Flora Vista
PARKING
Sandalwood
San Juan Country Club
Hwy 516
Rd 3000
River
Hwy 350
College
Lions Wilderness Park
Animas
Piñon Hills Blvd
San Juan College
Farmington
Bald
Mesa

FOOTHILLS DRIVE TRAILS

Farmington, NM (one hour south of Durango)

Description: The Foothills Drive trails are a mid-winter treat when trails in Durango are snowed in and muddy. These singletracks roll atop ridges with views of the La Plata Mountains, and swoop through gullies and Pinyon-juniper forest in the high desert. The rides begin on the moderate Kinsey Trail, and have only a few rocky sections. There are a few options for loops to either side of this trail. The trail along the top is recommended by locals as one-way only to avoid collisions, hence the parallel trails. The way back is fun, flowy track. The trails are short, but two loops can be added together for a longer ride, see Foothills Seven Sisters Loop, page 174. For a much longer ride in the same area, see the Road Apple Rally, page 175. The drawback of these trails is all the gas well drilling and roads.

Finding Route: Moderately difficult in places but these rides generally follow the ridge or loop back on either side of the ridge. There are lots of junctions and unsigned gas well roads. The trails are signed with carsonite signs with letters (almost no names of trails) and there are some Road Apple Rally symbols (a horse on a bike) on carsonite signs. Keep the main ridge in sight while exploring and follow the bike tracks. Be sure to bring this book.
Map: Singletrack Maps Phil's World has a helpful Farmington map. Some trails have disappeared with lack of use, and many roads have been recently built in the area.
Location: From Durango drive south 4.2 miles on Hwy 550 South/160 East and turn right on Hwy 550, up Farmington Hill. Drive 30 miles to Aztec. Go straight through Aztec onto Hwy 516 (Hwy 550 turns left at Main.) Continue 9 miles on Hwy 516 and turn right on Pinon Hills Drive in Farmington, just past the Ford dealership. Stay in the right lane and turn right in 1/10th mile on Foothills Drive. Stay on Foothills for 2 ½ miles to a T-intersection. Turn right, staying on Foothills Drive, and go 6/10ths mile to the junction with Colibri Street and the trailhead. On weekdays, park across the street in the dirt pullout.
Season: All year except for short periods in the winter after heavy precipitation. Hot in the summer.

FOOTHILLS KINSEY'S LOOP

★★★☆☆

Kinsey's, Rigor Mortis

Distance: 8.6 miles, 8 miles singletrack, 4/10ths mile doubletrack
Time: 1 hour or more, easy to add more loops.
Difficulty: Intermediate
Aerobic Effort: Low
Elevation: Top: 5,901' **Gain:** 450'

Mileage Log:

0.0 Ride through the yellow posts onto the singletrack, and stay right.

0.6 Cross a gas well road. The return route from the ride is to the left.

FOOTHILLS KINSEY'S LOOP

Kinsey's, Rigor Mortis

1.0 Ride left on the main trail, passing a singletrack spur to the right.

1.6 Ride very close to another trail, stay right and ride through a fence.

2.2 Cross a road and continue straight ahead, on the V route.

2.4 Ride past a spur to the left that heads back to the trailhead. In a short distance, stay left (straight) on the Y route at the next junction, passing the U route on the right (the Seven Sisters return route.)

3.1 Trail junction at a road crossing. Stay right (straight ahead) on the ridge on P. Left and across the road is R, which leads to Rigor Mortis.

3.4 Cross another road, ride straight ahead. There is a parallel singletrack to the left.

3.7 End signed Kinsey's at a several-way intersection. Turn left on the ridge on E, the Road Apply Rally, and ride through some sand. Seven Sisters is right, see loop below.

4.1 Junction. F and the Road Apple are right. Ride straight ahead (left) on G, and immediately left again on a singletrack with a brown carsonite marker. Follow the singletrack back toward the trailhead.

4.6 Cross a road. In 2/10ths mile cross another road.

5.0 Turn right at an intersection on Rigor Mortis. Left goes to the Kinsey Trail.

5.6 Merge onto a doubletrack at the end of the singletrack.

6.0 Turn left onto the signed singletrack and climb.

6.3 Intersect another trail, turn right. Left goes to Kinsey's.

7.0 Stay right as the trails come very close together. In ½ mile cross two roads.

8.0 Cross a road onto the trail through private property.

8.6 Back to the parking area.

FOOTHILLS SEVEN SISTERS LOOP

★★☆☆☆

Kinsey's, Seven Sisters, Rigor Mortis

Add the Seven Sister's loop to the loop above for a fun downhill and a bigger climb back to the ridge.

Distance: 10.8 miles, 10.4 miles singletrack, 4/10ths mile doubletrack.
Time: 1 ½ hours
Difficulty: Intermediate with a couple short advanced sections.
Aerobic Effort: Moderate
Elevation: Top: 5,901' **Gain:** 700'

FOOTHILLS SEVEN SISTERS LOOP

Kinsey's, Seven Sisters, Rigor Mortis

Mileage Log:

0.0 Follow the above directions to mile 3.7. Stay on the ridge and ride generally straight ahead at each junction.

3.7 End Kinsey's at a signed junction; turn right on Seven Sisters and swoop down the sub-ridge, over whoops and a couple steep descents. In 4/10ths mile the trails splits; take either, they rejoin.

4.3 Turn left and ride up a road, cross a cattleguard, and turn right onto the signed wide trail, which narrows soon.

5.1 Merge right onto a doubletrack, then left on singletrack marked with a cairn. Stay right on singletrack and climb.

5.4 Stay right at an intersection on T. C is left.

5.7 Climb to a hilltop above a motorcycle high pointing area, and ride back toward Kinsey's and the ridge.

5.9 Cross a road and climb.

6.4 Pass a right turn to S and climb a short steep hill on U. S is a short trail that ends on Kinsey's.

6.5 Back to the ridge and Kinsey's, turn right. V is left.

7.3 Cross the road to singletrack R and stay left when a singletrack forks right.

7.9 Merge onto a doubletrack at trail's end.

8.3 Turn left on the singletrack. In 3/10ths mile, turn right at a junction on singletrack.

9.3 Go through the yellow posts and stay right. In ½ mile cross two doubletracks.

10.2 Cross a road.

10.8 Merge with the outgoing trail and arrive at the parking area.

ROAD APPLE RALLY LOOP

★★☆☆☆

Farmington, NM

Description: The Road Apple Rally is a long loop in the rolling Pinyon- juniper forest and clay hills just outside of Farmington. This high desert loop is rideable nearly all winter. The climbs are mostly moderate, but there are fun and challenging sections of short, steep climbs and descents. End the ride with the Foothills Drive singletracks. The trails that make up the loop parallel both sides of the Chokecherry Wash on two ridges; connect the loop with a little paved and some dirt roads. Highlights of the loop are nice views of the surrounding desert country and the La Plata Mountains, many flowing sections and arroyos, narrow ridge sections, and lots of fun whoops. The drawbacks of the ride are the many gas wells and roads, some very wide and damaged motorized trail (poached by ATVs and trucks,) and at times dumping.

Distance: 27.4 mile loop, 19.7 miles of singletrack, 5.1 miles of dirt road and wider trail, 2.6 miles paved road.

Time: 3 ½ to 5 hours

Difficulty: Advanced intermediate with a few very short expert sections.

Aerobic Effort: Moderately high

Elevation: Top: 6,332' **Gain:** 1,476'

Finding Route: Difficult. There is a maze of gas well roads that makes route finding a challenge at the beginning of the ride, but the trail is well-used, has some signs and is fairly easy to follow once you find it. Likely you can follow the trail without reading the directions as much past mile 3.6.

Location: Park at the Lion's Wilderness Park Amphitheatre. Follow the directions, page 173 Location, to Pinon Hills Drive in Farmington and turn right. Get in the middle lane and continue on Pinon Hills past Foothills Drive. Turn right in 7/10ths mile on College. Follow College 1 mile to Sandalwood and turn right into the second entrance of Lion's Wilderness Park. There is a parking area immediately on the right, or you can continue downhill 4/10ths mile to Sandalwood Park on the left to park.

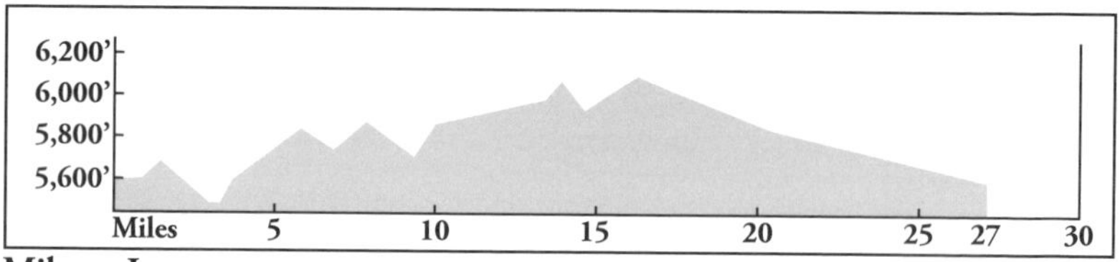

Mileage Log:

0.0 Ride out of the parking area and across to the northeast corner of College and Sandalwood. A small brown carsonite sign marks the start of the singletrack, through the fence. Turn right immediately at the fork in the singletrack. Follow the main trail through here.

1.3 The two trails merge. Go through the gate and left on paved Lakewood Drive (don't cross to the singletrack)! Ride straight across signed Hood Mesa onto a dirt road and gradually downhill, immediately passing a spur to the right. Ride straight out the dirt road, passing a spur road on the right in 3/10ths mile.

2.0 Swing left around a gas well, staying on the main road along the small rock bluff. Ride straight past a spur on the left in 3/10ths and a spur on the right in ½ mile.

2.7 Turn right as you arrive in the open sagebrush valley and ride up the wash. Next turn left, staying with the main road, and go straight across Chokecherry Wash to Glade Road.

3.2 Cross Glade Road and ride straight onto a spur road and uphill, under the powerline. Just to your left is a prominent but small yellow sandstone outcropping from the ridge.

3.6 At the crest of the hill take the signed "trail" (which is as wide as the road) to the right, through a cable fence. In 3/10ths mile cross a road to a gas well.

5.2 Turn left on a dirt road, and then right on the singletrack. In the next 1.1 miles, cross 3 more roads.

6.4 Turn right and descend a short, steep hill, next to a fence. Go through a gate, stay left, and then ride up a short steep hill and under the powerlines. Pass a spur road to the right and then to the left.

7.0 Cross a road. In 2/10ths mile, ride onto a hilltop road and straight (right) on narrow singletrack. This is a fun section with views of the La Plata Mountains.

8.4 Ride straight onto a road and left onto the singletrack. In 4/10ths miles cross a main road with a small powerline.

9.6 Cross a gated road to a well and climb. Stay right and climb, then swing right at the top.

10.0 Turn left passing a less used spur to the right, usually closed with sticks.

10.6 Turn right onto a road signed G and left on the singletrack, signed F and also with a small Road Apple symbol/sign (a horse on a bike.)

11.3 Cross a small cattleguard and road and climb steep singletrack. Cross a doubletrack and 2 more roads in the next 1 ½ miles. There are a few steep climbs and descents along here.

13.0 Stay left twice at a motorcycle high pointing area on a hill. Ribbons mark the turns. Stay left again as the trails merge on the other side of the hill.

13.3 Cross a small cattleguard and ride along a fence.

14.2 Turn right on paved Aztec Hwy 574 and stay on the shoulder. Pass Glade Road and a powerline road on the right in the low part of the valley and then climb.

15.6 Turn right on a dirt road at the top of the hill with a big Glade Run trailhead sign and a small carsonite Road Apple sign. The road forks behind the Glade sign; stay right and ride straight to the end.

16.0 Cross a steep little cattleguard and ride onto singletrack. Ride around a well site and cross a road.

18.3 Cross a road, then cross another at a junction. Ride straight ahead onto a spur road that starts at the crossing point. Continue on the spur road 4/10ths mile and turn left on signed singletrack.

18.8 Cross a road and ride along a fun ridge section.

19.6 Junction. Turn right and immediately left on singletrack signed with a brown carsonite marker. Left is signed E and is the traditional Road Apple race route and leads to a signed junction of Kinsey's and Seven Sisters loop, see page 174.

20.1 Cross a road. In 2/10ths mile cross another road.

20.5 Turn right at an intersection on Rigor Mortis. Left goes to the Kinsey Trail.

21.1 Merge right onto a doubletrack at the end of the singletrack.

21.5 Turn left onto the signed singletrack and climb.

21.8 Intersect another trail, turn right. Left goes to Kinsey's.

22.5 Stay right as the trails come very close. In ½ mile cross two doubletracks.

23.6 Cross a road onto the trail through private property.

24.1 End on Foothills Dr., go straight ahead and downhill.

24.7 Turn right on Hood Mesa, then turn left on Hood Mesa in 1/10th mile.

25.5 Turn left on the singletrack that may be marked with an arrow on the pavement. If you miss it, continue to Lakewood Drive, turn left, and then right on the singletrack, through a gate.

25.8 Cross Lakewood and stay to the right on the singletrack this time.

27.4 End at the corner of Sandalwood and College.

Road Apple Rally | *Holly Annala*

BIKE SHOPS, HUTS, TOURS, SHUTTLES AND OUTDOOR GEAR

DURANGO

HASSLE FREE SPORTS 970-259-3874
2615 Main Avenue. Full service bike shop and rentals. Durango's friendliest bike shop!

SAN JUAN CYCLES 970-247-6014
48 CR 250 Suite 1, next to Bread. Giant Bicycles. Great Service and Repair.

MOUNTAIN BIKE SPECIALISTS 970-247-4066
949 Main Avenue. Leading Durango in cycling for over 45 years! Specialized and Niner.

SECOND AVENUE SPORTS 970-247-4511
600 East 2nd Avenue. Full service bike shop. Top of the line retail and rentals.

DURANGO CYCLERY 970-247-0747
143 E 13th Street. Ride, Recycle, Hang Out, Drink Beer. Full service bike shop for 35 years!

VELORUTION CYCLES 970-259-1975
1077 Main Avenue. Bikes and gear for bikepacking, touring, fatbiking, commuting.

PEDAL THE PEAKS 970-259-6880
598B Main Avenue. Quality service. Mountain, downhill and BMX.

BACKCOUNTRY EXPERIENCE 970-247-5830
1205 Camino Del Rio. Backpacking, bike packing, travel gear, maps, more.

SAN JUAN HUT SYSTEM 970-626-3033
www.SanJuanHuts.com. Supported hut to hut bike packing on singletrack.

HERMOSA TOURS 877-765-5682
598 Main Ave., inside Pedal the peaks. info@hermosatours.net Guided tours and shuttles.

DURANGO MOUNTAIN BIKE TOURS 970-749-5528
Custom tours on Durango trails.

CORTEZ, DOLORES AND FARMINGTON

KOKOPELLI BIKES 970-565-4408
130 West Main Street Cortez. Full service, very friendly bike shop!

LIZARD HEAD CYCLES 970-394-4168
350 Railroad Avenue Dolores. Great service, new and used bikes and gear.

COTTONWOOD CYCLES 505-326-0429
4370 East Main Street Farmington, NM. The Four Corners Family Bicycle Center.

URGENT CARE SERVICES

DURANGO URGENT CARE 970-247-8382
2577 Main Avenue Durango Walk-In Urgent Care Clinic for Injuries & Illnesses.

ANIMAS URGENT CARE 970-385-2388
450 South Camino Del Rio/Hwy 550, next to Big 5. Walk-in care. 8:30 a.m.-7 p.m. daily

FOR FOREST SERVICE AND BUREAU OF LAND MANAGEMENT (BLM) INFORMATION:

SAN JUAN FOREST SERVICE: 970-247-4874

DOLORES PUBLIC LANDS OFFICE: 970-882-7296

ABOUT THE AUTHOR

Calico Trail | *Miko Meyer*

Holly Annala grew up on a small ranch in Durango, Colorado; riding horses until dark as often as possible, losing her boots in the mud, and getting cockleburs in her hair. This set her up for a lifetime of loving the outdoors and outdoor adventures. After high school she traded in the time she spent horseback riding for time on her first mountain bike, which she purchased at Durango Cyclery. She has been exploring trails around the west (and other places a bit farther away!) ever since. Holly has lived in Crested Butte, Colorado for 20 years with her husband Rob Mahedy. She is happiest when camping, riding bikes, backpacking and backcountry skiing with Rob and with friends from their wonderful community. She loves to know where every trail and drainage goes, what the name of every flower and bird is, and what is over the next ridge. Durango and the San Juan Mountains are still close to her heart. This is her fifth guidebook on mountain biking trails. She also teaches mountain biking and helps build trails with Crested Butte Mountain Bike Association.

Colorado Trail/Sliderock | *Scott DW Smith*

Bear Creek Trail | *Holly Annala*

Phil's World | *Scott DW Smith*

Dry Fork Trail | *Kennan Harvey*

Indian Ridge/Colorado Trail

Sharkstooth Trail | *Rob Mahedy*

Calico Trail | *Holly Annala*

Grindstone Trail | *Paul Adams*

La Plata Mountains/Indian Ridge | *Scott DW Smith*

Colorado Trail | *Holly Annala*

Groundhog Stock Driveway | *Holly Annala*

Pinkerton Flagstaff Trail | *Scott DW Smith*

Sand Canyon Trail | *Scott DW Smith*

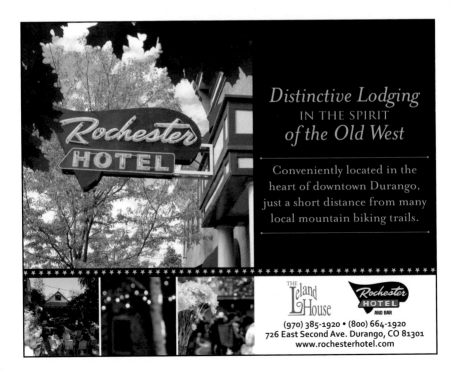

Boggy Draw | *Scott DW Smith*

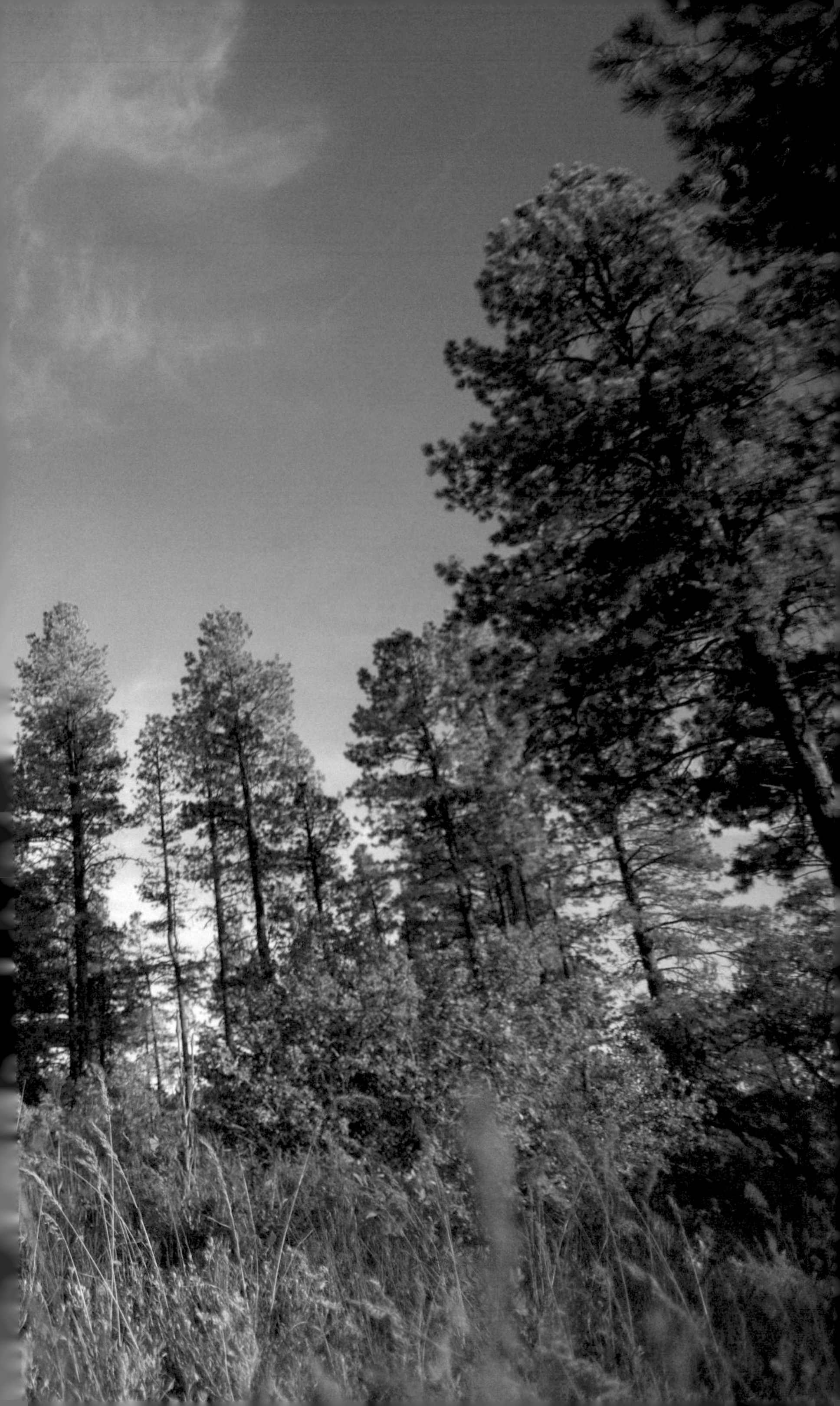

Colorado Trail/Indian Ridge | *Dodson Harper*

Snake Charmer Trail | *Trent Bona*

Elbert Creek Trail | *Scott DW Smith*

Engineer Mountain Trail | *Kennan Harvey*

Meadow Loop/Horse Gulch | *Scott DW Smith*